Killing Mr Lebanon

Killing Mr Lebanon

The assassination of Rafik Hariri and its impact on the Middle East

Nicholas Blanford

I.B. TAURIS
LONDON · NEW YORK

Published in 2006 by I.B.Tauris & Co Ltd

6 Salem Road, London W2 4BU
175 Fifth Avenue, New York NY 10010
www.ibtauris.com

In the United States of America and Canada distributed by
Palgrave Macmillan a division of St. Martin's Press
175 Fifth Avenue, New York NY 10010

ISBN 10: 1 84511 202 4 HB
ISBN 13: 978 1 84511 202 8 HB

A full CIP record for this book is available from the British Library
A full CIP record is available from the Library of Congress

Library of Congress Catalog Card Number: available

Typeset in Palatino by RefineCatch Limited, Bungay, Suffolk
Printed and bound in Great Britain by
TJ International Ltd, Padstow, Cornwall

Contents

Preface

I was working at home when the explosion that killed Rafik Hariri blasted through my quiet neighbourhood two kilometres from the St George Hotel, rattling windows and sending a few loose panes of glass smashing onto the street outside. I telephoned my United Nations peacekeeping contacts in south Lebanon, assuming that the thunderclap was produced by an Israeli Air Force jet flying a low-level supersonic run over Beirut, a muscle-flexing gesture that often meant trouble along Lebanon's southern border with Israel. But all was quiet in the south, they said, although they were hearing from their colleagues in Beirut that there was smoke rising from the hotel district on the downtown seafront.

Minutes later I was waving my Lebanese press card and pushing through the cordon of soldiers who were trying to seal off the site of the explosion. I had driven past the St George Hotel just an hour earlier with my wife and two children, a routine Monday morning trip to the Hamra shopping district in the western half of the city. But the carnage and chaos on the street outside the St George was anything but routine. For many in the West, the name Beirut may still conjure images of Hobbesian violence, but not for me. Beirut had been my home for over a decade. The 16-year civil war had ended in 1990, four years before I moved to Lebanon. Although blood continued to be shed throughout the 1990s in the stony hills and wadis of the south where Hizbullah's resistance fighters battled Israeli occupation forces, Beirut was a city at peace. Watching the firemen gently pry loose blackened, rubbery corpses from the smoking shell of a car and trying not to trip over the chunks of asphalt and clods of earth littering the road while blinking away the tears brought on by the acrid smoke, I was reminded not of Beirut but of Baghdad, or one of the bloodier days in south Lebanon in the 1990s.

There were only two people who could warrant a bomb assassination of this magnitude, so I thought – Walid Jumblatt, the head of the most prominent Druze dynasty and outspoken critic of Syria's long hegemony over Lebanon, or Sayyed Hassan Nasrallah, the secretary-general of Hizbullah. But Nasrallah rarely left his stronghold in the southern suburbs of Beirut, and the Beirut hotel district was an unlikely location to dispatch the leader of Hizbullah.

It was Mohammed Azakir, a veteran photographer for Reuters news agency, who told me. With an anguished look on his face, he said 'They got Hariri.'

Hariri? Gone? Impossible.

When I arrived in Lebanon, Rafik Hariri had been prime minister for two years, and his larger-than-life presence dominated the country. His national reconstruction programme was moving into action and Solidere, the private company reconstructing the city centre, had just begun dynamiting the war-scarred ruins of the old downtown. His energy and enthusiasm were obvious. When he opened the brand new Beirut International Airport terminal in 1998, I was one of a pack of reporters hurrying after Hariri as he marched around the empty gleaming halls and corridors, his entourage struggling to match his pace. Every now and then, he would stop to examine a new luggage conveyor belt, snip a ribbon, smile for the photographers and then march on. One could almost sense him mentally ticking off the airport from his list of 'things to do'.

In interviews, Hariri would give stock answers to political questions such as the Lebanon–Syria relationship or the resistance war in south Lebanon. But switch the conversation to reconstruction, and his eyes would light up. In 1996, in one of my interviews with Hariri, I asked him how he saw Lebanon at the turn of the century. This was the sort of question Hariri loved.

'The country's infrastructure will be finished,' he said with a broad, satisfied smile. 'I see lots of light industry in the free zones. I see the roads and hotels finished and the marinas functioning. I see Beirut as a jewel lit up at night.'

But the realisation of his vision was to be thwarted by the grinding political realities of Lebanon. From 2000 onwards, Hariri was locked into an increasingly fraught and bitter struggle for control of Lebanon, one pitting him against his nemesis, Emile Lahoud, the Lebanese president and former army commander, and the Syrian regime of President Bashar al-Assad.

The battle for Lebanon intensified with the onset of the Bush administration's 'war on terrorism' and the invasion of Iraq in 2003. With pressure mounting on Syria, Bashar adopted President Bush's maxim of 'either you are with us or against us', in his dealings with the Lebanese. Stoked by a pernicious whispering campaign by pro-Syrian Lebanese, the regime in Damascus increasingly came to regard Hariri as a threat, a powerful Sunni who was plotting with the Americans and French against Syria. But Hariri was a compromiser, an appeaser, who only sought to place relations between Beirut and Damascus on a more equitable footing and away from one dominated by the Syrian and Lebanese intelligence agencies. He cut a deal with Hizbullah over its weapons and was willing to use his international contacts to ease the pressure on Damascus. Hariri simply wanted to deal with fellow politicians in Damascus, not a general in the Syrian military intelligence headquarters in the Lebanese town of Anjar. Hariri wanted to be Syria's friend, but the Syrians believed he was their enemy.

The drama that unfolded was, at its heart, a Shakespearean tragedy of misunderstanding.

When I.B.Tauris and I first discussed the idea of a book on the Hariri assassination and its impact on Lebanon and beyond, Syrian troops were still on Lebanese soil and Lebanon's parliamentary elections were more than a month away. I would be writing the book as the story unfolded, but it was a compelling tale to relate, one which, although rooted in the tangled complexities of Levantine politics, contained universal themes of greed, power, fear, rivalry, suspicion and murder, fundamentals of the human condition which transcend region, language and culture.

I interviewed over 70 people for the book, many of them close to Hariri either professionally or personally. What became evident early on in my research was the remarkable effect Hariri had on those who knew him. Several interviewees wept when recalling their memories of Hariri; one broke down in tears in a café and sobbed quietly for several minutes; a serving cabinet minister choked up and called a halt to the interview. Even Hariri's staunch enemies would interject their criticisms of his economic and political policies with brief eulogies and assertions that they had always liked him on a personal level.

I would like to express my heart-felt thanks to all those who gave of their time to be interviewed for this book, both on and off the record, some of them over several sessions. The dates of the interviews appear in the notes to the text. I have not included the dates of my interviews with sources who requested anonymity to avoid identification.

Additionally, I would like to thank Shahir Idriss of Future Television who was enormously helpful and generous in unloading her impressive directory of contacts and helping facilitate interviews; I am also indebted to Amal Mudallali for helping arrange key interviews with the Hariri family and staff; enormous thanks go to Joshua Landis, professor of history at the University of Oklahoma and author of syriacomment.com, and Scott MacLeod, Middle East correspondent of *Time*, two good friends who doggedly waded through the manuscript chapter by chapter and provided solid advice, comments and corrections. Special thanks also to Abigail Fielding-Smith, my editor at I.B.Tauris, whose common sense and experience curbed my wilder flights of fancy and helped fashion what is hopefully a readable, informative and enjoyable book.

Thanks and apologies to my children, Yasmine and Alexander, who saw too little of their father in the eight months it took to write this book. Most of all, I would like to thank my wife, Reem. Without her unflinching support, patience and kindness, this book would not have been possible. It is to her that this book is dedicated.

Nicholas Blanford
Beirut

Countdown

Adnan Baba was feeling troubled.[1] For 28 years he had served as Rafik Hariri's personal secretary, handling the details of the billionaire politician's exhausting schedule, from organising overseas trips to selecting which tie he would wear each day. Baba spent more time with Hariri than with his own family, and knew his moods, tastes, habits and mannerisms intimately. But he had noticed to his unease that his employer and friend had changed. In the space of just one week, Hariri's thick dark hair and moustache, which had been steadily greying for years, had turned uniformly silver, a telling indicator, Baba thought, of the pressures Hariri was under.

Hariri had not slept well and was already awake when Baba tapped gently on the door of his bedroom on the seventh floor of the massive mansion that doubled as Hariri's home and headquarters in the Koreitem district of Beirut. He was in good spirits, though, and telephoned Hani Hammoud, a close advisor, to join him.

Hariri's wife, Nazek, was in Paris, so he ate breakfast alone, his usual light repast of thick strained yogurt mixed with olive oil known as labneh, a little toast, fresh tomatoes and cucumbers. He was trying to lose weight again and his doctors were always pestering him about his high blood pressure.

Riffling through a closet, Baba selected a dark blue suit, white shirt and striped blue and white tie for Hariri to wear. Hariri was sitting in the salon attached to the bedroom, sipping his customary double espresso and scanning the newspapers. He noticed that the scandal of the olive oil arrests had been given prominence on most front pages. Some workers at one of Hariri's charities had been arrested on Saturday and charged with bribing potential voters with bottles of olive oil four months before the scheduled parliamentary elections. His charity distributed food parcels, including bottles of olive oil, each year to needy families as a gift during the holy fasting month of Ramadan. In 2004, Ramadan fell during the olive harvest, so the food parcels had contained notes promising the oil would be delivered once prepared and bottled. Hariri considered the arrests ridiculous, a transparent and clumsy attempt by the authorities to further intimidate him. Even Sheikh Mohammed Qabbani, the highest Sunni authority in the country, had condemned the arrests.

But the incident reflected the escalating pressure he faced from his political opponents in the government and among Syria's Lebanese allies. In the past week, the hostility from the loyalist camp toward the opposition had reached new heights, particularly toward Hariri and his close ally Walid Jumblatt, head of the most prominent Druze dynasty in Lebanon. The intensity of the public attacks, coupled with repeated death threats and warnings from the international community, was creating genuine unease. Hariri laughed off the dangers in front of concerned friends, family and staff, but the stresses of the past months had taken a physical toll. Normally plump and jovial, he had became more thoughtful and was beginning to look his 60 years. And, as Baba had noted, his hair had turned silver almost overnight.

7.30 a.m.

Hariri's security team had already begun their first routine bomb sweep of the day as Amer Shehadi arrived at the mansion in Koreitem to report for duty. A tough, stocky man in his 40s with a clipped moustache and grizzled crew cut, Shehadi had worked for Hariri since 1983 when he had provided security at the Hariri Foundation headquarters in Beirut. The 100-strong security team was headed by Yehya Arab, more commonly known as Abu Tarek. Abu Tarek had served as Hariri's personal bodyguard since the late 1970s, a familiar figure to many Lebanese, forever shadowing his boss, unsmiling, his eyes hidden behind dark glasses. His team was responsible for protecting various members of the Hariri family as well as securing Hariri's residences in Lebanon – the Beirut home in Koreitem, the house in the mountain resort of Fakra, the beach chalet in Naameh, south of Beirut. Most of the bodyguards had years of experience and all of them were professionally trained by British, French and Jordanian police. Some of the team on duty that day had just completed a month-long refresher course of fitness and weapons training at the chalet in Naameh.

Shehadi was told he would be driving the lead vehicle when Hariri departed Koreitem later in the morning. As usual, Shehadi would not learn of their destination until the convoy was about to leave. But he knew that today was the first of a three-day session at parliament to discuss the electoral law under which the parliamentary elections would be held in May, and the boss would not want to miss that.

Hariri's mansion was in reality a fortress. The three-metre-high stone walls surrounding the building were topped with coiled barbed wire and canvas screens which, with a dense row of pine trees, prevented the curious from peering inside. Security cameras and floodlights maintained a 24-hour vigil on all the approach roads. Bodyguards accompanied by sniffer dogs paced slowly along the street, checking for hidden explosives. It was a task the team fulfilled at least three times a day, examining the entrances to the building and the surrounding streets for a distance of about 200 metres.

Hariri's personal vehicle, a black Mercedes S-600, was also searched inside and out and scanned with a chemical explosive detector. The armoured Mercedes was rated to the maximum B6/B7 protection level, its steel and hi-tech fibre armoured bodywork and layered polycarbonate windows capable of withstanding military-grade rifle fire with armour-piercing rounds, and blasts from hand grenades. It was also equipped with a self-sealing fuel tank and run-flat tyres allowing the vehicle to quickly escape an ambush even if the tyres were shot out. The bodyguards drove unarmoured Mercedes S-500s. Each of the three convoy protection vehicles carried four gigabyte jammers, the strongest available on the market to counter electronic signals which could be used to detonate bombs.

8.45 a.m.

Carole Farhat was 15 minutes late for work at the seafront St George Hotel in the Minet al-Hosn district of Beirut. She blamed the party she had attended the night before which had lasted until late. A slim woman in her late thirties with streaked blond hair, Carole entered her office on the first floor of the St George Annexe, a 10-storey building with a façade of flesh-coloured stone on the other side of the busy seafront road from the gutted ruins of the hotel. The St George was once the most famous hotel in Beirut, if not the Middle East, a legendary watering hole for diplomats, journalists, spies and assorted lowlifes who wheeled and dealed during Lebanon's golden years in the 1950s and 1960s. But the 1975–1990 war had left the hotel a bullet-scarred skeleton used as a billet by Syrian soldiers for most of the 1990s. The square, flat-roofed, five-storey building of dull pink walls and delicate, white-trellised balconies had yet to be restored, but the adjacent swimming pools and outdoor restaurant of the St George Yacht Club and Marina had resumed its pre-war role as the essential beach club for discerning Beirutis.

Carole was organising a St Valentine's Day dinner for 150 guests that evening. It would mark the first time the newly glassed-in pool-side restaurant had opened for business during the off-season winter months.

9.15 a.m.

Hariri took the lift from his private quarters on the seventh floor to his office on the fifth floor. A group of 10 to 15 people, mainly advisors and political colleagues, were waiting in the hall as they did every morning. Among them was Fadi Fawaz, a close aide who had been heavily involved in the post-war reconstruction process in the 1990s.

'He was in an excellent mood,' Fawaz recalls. 'He was smiling and talking about his latest diet and asking who would like to have lunch with him that day.'

They discussed the latest amendments to the electoral law and Hariri joked about the olive oil scandal.

'You do well in this country and they take you to court,' he told Fawaz with a smile. 'They have nothing on me now except this olive oil business.'

Basil Fleihan arrived at Koreitem at 10 a.m. A former economy minister under Hariri and a pillar of Lebanon's small Protestant community, Fleihan had returned to Beirut the night before from Geneva where his family had been staying as a consequence of the heightened political tension in Lebanon. His wife, Yasma, had urged him to stay in Switzerland, but he had wanted to attend the parliamentary session. He told Yasma he would return to Geneva in two weeks. At only 41, Fleihan was an accomplished and respected figure in Lebanon, an example of the smart technocratic Lebanese professional with whom Hariri liked to surround himself.

Hariri, his hands in his pockets, strode up and down the hallway, chatting to Fleihan before sitting down and having a cup of coffee.

'Adnan,' Hariri called to Baba. 'Do we have anything on Friday?'

Baba told him he had some appointments on Friday and Saturday.

'Hind's birthday is on Friday,' Hariri said, referring to his only daughter, who was staying with her mother in Paris. 'Cancel all my appointments and tell the captain to have the plane ready to fly to Paris on Friday for the weekend.'

Hariri looked at his watch. It was after 10.30 a.m. He asked Baba to alert the security detail to have his car ready to go to parliament. The parliamentary session was not due to start until noon, but Hariri wanted to arrive early. He turned to Fleihan and said with a smile, 'Come on, Basil, let's go to parliament and have some fun.'

10.35 a.m.

The security detail and sniffer dogs were still waiting on the street. They would stay there keeping an eye on the area until Hariri and his convoy had departed. Amer Shehadi was already at the steering wheel of the first Mercedes in the convoy when Hariri walked out of the upper entrance of the house accompanied by Basil Fleihan. The two men climbed into the armoured Mercedes, Hariri taking the driving seat as usual. He always drove himself, enjoying the feeling of independence. Baba hurried out of the house and handed Hariri his reading glasses which he had left on the desk in his office.

'I'll be back at one o'clock,' Hariri told Baba. He had invited some Beirut politicians to lunch.

'Maa Salameh' (Go in peace), Baba replied. The convoy swept through the front gate and sped along the narrow streets eastward toward the downtown district.

10.45 a.m.

Ghattas Khoury, a plump, bespectacled surgeon and MP for a Beirut constituency in Hariri's political bloc, drove to parliament in his wife's small blue Audi. It was a deliberately nondescript car that was less conspicuous than his usual black Mercedes saloon. Like many of Hariri's political allies, he and his wife had been receiving death threats for months. Khoury thought Hariri's sense of confidence was misplaced. After all, only four days earlier, Hariri had been warned by Terje Roed Larsen, a senior United Nations envoy, that the situation was very bad and that he should be careful. Also Basil Fleihan had told them on arriving in Beirut from Geneva the day before that he had heard of some fresh threats against Hariri and his allies.

11.00 a.m.

Abu Tarek, the chief bodyguard, mentioned to Hariri that Nejib Friji, the United Nations spokesman in Beirut, and some journalists were in Café de l'Etoile facing the parliament on the other side of the cobble-stoned Nijmeh Square. Hariri told Abu Tarek he would join them shortly. He was sitting in the main chamber of parliament with Marwan Hamade, a former minister and Druze MP close to Walid Jumblatt, and several other colleagues. Hamade still walked with a cane, a legacy of the injuries he had received in a car bomb assassination attempt four months earlier. The electoral law dominated conversation. The law was almost unchanged from the previous elections in 2000, except for a proposed amendment that would see Beirut split into three constituencies, a move that Hariri and his allies recognised as an attempt to dilute his representation in the capital.

Since Hariri had stepped down as prime minister in October, he had been building a nationwide network of political alliances ahead of the parliamentary elections. He had flirted with the Christian and Druze-led opposition, known as the Bristol Gathering, but until now had resisted openly siding with them, wary of losing the support of his Sunni constituency if he was seen moving too close to the more outspoken of Syria's Lebanese adversaries. Furthermore, Hariri was a man of compromise and, although his relations with Damascus had never been worse, he was still open to the possibility of a rapprochement. Indeed, there were three separate mediation efforts under way to achieve a reconciliation between Hariri and Bashar al-Assad, the Syrian president.

Even if a rapprochement was not possible, the Lebanese political landscape was likely to undergo a dramatic transformation at the elections. No matter how the government fixed the electoral law to suit loyalist candidates, all the data Hariri was receiving predicted a triumph for the opposition at the polls. If the pro-Syrian majority in parliament was overturned as expected, Syria would have little choice but to reach a new modus vivendi in its dealings with the Lebanese, one which should place bilateral relations on a more equitable footing.

Let the government produce any law they want, Hariri told his colleagues, we will still win.

12.00 p.m.

As Fady Khoury, the owner of the St George, approached the hotel, his chauffeur, Yussef Mezher, asked him 'Left or right?' Left would take him to the office in the St George Annexe or right to the beach club next to the hotel.

It was a beautiful day, brilliant sunshine, a deep-blue sky and mild for this time of year. The office could wait while he took a cup of coffee and observed the workmen putting the final touches to the newly renovated restaurant, his pet project during the winter months.

'Right,' Khoury said.

12.15 p.m.

Café de l'Etoile is a five-minute stroll from the modern, eight-storey, glass and stone United Nations headquarters. Nejib Friji, a dapper, cigar-smoking Tunisian who headed the UN Information Office, had arranged to meet some of Lebanon's top journalists to brief them on the results of a meeting in Damascus the previous Thursday between Terje Roed Larsen and President Bashar al-Assad. Larsen was tasked by the UN with overseeing the implementation of UN Security Council Resolution 1559. The US- and French-sponsored resolution included demands for a free and fair Lebanese presidential election, a withdrawal of Syrian troops from Lebanon and the disarming of the Shiite Hizbullah organisation. It was adopted by the UN Security Council in early September, 24 hours before the Lebanese parliament rubber-stamped a three-year extension to the mandate of Emile Lahoud, the Lebanese president and Hariri's political nemesis. Resolution 1559 was deeply controversial in Lebanon, with its critics insisting that it represented an unwarranted interference in Lebanese affairs.

Sitting around the table with Friji were four prominent journalists, among them Ali Hamade of Lebanon's *An Nahar* newspaper, the brother of Marwan Hamade, and Walid Choucair of *Al-Hayat*. As they chatted, Abu Tarek, Hariri's bodyguard, entered the café and told Friji that Hariri would be with them in a few minutes. Friji and Hariri occasionally took advantage of chance meetings to compare notes and swap information. Friji thought it would be a good opportunity to ask Hariri's advice on a couple of pressing issues.

12.25 p.m.

Ghattas Khoury walked out of the parliament building with Hariri into Nijmeh Square where they stopped briefly to discuss the possibility of setting up a meeting with the Bristol Gathering to elicit its support over the olive oil arrests. Hariri agreed and asked where the meeting should be held.

'What about the Tayyar Mustaqbal office?' Khoury suggested, referring to the headquarters of Hariri's 'Future Tide' political movement.

Hariri grimaced. He was preparing to formally announce his alliance with the opposition, but the timing was not yet right to host a meeting at his political headquarters. Was there not a more neutral setting where they could meet? Khoury insisted on the Tayyar Mustaqbal office, and Hariri said they would discuss the matter again later. Khoury departed for the American University Hospital where a patient with a perforated stomach ulcer was awaiting his attention.

12.30 p.m.

It was the first time Samer Rida had been in the St George neighbour-hood for a month. A slim, dark-haired, 25-year-old supervisor at the distribution department of *Al-Wasit*, a free weekly newspaper carrying classified adverts, Rida was showing a trainee the delivery route in the area. They stopped off at several shops along Phoenicia Street facing the towering Phoenicia Hotel before turning right down a small lane past a branch of HSBC bank toward the seafront road and the St George Hotel.

12.35 p.m.

Hariri walked across Nijmeh Square to the Café de l'Etoile, pausing momentarily to chat to a group of women who were lobbying for greater female representation in parliament. As he entered the café, two of the reporters who were sitting with Friji moved to another table, hoping Hariri would join them.

Walid Choucair, the *Al-Hayat* correspondent, turned to Hariri and, pointing at Friji, said playfully 'If you sit with him, it means you are with Resolution 1559. But if you sit with them,' he said indicating the Lebanese journalists at the other table, 'you are with Taif', the 1989 accord that helped end the Lebanese civil war and paved the way for Syria's domination of Lebanon.

Hariri smiled and walked over to a third table lying between the other two and sat down, whereupon Friji and the four journalists joined him. Hariri enjoyed the company of reporters. When he had been prime minister, sometimes he could be found in the evenings spending more time deliberating on the content of his *Al-Mustaqbal* newspaper than concentrating on affairs of state.

They discussed the coming elections and the tensions in the country. Hariri told them that he was dropping from his parliamentary bloc several pro-Syrian MPs that he had been obliged to include in 2000, the 'back-stabbers', he called them. It was a bold move and reiterated to Friji just how sour relations had grown between Hariri and the Syrians.

'All I need are seven solid MPs on my list and the rest will join us,' Hariri said.

He motioned to Friji that he wanted to speak to him alone. The two men stepped outside and sat at an empty table.

Friji asked Hariri for some advice on an awkward diplomatic incident that had occurred on the sidelines of Larsen's meeting with Bashar al-Assad four days earlier involving Major General Rustom Ghazaleh, the head of Syrian military intelligence in Lebanon and as such Damascus's most powerful representative. Hariri listened to Friji's account of what had happened, and then said, 'Forget about Ghazaleh. Don't give him any importance. Don't go and see him. He's useless.'

Friji then changed the conversation to Hizbullah, which was obliged to dismantle its military wing under Resolution 1559. Hariri advised Friji that the UN should deal directly with the Shiite group. Even though much of the West considered Hizbullah a terrorist organisation, it was an important political actor in Lebanon and should be treated carefully.

'Make sure that you tell the Americans before you go; otherwise they will be upset,' Hariri said. 'But definitely you should speak to Hizbullah.'

The two men returned inside the café and were joined by Basil Fleihan and Samir Jisr, a Sunni MP from Tripoli in the north and an ally of Hariri.

Hariri made a brief phone call asking to meet with an advisor before lunch and then notified the security team he was ready to leave.

12.48 p.m.

The convoy was waiting on a side street beside the parliament building. Abu Tarek briefly discussed with the police escort and his assistant Talal Nasser which route to take back to Koreitem. They had three choices. The first was the longest, heading south out of Nijmeh Square and following the highway toward the airport before looping around the western half of the city to the mansion in Koreitem. The second route took the convoy due west, next to the restored Ottoman-era military barracks that now housed the prime minister's offices, then past the derelict 32-storey Murr Tower, once a favourite vantage point for snipers during the war. The convoy would then head into the busy Hamra shopping district before reaching Koreitem. The third route ran along the coast, north of Nijmeh Square, past the new marina and the St George Hotel along the seafront corniche. They picked the seaside route. It was a little longer than heading through Hamra but the boss wanted to be back at Koreitem by 1 p.m. and at this time of day it would be faster.

The convoy eased out of the side street and took up position on the cobble-stoned square beside the café.

12.53 p.m.

The conversation in Café de l'Etoile broke up and Hariri, accompanied by Basil Fleihan, walked outside to the waiting convoy. Fleihan climbed into the Mercedes' passenger seat as Hariri paused to smile and wave at Friji and the reporters.

Friji remarked to Ali Hamade on the peculiar black hearse-like vehicle waiting at the rear of Hariri's six-car convoy.

'That's no hearse,' Hamade said. 'That's one of the most sophisticated ambulances in the world.'

In the back of the ambulance, a converted Chevrolet, sat Rashid Hammoud. A respiratory therapist with the American University Hospital in Beirut, he had served as a paramedic on Hariri's medical team since 1993. A wooden board separated him from the front compartment, although through a narrow opening he could see Mohammed Awayni, the driver, and Mazen Zahabi, the second paramedic, who had begun working with the team just three months earlier. The ambulance was always located at the rear of the convoy and when moving it would hang back, where traffic allowed, about 30 metres. If the convoy ran into an ambush, it was essential for the ambulance to remain out of harm's way.

The lead vehicle in the convoy was a Toyota Land Cruiser carrying four policemen from the Internal Security Forces followed by the Mercedes driven by Amer Shehadi who was accompanied by two bodyguards, Mohammed Dia in the passenger seat and Hassan Ajouz in the back. Hariri's armoured vehicle was third, followed by two more Mercedes carrying another three bodyguards each. Abu Tarek sat in the passenger seat of the fourth vehicle, which was tasked with covering the right flank of Hariri's car. The fifth Mercedes hung to the left-hand side of the road to protect Hariri's left flank. The three bodyguards sitting in the passenger seats carried Heckler & Koch MP5 machine pistols, small, lightweight weapons with collapsible stocks that could be discreetly hidden beneath a suit jacket. The other three men sitting in the rear seats of the convoy protection vehicles were armed with heavier M-16 rifles. Each bodyguard carried a 9mm automatic pistol in a shoulder holster, a choice of either a Beretta or a Glock with which they practised at least twice a week at the shooting range in Naameh. All the security team carried four magazines of ammunition for each weapon, one loaded and three spares.

There was no internal chit-chat over the short-wave radio when the convoy was on the move. Radio silence was strictly observed although the powerful electronic jammers in the boots of the three Mercedes S-500s made communication difficult anyway.

As the convoy swung around the clock tower in the centre of the square and headed down the street beside the Italian embassy toward the seafront, a pair of eyes noted the direction and a telephone number was punched into a mobile phone, the first of four calls the watcher would make in the next few seconds.[2] All the recipients were in the vicinity, covering Hariri's potential routes to Koreitem. The watcher's pre-paid mobile phone line was one of eight activated just over a month earlier and since then the only calls they had made were to each other. And when these calls were concluded, the lines would never be used again.

Fady Khoury at the St George glanced at his watch. It was almost 1 p.m. He had spent long enough enjoying the sunshine at the restaurant. He called to Youssef, his chauffeur, and to Carole Farhat to accompany him to the office on the other side of the busy road. Carole had finished preparations for the evening's dinner. She picked up her bag and some files to work on in the office. Maria Deeb, her sister-in-law and close friend, had already gone ahead.

Clutching a bundle of newspapers, Samer Rida and his trainee walked down the short staircase leading from the main road into the St George beach club. He handed a copy to one of the staff and then turned to go back up the stairs.

One of the four people contacted by the watcher in Nijmeh Square was the driver of a white Mitsubishi Canter van who had been lingering near the St George Hotel while awaiting the call. Now the van inched slowly down the main road, cars and trucks whipping past as the driver hugged the right-hand side travelling at a mere 8 kilometres per hour. A grey sheet shrouded the contents in the back of the fully laden vehicle. It passed the small covered entrance leading to the St George beach club, and came to a halt a few metres further on, double-parking beside a line of cars.

As Fady Khoury and Carole Farhat began climbing the stairs from the beach club to the main road above, Khoury's mobile phone rang. He asked Carole to wait while he took the call, but Carole guessed he would be chatting for several minutes and she was weighed down by her bag and several heavy files.

'I'll see you in the office,' she said.

Khoury nodded and turned his attention to the phone call.

Hassan Ajouz, the bodyguard, sitting in the rear of the first Mercedes S-500, saw a car edging too close to the approaching convoy. One of his responsibilities when in the rear seat was to keep other vehicles away from the convoy. Ajouz thrust his arm out of the window and gestured aggressively for the motorist to move out of the way. The motorist mouthed a curse as he braked and swung his car out of the path of the convoy.

12.55 p.m.

Carole Farhat stepped onto the road and noticed to her right a light-coloured, commercial-looking van. Curiously, the driver had chosen to double park beside the only car parked next to the hotel, so the van protruded unnecessarily into the busy street. Its presence puzzled her briefly; she was not expecting any more deliveries for the dinner.

She hurried across the broad busy street to the Annexe building on the other side. As she crossed the sand verge before the entrance to the Annexe, she missed seeing to her left a line of sleek black Mercedes limousines racing toward the St George Hotel.

But another pair of eyes saw the convoy, a pair of eyes belonging to the driver of the white Mitsubishi van who would have been staring intently at the left-hand wing mirror from the moment he parked beside the St George Hotel less than two minutes earlier. The driver would have seen the policemen's grey Toyota Land Cruiser first, growing larger in his wing mirror as it sped around the broad sweep of road beside the St George marina and flashed past his van, followed a fraction of a second later by Amer Shehadi's Mercedes. The next car to pass the van, the third in the convoy, was Hariri's Mercedes, the armoured S-600 model which its makers boasted could withstand blasts from hand grenades. As it drew alongside, an unseen hand pressed a switch, a simple physical gesture that was about to alter the course of Lebanese history.

The fixer

'This area once was all orchards,' says a wistful Ibrahim Antar, sitting beneath a trellis of grape vines that shaded the courtyard of his home in Sidon from the intense summer sun.[1] 'Just trees with a few small houses where the farmers and their families lived. We grew everything, oranges, lemons, grapes, mandarins, clementines. Life was much better back then.'

A paunchy man in his sixties wearing a white vest and blue tracksuit trousers, Antar ruffles the head of his three-year-old granddaughter as he reminisces.

'You want to know where President Hariri was born?' he asks, using the Arabic term, 'rais', to describe the former premier. 'Look.' He indicates a spot lying 50 metres away on the other side of his small orchard of fruit trees. 'That's where Hariri's house stood. We were the only two families around here.'

The flat-roofed, two-storey stone building where Rafik Hariri spent his childhood disappeared long ago, as have all the orchards and along with them Sidon's former agrarian way of life. Today, where the Hariri home once stood, there is a telephone exchange, a squat ugly building with a façade of blue tiles and an imposing tower of bare concrete surmounted by antennae and satellite dishes. The surrounding streets are choked with traffic and lined with drab multi-storey buildings, occupied by banks and trading companies. The ground-floor shops sell cheap furniture or plastic household goods, such as mops, buckets, fans and brooms, which spill out onto the pavement. Rows of uninspiring apartment blocks lie next to each other in uncomfortable proximity, like so many bowling pins, balconies either shaded by ubiquitous green and white striped curtains or festooned with laundry hanging limply in the humid air.

The distant hills overlooking the coastal city are barely visible through the midsummer haze of dust and exhaust fumes.

Antar's house is one of the few surviving farm dwellings that once dotted the thick, verdant belt of orchards that ringed the old port town of Sidon 60 years ago. His home is protected from the urban sprawl by towering eucalyptus trees and an empty car park flanked by thick undergrowth. The scent of roses, gardenias and jasmine floats through the courtyard, and it is just possible to imagine how the area might have looked more than half a century ago.

'This jasmine bush belonged to the Hariris,' Antar says, plucking a slender white flower and sniffing it appreciatively. 'I replanted it here when their old home was torn down.'

Lebanon was days away from marking its first year of independence when Rafik Hariri was born on November 1, 1944, the eldest of three children. Raised in an environment of hardship and poverty, the family – Rafik, his sister Bahiya, brother Shafik and their parents – shared two small rooms on the upper floor of their rented home while the ground floor housed cows and chickens. His father, Bahieddine, was a farmer who worked two orange orchards, one he owned, the other he rented. He earned just enough money to provide for his family and satisfy an unsympathetic landlord, but it was a precarious living and subject to the whims of nature. After one particularly bad harvest, Bahieddine was forced to give up the rented property and earn extra income as a labourer in other orchards. Many years later, Hariri would purchase all those orchards and hand them to his father as a gift.

Hariri was a gregarious child and quick to make friends. The orange groves which surrounded his home were his backyard where he and his friends played, scampering along the dusty paths that criss-crossed the orchards. During the hot, languid days of late summer, he and his friends headed to the Iqlim al-Touffah, or Apple Province, in the mountains east of Sidon, where he would camp out and earn money picking fruit.

He excelled at the King Faisal I school in Sidon, becoming one of three students to win a high school scholarship from the Makassed Islamic Philanthropic Association.

Politics took hold of Hariri at a young age. By the time he was 13, Hariri, like many of his Muslim contemporaries in the 1950s, became captivated by the revolutionary zeal of Arab nationalism, a powerful new force preaching self-determination and unity which was sweeping through the Middle East toppling monarchies and ousting the lingering influence of Europe's colonial powers.

Sidon in the 1950s was particularly susceptible to the clarion call of Arab nationalism because of its traditionally intimate relationship with Palestine and sympathy for the some 110,000 Palestinian refugees who had fled their homes during the Arab–Israeli war of 1948 when the Jewish state was established. Some 5,000 Palestinian refugees had settled in a makeshift camp three kilometres south of Sidon among the orange trees and banana groves of an area called Ain al-Hilweh. Hundreds of other more fortunate refugees had moved in with friends and relatives in the town.

The arrival of the Palestinian refugees and the growing support for Arab nationalism, particularly among Lebanon's Muslims, began to strain the National Pact, the delicate sectarian power-sharing system under which Lebanon had been governed since independence in 1943.

The National Pact was an unwritten modus vivendi reached between Lebanon's Maronite and Sunni leadership shortly before independence from France. It essentially allocated key positions within the state to different sects on a proportional basis using a 1932 census as a guide. The census – which to this day has never been officially updated – recorded that 51 per cent of the population was Christian and 49 per cent Muslim with the Maronites representing the largest confession – or sect – at 29 per cent, followed by the Sunnis and Shiites at 22 per cent and 20 per cent respectively. Accordingly, the powerful presidency and the key security positions were given to the Maronites while the premiership fell to the Sunnis and the parliamentary speakership to the Shiites.

The National Pact was a fragile system of checks and balances that allayed Christian fears of being overwhelmed and marginalized in a predominantly Islamic region, and reassured Muslims of Lebanon's 'Arab face' and freedom from Western interference. The flaw in Lebanon's unique political model was that it lacked a mechanism enabling it to adapt to evolving population demographics. Lebanon's greatest export is its people. The tiny nation has been haemorrhaging its population since the nineteenth century, mainly Maronites who sought a better life in the United States, South America and Africa. Christian emigration combined with a higher Muslim birth rate gradually eroded the demographic advantage of the Maronites. Consequently, it was no oversight that the 1932 census was the last held by any government. The Maronites feared that their privileges in time would be stripped from them if it was confirmed that their percentage of the overall population had declined compared to that of the Sunnis and Shiites.

During the early post-independence years, the National Pact held together, but by the mid-1950s the arrangement was beginning to buckle under the burden of its inherent inequities aggravated by the stresses of regional developments.

In the mid-1950s, Lebanon found itself drifting closer to the Western orbit, partly in reaction to what many Lebanese Christians regarded as the threat posed by the radicalism of the emerging Arab republics in Egypt and Syria. Lebanese Muslims, however, drew inspiration from the example of Jamal Abed al-Nasser, a colonel in the Egyptian army who seized power in 1952 and articulated a populist anti-Western, anti-colonial rhetoric.

Lebanon's crisis came to a head in 1958 when Syria and Egypt merged to form the United Arab Republic, galvanising Lebanese Muslims who favoured joining the UAR. Street battles erupted in the northern city of Tripoli and Muslim areas of Beirut, pitching the mainly Muslim Arab nationalists against Christian parties.

The presence of a Palestinian refugee population radicalised by the experience of 1948 had a powerful influence on Sidon's young Sunnis, many of whom were enthusiastic recruits for the numerous political parties spawned by Arab nationalism.

'We were the generation of 1958,' recalls Adnan Zibawi, a childhood friend of Hariri who still lives in Sidon.[2] 'We were only 12 or 13 but it was impossible not to get caught up in the atmosphere.'

Hariri and Zibawi were both members of the Arab Nationalist Movement (ANM) founded by George Habash, a Palestinian student at the American University of Beirut who would later achieve fame and notoriety as the leader of the Popular Front for the Liberation of Palestine. The two teenagers absorbed politics, discussing the latest developments at the Jihad Club, a venue for ANM members. They went out into the streets ostensibly to teach Arabic to illiterate bakers and fishermen, but quickly turned each language lesson into political instruction, spreading the gospel of Arab unity.

'Politics was in his heart and blood from his early teens. Until the day he died he believed in the Arab cause and the cause of Palestine,' says Samir Bsat, a journalist and a contemporary of Hariri from Sidon.[3] 'He would become so excited at demonstrations that his friends would carry him on their shoulders as he yelled out slogans of support for Palestine.'

But as Hariri grew older, he was forced to temper his political activism so that he could concentrate on his school studies. Given his poor background, politics was a luxury he could ill afford. Family and friends recall that, even at a young age, Hariri was driven by ambition and a determination to escape his destitute childhood.

'His mind was very clear,' recalls Fouad Siniora, a classmate of Hariri at the King Faisal I School and fellow member of the Arab Nationalist

Movement.[4] 'He had a very strong character. He was highly outspoken and determined.'

Hariri's parents encouraged his studies, instilling in the teenager the importance of education as a means of widening his future prospects. It was a lesson that Hariri appeared to take to heart and in later years spurred the establishment of the Hariri Foundation which awarded scholarships to Lebanese students to study at universities overseas. A school report for 1958 records Hariri as one of three students in his class of 33 whose academic performance for the year was marked as 'very good'. He graduated from the Makassed school four years later.

Hariri left Sidon and enrolled at the Arab University in Beirut where he studied accountancy. Here he fell in love with Nida Boustani, an Iraqi student, whom he married while still at the university.

'He was shocked when he realised that he had to start making some money, especially after his wife got pregnant,' Adnan Zibawi recalls.[5]

Hariri juggled his university studies with proof-reading jobs at *Al-Sayyad* magazine published by *Al-Anwar* daily and with *Al-Hurriyeh* magazine. But there was little money to be made in journalism, so Hariri abandoned his university studies in 1964 and like many other Lebanese left his family in Beirut and moved to Saudi Arabia hoping to earn a steady living in the Gulf kingdom.

They were lean years for Hariri and his family in Beirut whom he would visit every six months. He taught mathematics in Jeddah and worked as an accountant before taking on small subcontracting jobs and then setting up his own company, CICONEST, in 1969. Hariri's marriage to Nida eventually fell victim to his long absences, and in 1976 he married Nazek Audi, a Palestininan Lebanese whom he met in Saudi Arabia.

The modest fortunes of CICONEST and another firm in which he was partner, the Saudi Establishment for Roads and Buildings (SERB), were badly hit by the oil boom in 1973 which brought a massive cash bonanza to Saudi Arabia. The desert kingdom became one of the fastest-growing economies in the world, with the oil profits used to fund a series of multi-billion-dollar development programmes. Despite the construction boom, however, Hariri's companies saw profit margins tumble due to the rapid rise in the costs of raw materials such as cement and steel, which tripled and quadrupled in price.

'They were very tough circumstances,' recalls Farid Makari, a Lebanese engineer employed by Hariri in 1974.[6] 'We were not really making any money because we had signed our contracts before the prices of raw materials soared.'

The determination to overcome the financial hurdles in Saudi Arabia meant that Hariri saw little of his growing family in Lebanon. His children, Bahaa, Saad and Hussam, lived in Sidon in a two-bedroom apartment with their grandparents, an aunt and an uncle.

'We used to heat the water over a charcoal fire. It was before my father made it [financially],' recalls Saad Hariri, Rafik's second son.[7] 'It was actually nice because we didn't have to worry about much.'

Hariri's luck began to change from 1976 when he teamed up with Nasser Rashid, a construction tycoon who was close to the Saudi royal family, to build three luxury blocks in Riyadh for the wife of Saudi King Khaled. The profits from that project allowed Hariri to repay all his debts and purchase his first private jet.

At the end of 1976, King Khaled asked Rashid to build the Massara hotel in the resort city of Taif. The monarch told Rashid that he planned to spend the summer in Taif and before he returned to Riyadh wanted to officially open the hotel in time for an Islamic summit.

Rashid discussed the project with Hariri who recognised that if the perilously short nine-month deadline could be met he would win the favour of the royal family, opening up a limitless horizon of opportunities. Hariri approached an ailing French construction company called Oger and proposed it handle the $100 million project. Oger's parent company approved the deal, considering it a final, make-or-break chance for its subsidiary.

'We worked 24 hours a day, shipping materials in by air, no expense spared,' says Farid Makari, who was the project manager.[8] 'Hariri knew how to seize an opportunity.'

The construction of the hotel, which was completed less than a week before the expiry of the nine-month deadline, marked a turning point in Hariri's life. A grateful King Khaled bestowed upon Hariri the rare honour of Saudi nationality and handed him more construction projects. In 1978, Hariri and Oger formed a partnership, Saudi Oger, to handle the lucrative new projects. The following year, Hariri bought out his French partners, merging Oger and Saudi Oger to form Oger International, through which in a stunningly short period of time he accumulated enormous wealth.

'It was his moment,' Fouad Siniora recalls.[9] 'He was at the station when his train came in. If he had been a minute late, it could all have been different.'

By 1982, just five years after the Taif hotel contract, Hariri had emerged as one of the richest men in the world, a multi-billionaire presiding over a business empire which ranged from banks and construction companies to light industry and publishing. But developments in Lebanon during the late spring of 1982 would spur Hariri to refocus his energies on his homeland, gradually kindling his dormant political ambitions and within a decade propelling him from relative obscurity to the perceived saviour of Lebanon.

While Hariri had been building his fortune in Saudi Arabia in the latter half of the 1970s, Lebanon had collapsed into a bitter and bloody conflict that by 1982 had cost thousands of lives, destroyed the infrastructure and partitioned the country into militia-controlled cantons.

The catalyst for the outbreak of war in April 1975 was the Palestinian presence in Lebanon, in particular the thousands of armed Palestine Liberation Organisation fighters. The Palestinian population had swelled to around 400,000 by 1975, the result of immigration and natural growth. Lebanese Muslims were sympathetic to the mainly Sunni Palestinians, regarding the growing power of the PLO as potential leverage in pressing for greater representation and political reforms. The Maronites naturally feared that the absorption of hundreds of thousands of Palestinians would upset Lebanon's delicate sectarian balance to Muslim advantage. Lebanon's unbridgeable sectarian divisions, exacerbated by worsening socio-economic conditions, plunged the country into war in April 1975. What the Lebanese refer to as the 'civil war' lasted from April 1975 to October 1976 and pitted the National Movement composed of leftist groups led by Druze leader Kamal Jumblatt and their PLO allies against the Phalange party of Pierre Gemayel and other Christian militias.

The savagery of the conflict reached its apogee in a series of brutal massacres in late 1975 and 1976 during a bloody process of cantonisation that cemented the sectarian fissures running through the country. By March 1976, the Christian militias were losing ground to the National Movement. They were driven eastward from their stronghold in central Beirut and their leftist enemies were advancing northward into Christian areas of Mount Lebanon.

In neighbouring Syria, developments in Lebanon were being closely scrutinised by Hafez al-Assad, the shrewd, patient, yet ruthless, 45-year-old president. Assad had snatched power from his rivals in the ruling Baath party in 1970 and since then had achieved some welcome stability in Syria after three decades of political upheaval and recurrent coups. Assad recognised that the turmoil in Lebanon represented both a threat and an opportunity. His chief concern was that Israel might be tempted to intervene on behalf of the Christians, who were dangerously close to defeat. Damascus lay only 30 kilometres from the Lebanese border and Assad was forever wary of Israel launching a flanking attack on his capital via Lebanon. On the other hand, he saw an opportunity to exert influence over Lebanon which would have a practical value in thwarting Israeli designs and an ideological bonus of restoring the errant Lebanese state to the Syrian motherland.

Although the state of Syria within its current borders was as much a creation of the European mandatory powers as the state of Greater Lebanon, Syria's rulers never accepted the notion of an independent Lebanon. What had become the Republic of Lebanon, they claimed, was in fact no more than a small component of Bilad ash-Sham, the traditional name given to the culturally and geographically homogeneous region bordered by the Taurus mountains to the north, the Euphrates river to the east, the Arabian desert to the south and the Mediterranean to the west. The state of Greater Lebanon was an aberration, they argued, a result of Maronite particularism and French indulgence that was not even accepted initially by many of its citizens. That Syrian view of Lebanon hardened when the Baath party – which espouses a secular, socialist Arab nationalism – took power in 1963.

Assad tried diplomatic means to resolve the crisis in Lebanon, exhorting Kamal Jumblatt to ease his military campaign against the Christians. But Jumblatt, scenting victory, was determined to smash the Christians into submission as a means of forcing through comprehensive political changes.

Syria intervened militarily after receiving approval from the US, the consent of Suleiman Frangieh, the Lebanese president, and the grudging acquiesence of Israel, which insisted that Damascus observe some 'red lines' – no troops south of Sidon, no use of aircraft in Lebanon and no deployment of anti-aircraft missile batteries. Syrian troops entered Lebanon on the night of May 31, 1976, and swiftly gained the upper hand against the National Movement and its Palestinian allies. But it cost Assad significant political capital in the Arab world. Critics claimed Assad's onslaught against the PLO was intended to benefit Western-leaning Maronites, a group which aroused little sympathy among Muslim Arabs.

By October, the Lebanese leftists and the PLO were defeated and the Syrian military presence legitimised by the Arab League as part of a 30,000-strong Arab Deterrent Force (ADF) to help restore the Lebanese government's authority over the country. Although the ADF was supposed to be a temporary measure, it would be 29 years before the last Syrian troops departed Lebanese soil.

A semblance of normality slowly returned to Lebanon over the following months. In January 1977, banks re-opened for the first time in 10 months, foreign diplomats returned, reconstruction aid poured in, and the government announced the establishment of the Council for Development and Reconstruction to repair and upgrade the war-damaged infrastructure. But the return of stability was pricked by occasional bursts of violence, including car bombs and assassination attempts. In April 1977, Kamal Jumblatt was murdered near his ancestral home in the Chouf mountains. His death, which was widely blamed on Damascus, effectively ended the last anti-Syrian opposition.

As Hariri's wealth increased in the late 1970s, he began playing a public role in Lebanon, although it remained humanitarian in nature rather than political. After earning his first million Saudi riyals (about $300,000), he rebuilt his old school in Sidon, and in 1979 founded the Islamic Institute for Culture and Higher Education, a non-profit institution that offered loans to Lebanese university students to pay tuition costs. The Institute, which five years later was renamed the Hariri Foundation, would become the cornerstone of Hariri's extensive charitable endeavours, helping educate over the next two decades more than 35,000 students in Lebanese and foreign universities. The same year, Hariri began construction on an ambitious $150 million educational and vocational training complex on 2 million square metres of land near Kfar Falous, a small village in the hills east of Sidon. The Kfar Falous project was to include a teaching hospital, a university and schools. The location was chosen deliberately because it lay between Sunni Sidon, the Shiite south, the Christian Jezzine district to the east and the Druze Chouf mountains to the north. It was to be a melting pot of Lebanese confessions where students from all over the country could learn and interact with each other in a non-sectarian environment.

'He felt a social responsibility because he was born into a poor background,' says Adnan Zibawi, Hariri's childhood friend.[10] 'He went to poor schools and knew the importance of a good education. That's why he began giving scholarships and building the Kfar Falous project.'

Although Hariri took an interest in the tangled and violent politics of Lebanon, his involvement remained limited to discussing general ideas to end the war and using his contacts with Muslims and Christians to win the release of hostages kidnapped by rival militias. Hariri's emerging profile in Lebanon was the subject of much debate. Who was this fabulously wealthy Sunni businessman from Sidon with close ties to the Saudi royal family and what did he want? By 1982, Hariri had piqued the interest of Bashir Gemayel, a charismatic and ruthless young man who had clawed his way to power over the bodies of his rivals to head the Lebanese Forces, grouping several Christian militias. In January 1982, Gemayel dispatched to Paris two aides to learn more about Hariri.

'We had dinner with Hariri and then he drove us back to a hotel and he talked throughout the night, until 4 a.m., telling us his origins and how he had made his money, his beliefs, his relations with the Saudis, everything,' recalls Michel Samaha, one of Gemayel's envoys.[11]

By the spring of 1982, Lebanon was bracing itself for what looked like an inevitable full-scale invasion by Israel organised by Ariel Sharon, a headstrong and rash yet occasionally brilliant former general in the Israeli Army whom many Israelis revered as a national hero. Sharon devised a bold plan to invade Lebanon, crush the PLO, force out the Syrian Army, and hand the presidency to Bashir Gemayel. In exchange for the presidency, Gemayel would sign a peace treaty with Israel, thus securing Israel's northern front. It was an audacious scheme that possessed a fatal flaw: success depended entirely on Gemayel. Sharon had no Plan B if Gemayel was to die or turn on his Israeli allies.

After months of rising tension, Israel launched the invasion on June 6, 1982, seizing upon the shooting of an Israeli diplomat in London to justify the assault. Outnumbered and outgunned, most PLO units in the deep south simply fled north. On June 13, Israeli forces linked up with Gemayel's militiamen at the presidential palace in Baabda in the hills overlooking Beirut. With the encirclement of Beirut complete, the siege began of the western half of the city where the PLO was holed up.

Sidon was badly damaged during the invasion. Some 1,500 residents died in the city of 180,000, with an estimated 4,000 homes destroyed in the Sidon region and damage totalling at least $300 million. Hariri's Kfar Falous development was destroyed in the fighting, just one year after the university, teaching hospital and school had opened. The Israeli Army was ill prepared to handle the humanitarian needs of the city, and there was unlikely to be any Lebanese government assistance until at least after the siege of Beirut had been lifted. Hariri saw that his financial and logistical resources could be used to help alleviate the dire humanitarian conditions in besieged west Beirut as well as Sidon where his children were living with their aunts in the new Hariri family home which had become a refuge for homeless Sidonians.

'We used to have as many as 1,500 people staying with us,' recalls Saad Hariri.[12] 'It was exciting in a way. We were young and didn't feel the fear that other people did. There were always other children running around the house. It was only scary when the Israelis came to search the house.'

During that long, hot summer, Hariri repeatedly telephoned Lebanese officials with offers of material and financial aid or Saudi diplomatic assistance to persuade the Israelis to allow water and food supplies to the civilians under siege.

He purchased 700 tons of food and blankets and organised a ship to carry the supplies from Limassol in Cyprus to Sidon. But the Israelis refused to allow the ship to dock in Sidon's port. Undaunted, Hariri telephoned Ghassan Tueni, Lebanon's ambassador at the United Nations, and asked for his help.

Could Tueni persuade the UN secretary-general to authorise the delivery or reflag the ship under the UN colours? Tueni said he would try. Kurt Waldheim, the UN secretary-general, accepted Tueni's proposal. The ship was fitted with the UN flag and sailed that day from Cyprus for Sidon. This time, the Israelis gave permission for it to dock in the port and unload its supplies.

In the middle of August, the siege of Beirut drew to an end with the evacuation of the PLO under the protection of a three-nation Multi-National Force. With the PLO removed from Beirut, the second stage of Ariel Sharon's masterplan began to unfold with the election of his Maronite ally Bashir Gemayel as the new Lebanese president.

Hariri believed, however, that electing Gemayel under the protection of Israeli guns would only perpetuate the violence. On his own initiative, he began exploring the feasibility of extending the mandate of President Elias Sarkis and establishing a government of national unity.

Johnny Abdo, the head of Lebanese military intelligence in 1982, recalls listening to a recording of a phone conversation in which Hariri was trying to persuade Saeb Salam, a former Lebanese prime minister and head of a powerful Sunni family in Beirut, against supporting Gemayel's presidency.

'I got the impression that he might be a tough adversary against Bashir Gemayel, using his Saudi influence to pressure Saeb Salam and other Sunni MPs. I later realised that this was an incorrect image after I listened to several more telephone calls, and I thought that he could be one of the most important Sunni leaders,' he says.[13]

Gemayel was duly elected president on August 23 and, with the PLO departing Beirut, Lebanon appeared to be on the verge of a new era of stability. But just as Israel's fortunes seemed to be at their zenith, the flaw in Sharon's grand plan was exposed. On September 14, Gemayel was killed in a bomb blast. The bomb was planted and detonated by a pro-Syrian activist. It appeared that Assad, whose strategic position in Lebanon had eroded with the Israeli invasion, had found and exploited Israel's Achilles heel. In that one instant, Sharon's ambitions in Lebanon collapsed. The gamble had failed to pay off and Israel began its long painful retreat from Lebanon, one that would take another 18 years to complete.

Following Gemayel's death, Israeli troops moved into west Beirut accompanied by their Christian militia allies. Ordered into the Sabra/ Shatila Palestinian refugee camps, the militiamen, fuelled by revenge for their slain commander, embarked on a three-day orgy of killing in which over 1,000 Palestinian and Lebanese residents were slaughtered.

The massacre shocked the world and compelled the return of the Multi-National Force which had departed two weeks earlier after the last PLO fighters left Beirut. Amine Gemayel, Bashir's older brother, was elected president on September 23 and, after the trauma of the previous two weeks, Lebanon set its sights once more on the future.

Hariri offered his services to the president, bringing in dozens of bull-dozers and trucks and employing hundreds of workers to clear the streets of central Beirut of the detritus of seven years of war.

Elie Salem, the foreign minister in the new government established in October 1982, recalls Hariri arriving at the presidential palace in Baabda and unloading from the back of a truck a scale model of downtown Beirut.[14]

'What's that?' Salem asked.

'It's my plan for the city centre,' Hariri replied. Hariri's attachment to his model of central Beirut would bemuse friends and colleagues in the following years who would come across it variously in the tycoon's homes in France and Saudi Arabia and even on his private jet.

Salem remembers Hariri as a 'very strange man'.

'He was very self-confident. Lebanon was and remains a series of problems and Rafik was the kind of guy who wanted to be involved in every problem with a view to solving it,' he says.

On December 28, Lebanese and Israeli negotiators began discussing an agreement that would allow for the withdrawal of Israeli troops. The Israelis wanted a deal that was a peace agreement in all but name that would justify the costly and domestically unpopular invasion. But the Lebanese government was being squeezed by a resurgent Syria and its allies in Lebanon who rejected the notion of any arrangement that rewarded Israel.

'We were under a very heavy American pressure to sign the agreement,' says Gemayel.[15] The hapless president desperately wanted the Americans to stay involved in Lebanon because he knew that the country was too weak to stand up to the Syrians and Israelis alone. But Israel and Syria resented US influence in Lebanon, believing it undermined their own separate interests.

Time was running out for the Reagan administration's Lebanon policy. On April 18, 1983, a truck bomber destroyed the American embassy in

Beirut, killing 63 people, a stark warning that the US was becoming increasingly unwelcome in Lebanon. Like the Israelis, the Americans also needed a deal.

In early May, the Israeli government agreed to a US-brokered arrangement and it was signed on May 17. Yet, at the last moment, the Israelis introduced a side letter that effectively killed the agreement at birth. The side letter stated that Israel would only withdraw its troops after the Syrian Army had pulled out from Lebanon. That gave Assad an effective veto over the agreement's implementation. If Assad refused to withdraw his forces, then the Israelis would stay and months of tedious and frustrating negotiations would come to naught.

Syria mobilised its Lebanese allies against the May 17 accord and during the summer fierce fighting flared in the northern Chouf between Christian and Druze militias. King Fahd of Saudi Arabia formally appointed Hariri his envoy, an indication of the close relationship which had developed between the two men since Hariri had become the chief construction agent for the royal family. With his new appointment, Hariri's role in Lebanon began to shift from reconstruction to mediating between the warring parties. He brokered ceasefires around Beirut International Airport after artillery barrages between the warring militias in the overlooking mountains forced the closure of the runways and endangered the US marines who were deployed there. According to Elie Salem, Hariri's principal motivation for keeping the airport open was so that he could fly between Beirut and Riyadh in his private jet to consult with King Fahd and bring fresh ideas back to Lebanon. At the end of August, Israel began preparing to withdraw its forces from the Chouf southward to Sidon. The Israeli withdrawal threatened to create a security vacuum in the Chouf which would be filled by the Druze militia of Walid Jumblatt, son and heir of the slain Kamal Jumblatt, and the Christian Lebanese Forces. Hariri arranged a meeting in Paris between President Gemayel and Jumblatt but was unable to broker an agreement between the two rivals. On September 1, the so-called Mountain War began in earnest, pitting Jumblatt's Druze against the Lebanese Forces and units of the Lebanese Army in one of the bloodiest episodes of the war.

Believing that the Americans were losing interest in Lebanon, Gemayel switched to the Saudis, beseeching King Fahd to help resolve the mess. Braving intense artillery fire around the airport, Hariri returned by helicopter from Cyprus to Beirut in early September accompanied by Prince Bandar bin Sultan, a favourite nephew of King Fahd who was at the forefront of a new Saudi peace drive.

Two weeks of intense shuttling and negotiation between Beirut and Damascus resulted in a ceasefire in the Chouf and a promise of a Saudi-sponsored national reconciliation conference. But even deciding on the location of the conference proved to be problematic and took up much of Hariri's time following Bandar's departure to Washington to take up the Saudi ambassadorship. The original site for the conference in Saudi Arabia was changed to Beirut International Airport. But Jumblatt rejected the airport, saying it would not be safe 'and wouldn't be relaxed with all those planes coming and going'. Gemayel suggested the presidential palace, and Rashid Karami, a former prime minister from Tripoli in the north, recommended a boat. Hariri won a consensus for the Intercontinental Hotel in Geneva as the venue and he arranged all the logistics, including travel and accommodation. The conference opened on October 31 amid tension and distrust. Although the Saudis were formally represented by a minister of state, none of the attendees were in any doubt that Hariri was the real voice of King Fahd. He proved a tireless negotiator, 'commuting from room to room 24 hours a day trying to convince the various partners to take a conciliatory position', Gemayel says.[16]

Five days of negotiations ended with Gemayel pledging to find a new formula for an Israeli withdrawal in exchange for recognition of his presidency by his Lebanese opponents. Reagan was reluctant to give a *coup de grâce* to the only political 'success' his administration could point to in Lebanon. But Washington's ability to influence events in Lebanon was steadily waning. The US Marine barracks at Beirut International Airport had been destroyed in October in a massive suicide truck bomb blast in which 241 American servicemen perished. Then on February 6, the Lebanese Army collapsed in west Beirut, the soldiers deserting to join their co-religionists in the militias of the Shiite Amal movement led by Nabih Berri and Jumblatt's Druze, which overran the western half of the city, cutting off the US marines who were dug in around the airport. Hours later, Reagan decided to pull the plug on his Lebanon debacle. Eleven days later, the last US marines departed Lebanon, bringing an end to what Caspar Weinberger, the US defence secretary, called 'a particularly miserable assignment'.

For Hafez al-Assad, the collapse of Washington's Lebanon policy was a moment of triumph after the tribulations of the previous two years. The 1979 Israeli–Egyptian peace agreement had isolated and weakened him regionally at a time when he was facing mounting domestic pressure from the rebellious Muslim Brotherhood which was waging a campaign of bomb attacks and assassinations against Baathist rule. He crushed the Muslim Brotherhood's rebellion in early 1982 and then had to contend with Israel's invasion just four months later. In November 1983, when the struggle against the Americans for Lebanon was at its height, he had collapsed from nervous exhaustion, spurring his younger brother, Rifaat, to lead an attempted coup, believing Assad was incapacitated by a heart attack. It took Assad until April to head off Rifaat's challenge, by which time the battle against the Americans in Lebanon was won, allowing him the opportunity to enjoy the ignominious departure of the US from Lebanon and gleefully watch his Israeli enemy become further ensnared in the quagmire of south Lebanon where a Shiite resistance was inflicting ever deadlier blows. Now operating from a position of strength, Assad rejected a Saudi peace initiative that called for the abrogation of the May 17 Agreement and for the withdrawal of Israeli and Syrian troops (he saw no reason why he should withdraw his forces), and pressured Gemayel into meeting him in Damascus in an act of public submission. Gemayel bowed to the inevitable. On February 29 he travelled to Damascus and promised to annul the May 17 Agreement in return for Syrian support for his presidency.

Hariri teamed up with Elie Salem, the foreign minister, to craft a document that would terminate May 17 to Syria's satisfaction.

'We had to abrogate the agreement because we couldn't do anything without Syria's permission at that time or we would reap very bad results on the ground,' Salem says.[17]

Hariri shuttled between Beirut and Damascus, consulting with Abdel-Halim Khaddam, a tough Sunni from the small coastal town of Banyas who had been a childhood friend of Assad and was in charge of Syria's Lebanon portfolio. After 11 years as foreign minister, Khaddam had just been promoted to vice-president. Within days, the Syrians were satisfied and Gemayel signed the abrogation.

Hariri, pleased at the result of his arbitration, wanted to take the document to Damascus straight away to show Assad, according to Elie Salem.[18] He contacted the American ambassador in Beirut and asked to borrow a helicopter to fly to Damascus. Taken aback by the request, the ambassador said it was impossible. He would have to call the State Department, which would have to contact the Pentagon, which would have to call the Sixth Fleet in the Mediterranean. Undaunted, Hariri offered to buy three US military helicopters there and then and have them stationed at Beirut International Airport. He would also pay to have three helicopter crews permanently on standby. The ambassador stared at Hariri incredulously. 'You are a one-armed bandit,' he said.

Hariri helped organise a second reconciliation conference in Lausanne on March 12, seven days after the Lebanese government formally abrogated the May 17 Agreement. But the Lausanne conference was a tense, unhappy affair and, after 12 days of bickering, it ended without agreement.

One evening toward the end of the conference, Hariri left the room where the delegates were arguing and headed back to his suite. He was joined by Sarkis Naoum, a Lebanese journalist who was covering the conference for his paper, *An Nahar*. As they entered the hotel suite, Hariri took off his jacket, sat down and began to weep. An embarrassed Naoum asked what was the matter. But instead of replying, Hariri continued crying and then began talking to himself.

'What are these people doing?' he sobbed, shaking his head slowly. 'Don't they realise they are destroying the country? What's the matter with these people?'

'Two things became clear to me then,' Naoum recalls.[19] 'First that the Lebanese were not yet ready to reach a compromise to end the war. The second thing was that I realised that Rafik was not doing this for prestige or to get a position. He was genuinely sincere in wanting to end the war.'

Despite the failure at Lausanne, Hariri was fast proving himself an indispensable component of wartime mediation. He commanded respect and attention by virtue of his connection to King Fahd, as well as his wealth.

'Hariri had real power,' recalls Elie Salem.[20] 'When Hariri was talking it was King Fahd talking. He would come up with ideas that were very forceful and say that this is what King Fahd wants. And what Fahd wants is what Hariri tells him. Fahd, of course, was not interested in the details. Any other person might have made nothing out of it. But Hariri was a catalyst in Lebanese politics. He befriended everybody, through me Gemayel, Berri, Jumblatt. He was very close to the Syrians. He was always playing the role of conciliator to bring consensus.'

Hariri had concluded from the collapse of the Lausanne conference that the war could not end and no meaningful constitutional reforms could be implemented unless the three main militias – the Lebanese Forces, headed by Elie Hobeika, the Amal Movement of Nabih Berri and Walid Jumblatt's Druze Progressive Socialist Party – could be persuaded to cease fighting and disarm. He badgered friends and colleagues for ideas, distributing paper and pencils at brainstorming sessions so they could jot down their thoughts and proposals.

'He was a man who would never accept defeat,' recalls Fouad Siniora, his childhood friend who by 1982 was running Hariri's Groupe

Mediterranee banking interests.[21] 'If he doesn't succeed in one way, he goes around it, tries to develop other ways and means to re-explain his point of view. He would always try and find some way around a problem. That really was a very important trait in him. And that's how he dealt with Lebanon's problems.'

Syria already had Walid Jumblatt and Nabih Berri as loyal allies, but Hariri spent months coaxing the suspicious Elie Hobeika into accepting an alliance with Damascus, arranging for the exchange of letters between the militia leader and Abdel-Halim Khaddam, hosting secret meetings in Crete and his residence in Paris and sweetening the negotiations with millions of dollars. Hobeika finally accepted the rapprochement with Damascus, which led to a series of 'tripartite' negotiations with Berri and Jumblatt which were supposed to end the war.

'Of course, Hariri followed up every bit of the agreement,' says Marwan Hamade, who was Jumblatt's representative at the talks.[22] 'Most of the text of the agreement was written in his house, often in his own handwriting. He was always trying to accommodate things.'

The Tripartite Accord was signed on December 28, but lasted less than three weeks. It was bitterly opposed by the traditional political class, who resented the infringement of the militia upstarts. Many in the Lebanese Forces also were deeply unhappy with what they thought was Hobeika's sell-out to the Syrians and in a bloody coup evicted Hobeika from the leadership, shattering the Tripartite Agreement and leaving months of intensive negotiations in ruins.

The collapse of the Tripartite Accord was another bitter disappointment for Hariri, but after three years of close involvement in Lebanon's tortured and unforgiving political environment he was hooked.

Abdullah Bouhabib, the then Lebanese ambassador to the US, remembers meeting Hariri in New York in early 1983 and listening to the tycoon enthusiastically describe his reconstruction activities in Lebanon. When the conversation turned to politics, Hariri fell silent, but by 1985 'it was all politics with him'.

'Politics in Lebanon is like an addiction. Once you are in, you cannot leave,' Bouhabib says.[23]

Yet many of his interlocutors in Lebanon could not understand why someone as rich and powerful as Hariri would persist with the thankless and dangerous task of Lebanese peacemaking. It was a question that was once put to Hariri by Johnny Abdo, who was Lebanese ambassador to Switzerland and then France after retiring as head of military intelligence in 1983.

'I once spoke to Hariri using coarse Arabic to say that Lebanon is like a pool of shit and why did he insist in swimming in it when he didn't have to,' Abdo recalls.[24]

Hariri replied by asking Abdo how many years he had served Lebanon in the military and then as a diplomat.

'Ten or 11 years. Why?' Abdo said.

'What are your dreams now? To earn maybe $10 million?' Hariri asked.

'Sure. Why not.'

'Well, I have one hundred times your dream, so why shouldn't I now follow my dream of helping Lebanon as you have already done?'

'I accepted the logic of what he said but I told him that Lebanese politics can be very dangerous,' Abdo says.

Friends and colleagues maintain that Hariri's initial motivation to intervene in Lebanon's war stemmed from memories of his humble childhood among the orange groves of Sidon and the Arab nationalist ideology that he absorbed in his teenage years. He also took his religious obligations as a Muslim seriously, which served as further stimulus to help resolve Lebanon's problems. Marwan Hamade recalls Hariri telling him that, after making his first million dollars, he had looked at himself in the mirror and said 'Rafik, you are a millionaire now. You are a millionaire, but you are still Rafik Hariri.'[25]

'What distinguished Hariri from all the other Lebanese millionaires . . . was that he never forgot his modest origins and he used to talk with some nostalgia about the times he was in the mountains carrying boxes of apples for five Lebanese lira a day,' says Marwan Hamade. He was motivated by 'religious belief, Arab nationalism and a sense that some of his money was owed to the people'.

Indeed, money was one of Hariri's most useful assets in his mediation efforts. A few suitcases stuffed with US dollars were often more persuasive and achieved swifter results than patient dialogue. For Hariri, money was a tool in negotiation much as a plumber uses a wrench to stop a leak or a sculptor uses a chisel to fashion a block of wood.

'He was a corrupter, rather than corrupt,' says one acquaintance from the 1980s.[26]

Hariri distributed his own funds lavishly on his philanthropic projects and had a reputation for personal generosity, although others would say he was a 'soft touch'. Explaining once the purpose of his largesse to a Lebanese politician,[27] Hariri asked what he would gain if he had $100 million and gave $50 million to his family and the other $50 million to help people. A lot of friends, the politician replied. Exactly, Hariri said. And Hariri was winning a lot of powerful friends – presidents, kings, politicians, warlords, statesmen and diplomats from the Arab world to Europe, the Far East and the United States. In Paris, he had befriended the charismatic mayor, Jacques Chirac, to whom he had proved useful in buying up ailing French companies or helping them secure lucrative contracts in Saudi Arabia.

In Damascus, Hariri was forging close ties to some members of the regime. He attempted to ingratiate himself with Assad by building him a luxurious palace on the airport road, but the unimpressed Syrian president chose to remain in his smaller Rowda palace and turned Hariri's gift into a hotel. Hariri developed a good working relationship with Abdel-Halim Khaddam and with Hikmat Shehabi, the Syrian Army chief of staff, a relationship allegedly cemented by extensive financial contributions. Like Hariri, his two main Syrian interlocutors were Sunnis, among the most senior in the Alawite-dominated regime.

'He was closer to Khaddam than Shehabi because Shehabi was a military man and it was impossible to have the same warmth of relationship,' says Nohad Mashnouq, a close advisor to Hariri in the 1990s.[28] 'Shehabi was used to deliver the tough message from Damascus and Khaddam delivered the softer normal message.'

The Saudis traditionally relied on middlemen to 'buy' Lebanese politicians and journalists – the 'Saudi way' of doing business, as one former Lebanese official put it. But Hariri soon became the sole conduit of Saudi funds in Lebanon, which increased his value as a serious negotiator. Hariri used cash and gifts to build a network of informants, becoming a 'one-man mukhabarat,' according to Gemayel, with information on everyone.[29] Secretaries of powerful figures would receive gifts of new cars or jewellery so that Hariri could be assured of a sympathetic ear when he telephoned to speak to their employers.

His wealth and prestige also underpinned an extensive logistics network which helped facilitate his mediation.

'He established an infrastructure of capable men, political scientists, economists and so on to advise him and write position papers,' Gemayel says.[30] 'It was essential to have someone who could talk to everyone, Christians, Muslims, the left and the right.'

Elie Salem recalls being at the Lebanese embassy in Paris when Hariri telephoned to say he had an important message for him from King Fahd.[31] Would Salem come down to Monaco where Hariri was staying on his yacht? Salem said he would, but he had to be back in Beirut the next day. No problem, said Hariri. There would be a car waiting for Salem outside the embassy in ten minutes. The car arrived on time and Salem was driven to the airport. He was ushered onto Hariri's private jet which took off for Nice. On arrival in the south of France, he was picked up in a white helicopter for the short flight to Monaco. When Salem landed at Monaco, there was a white Rolls-Royce and two of Hariri's staff dressed in white waiting on the runway to collect him. They drove the bemused foreign minister to the yacht where Hariri, also dressed in white, was waiting to greet him.

'How could anyone from Sidon have such a system?' Salem asked Hariri.

'This is not a Sidon system. It's the Hariri system,' he replied. 'If it's not done this way, it will never work.'

During his premiership in the 1990s, Hariri's critics would accuse him of having deliberately funded rival militias to prolong the war and the destruction of Beirut so that he could profit from post-war reconstruction. Certainly, many political figures, including Elie Hobeika of the Lebanese Forces, benefited from Hariri's financial largesse, although Hariri maintained that the money he distributed was not intended to perpetuate the war but to bring it to an end. Despite being the Saudi envoy of King Fahd, the only way Hariri was going to get a seat at the table with the high rollers was if he could bring a very large bag of cash with him. After all, the respect for King Fahd in Lebanon was not down to his personal charm and ability to tell a good joke. It was because his kingdom sat on the largest deposits of oil on earth.

'You want to operate in this country, you have got to pay, otherwise you can't come in,' says Abdullah Bouhabib, Lebanon's then ambassador to Washington.[32] 'You had to pay Berri, Jumblatt, the Lebanese Forces, everybody. Hariri couldn't come to Lebanon without paying everyone.'

The funds allocated by the Saudis were scrupulously recorded by Hariri in a ledger. 'King Fahd won't open it, but I have to keep the book to maintain his confidence. And it's accurate,' he told a friend.[33] 'That's why I love them and they love me.' It was a relationship of 'absolute clarity, loyalty and respect' for the Saudi royal family.

Not all the Saudi funds were distributed as sweeteners to politicians and militia leaders. King Fahd donated millions of dollars to charity and helped prop up the ailing Lebanese pound with huge transfers of cash to the Banque du Liban, the central bank. In February 1985, Hariri arranged for $500 million of Saudi money to be pumped into the Lebanese treasury after the pound, buckling under the strain of 10 years of war, dropped 16 per cent in value to the dollar in a single day.

According to Johnny Abdo, Hariri channelled $500,000 a month to the Lebanese Army to help pay the salaries of soldiers to prevent them deserting and joining militias.[34] Fouad Siniora says that, by the late 1980s,

Hariri was buying schools to keep them open and paying the salaries of university professors and tuition fees of students at the American University of Beirut, and Beirut University College (now called the Lebanese American University).[35]

By the mid-1980s, however, it was clear to those close to Hariri that he had his eye on the premiership. He was a wealthy Sunni with a powerful patron in King Fahd who enjoyed extensive contacts across the sectarian divide in Lebanon and friendships in Syria and the West and was untarnished by affiliation to any particular militia. Hariri saw himself as an ideal candidate for the premiership. The same drive that had sustained him during the difficult years in Saudi Arabia also underpinned his political ambitions which, in the view of many of those who worked with him, made him overly susceptible to compromise.

'He was very ambitious and he knew he couldn't be prime minister without the Syrians,' says Gemayel.[36] 'The ambition factor was essential with Rafik Hariri and it led him to make many compromises at the expense of the national interest.'

Abdullah Bouhabib, the Lebanese ambassador to Washington, recalls dining with Hariri in the south of France in August 1987 during which the tycoon aired a bold ploy to end the war in one fell swoop.[37] Amine Gemayel, Hariri said, would be offered $30 million to resign the presidency in favour of Johnny Abdo, then the Lebanese ambassador in Switzerland. Hariri would be appointed prime minister under Abdo.

Bouhabib expressed scepticism and doubted that Gemayel would accept the proposal. But Hariri said that with another $500 million he could dissolve the militias, satisfy the Syrians and retain the presidency for the Maronites. If Gemayel agreed to the plan, Hariri added, he would bring King Fahd of Saudi Arabia to Damascus to persuade the Syrians.

Gemayel says he learned of Hariri's proposal but ignored it and nothing more was said. Abdo, however, insists that the offer was not serious and that the tale was an example of Hariri's political immaturity.

'He repeated the same story to me in Basel,' Abdo recalls.[38] 'It was a joke. He was a beginner in politics at that time. People used to call him "the Cheque Book".'

Four years later the conversation came back to haunt Hariri when Abdullah Bouhabib referred to it in his memoirs.[39] According to Bouhabib, King Fahd allegedly refused to talk to Hariri for three months after the book was published, insulted by the notion that he was at the beck and call of his Lebanese envoy.[40]

Syria, meanwhile, was reasserting itself in Beirut. In February 1987, some 7,000 Syrian troops entered the city for the first time since Israel's invasion five years earlier. The Syrians stamped out fighting between warring militias, and a semblance of calm descended over the western half of the capital.

General Ghazi Kanaan, the Syrian military intelligence commander who would play a key role in future developments between Hariri and Syria, called for the re-opening of embassies and the return of foreigners, most of whom had fled with the beginning of a kidnapping campaign by Shiite militants. 'Your ordeal is over,' he said in a radio message to Beirut's residents, promising that the stabilising Syrian troop presence was open-ended. Kanaan even went jogging along the seafront corniche each day without bodyguards to demonstrate just how safe Beirut had become under Pax Syriana.

A tough and wily Alawite from the sect's stronghold in the coastal mountains of western Syria, Kanaan was a rising star in the Syrian military. He had commanded an army unit on the Golan Heights in the 1973 Arab–Israeli war. He was promoted colonel and served as head of military intelligence in the Syrian city of Homs. When the Muslim Brotherhood rebellion erupted in early 1982, he calmed the seething tensions in Homs by striking a deal with the Sunni militants. In contrast, the rebels in the neighbouring city of Hama were crushed with ruthless excess by an elite Syrian Army brigade in which as many as 20,000 people died and large areas of the city were razed to the ground. Kanaan was appointed military intelligence chief in Lebanon following the Israeli invasion months later.

Syria's strengthening grip on Lebanon failed to bring the war to an end, however, with sporadic negotiations invariably ending in deadlock and acrimony.

In June 1987, Hariri persuaded Elie Salem and a reluctant Amine Gemayel to join him in an overnight session to discuss some proposals from Saudi King Fahd on board his private jet as it ploughed through thunderstorms high above the Mediterranean Sea. The document that emerged, known as the Hariri Working Paper, included agreements on key points of contention such as the Arab identity of Lebanon, equal representation in parliament between Christians and Muslims, a phased removal of sectarianism, disbanding the militias and ending the war, with 'the assistance of sister Syria in the realisation of all these objectives'. Although the agreement hammered out on Hariri's jet won Assad's tepid endorsement, it was not translated into action.

In September 1989, Amine Gemayel's six-year term came to an end amid political deadlock over the choice of a suitable successor. Minutes before his term expired at midnight on September 22, Gemayel appointed

General Michel Aoun, the commander of the Lebanese Army, to head an interim six-man military government pending presidential elections. Gemayel's departing decision was rejected by the Lebanese government headed by Salim Hoss in west Beirut. Several other senior army officers refused to side with Aoun, including General Emile Lahoud, the head of operations at the defence ministry. The city was split between a Syrian-controlled western half and a Christian enclave centred around Baabda presidential palace where Aoun set up his headquarters.

Aoun was a unique phenomenon during the war. His unflinching nationalism and 'clean' reputation resonated with many Lebanese who had grown revolted at the brutality and cynicism of the militias and weary of the toothless and moribund political class. A populist who evoked passionate support from his followers, Aoun lacked the necessary pragmatism and guile to fulfil his ambition of breaking the power of the militias and removing Syrian troops from Lebanon. He moved against the Lebanese Forces in early 1989, uprooting the militia from parts of east Beirut and closing its illegal port. He then imposed a blockade on the illegal Druze- and Shiite-run ports in west Beirut. Alarmed at Aoun's boldness, the Syrians began shelling his east Beirut enclave in a bid to break his will. Instead, Aoun responded by launching his 'war of liberation' in March, a quixotic bid to drive the Syrian Army out of Lebanon in which the two sides traded artillery fire and skirmished along the edges of the enclave for seven months at a cost of 1,000 lives.

The fighting between Aoun's forces and the Syrians came amid renewed Arab diplomatic efforts to bring the war to an end. Relations between Damascus and other Arab states were fragile in 1989, a consequence of Arab irritation at Syria's transparent ambitions in Lebanon and its support for Iran against Iraq during the 1980–1988 Gulf War. Assad, feeling squeezed by Aoun's durability and the unwanted Arab diplomatic intervention, dug in his heels, determined to repulse all challenges over Lebanon. He had thwarted Israel's ambitions in Lebanon and foiled the American intervention in 1983. Both had represented far graver challenges to Assad than Arab displeasure at Syria's behaviour in Lebanon. Aoun represented the last obstacle to Assad exerting full control over Lebanon, and it was unthinkable that at this late stage the Syrian leader would yield to the will of the Arabs, particularly to his arch-enemy Saddam Hussein of Iraq who was gleefully supplying Aoun and the Lebanese Forces with heavy weapons to use against the Syrians.

Assad's persistence paid off. The Arabs dropped a demand for a Syrian troop withdrawal from Lebanon and called instead for a ceasefire followed by a reconciliation conference in the Saudi Red Sea resort of Taif.

Hariri played an instrumental role in the logistics of the conference, arranging for the ageing members of the Lebanese parliament to be flown to Saudi Arabia while he shuttled back and forth to Damascus with Saudi foreign minister Prince Saud al-Faisal to relay developments to Assad. Of Lebanon's original 99 MPs elected in 1972, only 62 survived, 20 of them very old or sick. Corralled in a hotel in Taif, denied access to the media and with former prime minister Saeb Salam's warning that 'failure is not permissible' ringing in their ears, the parliamentarians spent an acrimonious month arguing over a charter for national reconciliation drawn up by Lakhdar Brahimi, the secretary-general of the Arab League, based largely on Hariri's Working Paper. After 22 days, they reached an agreement and the National Reconciliation Accord, known as the Taif Accord, was born. The Taif Accord was the most important political agreement since the National Pact of 1943 and would provide the constitutional foundation for post-war Lebanon. Among its provisions, the accord called for the phased abolition of political sectarianism, but set no deadlines, leaving its implementation open-ended. Indeed, the 1943 power-sharing agreement was implicitly enshrined by Taif through a more equitable distribution of parliamentary and cabinet seats where representation went from a 6 to 5 ratio in favour of the Christians to a 50:50 balance. Executive power was transferred from the presidency to the cabinet in an attempt to whittle away a key Maronite privilege. The increased powers of the Sunni premier and Shiite parliamentary speaker at the expense of the Maronite president effectively produced a troika system of rule comprising the three most powerful positions in the country.

Crucially, Syria's role in Lebanon was enshrined by the accord. It stated that Syrian forces would assist the Lebanese government in restoring sovereignty throughout the country. Two years after the ratification of the accord, Syrian troops would redeploy from the coastal littoral to the Bekaa. The timeframe and extent of further redeployments would be decided by a Lebanese and Syrian military committee. But the accord hinted at deeper ties between the two countries. The 'distinguished relations' between Lebanon and Syria and the 'roots of kinship, history and common fraternal interests' would be manifested in 'agreements . . . in various domains'.

Aoun rejected the Taif Accord, describing it as an 'unforgivable crime' for not defining a clear timetable for a Syrian troop withdrawal. But most Lebanese generally welcomed the agreement, seeing it as the most realistic means of ending the bloodshed. After 14 years of war, there was a recognition that Lebanon's woes could not be unpicked from the

Gordian knot of the Arab–Israeli conflict and inter-Arab relations and that temporary Syrian hegemony was an acceptable price for stability.

On November 5, Rene Mouawad, a veteran MP and former minister from the northern village of Zghorta, was elected president, ending a presidential vacuum of over a year. Hariri, who was angling for the premiership, gave Mouawad the use of his Oger building in west Beirut as a temporary presidential residence while Aoun clung to the shell-pocked Baabda palace. He also handed Mouawad an armour-plated Mercedes to travel the violent streets of Beirut. Abdel-Halim Khaddam, the then Syrian vice-president, recalls Hariri's name coming up for the first time in Damascus as a serious contender for the premiership.

'It was decided that it would be better to make him prime minister after legislative elections had been held in Lebanon,' Khaddam recalls.[41]

Mouawad told Hariri that his organisational talents were needed to run the Council for Development and Reconstruction which would play a pivotal role in the post-war redevelopment of Lebanon.

'Don't worry, Rafik, your time will come,' he reassured Hariri.

However, on November 22, Lebanese independence day, and just 17 days after being elected, Mouawad was killed in a bomb blast which struck his motorcade as it passed through the Sanayeh district of Beirut en route to his residence in the Oger building. Although Mouawad's security team had cleared all parked cars from the streets along the motorcade's route, the assassins had come up with an ingenious trick of planting the 350-kilogramme shaped-charge bomb in a small building separated from the street by a tall concrete wall. The killer triggered the blast by remote radio control from the roof of a building overlooking the street below. The shaped explosive charge concentrated the blast in a single direction, smashing through the wall and cutting Mouawad's armour-plated Mercedes in half, hurling the president's mutilated body 50 metres down the road. It was a chillingly proficient assassination and the latest to join a long list of unresolved political murders in Lebanon. Travelling in the lead vehicle, some 200 metres in front of the convoy, was a major in Syrian military intelligence called Jamaa Jamaa. As future deputy chief of Syrian intelligence in Lebanon, Jamaa's name would become linked to the equally professional and ruthless assassination of Rafik Hariri.

Mouawad's murder was a devastating blow to those in Lebanon and around the world who believed that the country was on the road to recovery.

'Whenever we take one step forward, we take five steps back,' said a despairing Arab League ambassador.

Elias Hrawi, an MP from the Bekaa town of Zahle, was elected president two days later and he re-appointed Salim Hoss as prime minister. Hrawi formally dissolved Aoun's government and ordered the maverick general to depart from Baabda palace. Aoun refused and a tense stand-off marked the following months. Ultimately, the event that precipitated Aoun's downfall did not occur in Lebanon but several thousand kilometres away in the Gulf where on August 2, 1990 Saddam Hussein launched his invasion of Kuwait.

For Assad, the timing of Iraq's invasion was fortuitous. The Iraqi invasion marked a juncture for the converging interests of the US and Syria. Assad understood that, with the decline of his Soviet backer, he would have to undertake a major strategic realignment involving cooperation with the United States. Following the election in 1988 of President George H.W. Bush, the cold, distrustful relations of the mid-1980s had improved, with Assad encouraged by Washington's support for the Taif Accord and opposition to Aoun's obstinate hold-out.

The Bush administration, on the other hand, had come to accept that Syrian involvement in Lebanon was unavoidable if the country was to achieve any long-term stability. Damascus remained key to securing the release of the American hostages held in Lebanon by Shiite groups. Furthermore, if Syrian support could be harnessed against Iraq, it would give added credibility to the international coalition being assembled against Saddam Hussein.

At the request of the US, Assad dispatched an initial 3,000 troops to Saudi Arabia and another 1,000 to the United Arab Emirates followed by a 9,000-strong mechanised division to the Gulf. The decision provoked some domestic opposition. Many Syrians sympathised with Iraq, particularly the tribal areas in the east whose territory spanned the border with Iraq and whose Sunni inhabitants shared the same roots. In the border town of Abu Kamal, midway along the remote 400-mile border, a mini insurrection broke out with residents chanting 'Long live Saddam Hussein. Long live Iraq.' Assad deployed an armoured division to crush the protests, and dozens were rumoured to have been killed and many more arrested. The hostility shown by the inhabitants of eastern Syria in 1991 toward foreign aggression against their Iraqi neighbours was a foretaste of what was to come when America launched its second war against Iraq 15 years later.

Assad was rewarded for his commitment to the coalition by tacit US approval for Syria and the Lebanese Army units loyal to Elias Hrawi to move against the Aoun enclave, expelling the general from Baabda and reuniting the two halves of Beirut.

What would be the last major battle of the war began at dawn on October 13 with an air raid by Syrian jets against Baabda palace and the nearby defence ministry in Yarze. Aoun, who a day earlier had pledged to fight to the death, fled from Baabda and sought refuge in the French embassy. To avoid further bloodshed, he contacted his commanders and told them to surrender to the Lebanese Army. But it was a grim and bloody conclusion to Aoun's adventure. Syrian troops committed a number of atrocities when they overran positions held by Aoun's soldiers, killing dozens, perhaps hundreds, of Aounist soldiers as well as civilians. Another 200 residents of the Aoun enclave simply disappeared. The bloody legacy of the war's denouement would fester over the next 15 years, an open wound for Christian opponents of Syrian tutelage.

Aoun remained in the French embassy for another 10 months before being granted asylum in France. But his expulsion from Baabda signalled the end of the war and the dawn of the Pax Syriana era in Lebanon.

It had been a long and bitter struggle, but it was a moment of triumph that perhaps Assad quietly savoured in the Rowda presidential palace in Damascus. Since his 1976 intercession in Lebanon, Assad had faced numerous challenges to his usurpation of Lebanon but had repulsed them all through a combination of perseverance, guile, determination and luck. The decisive routing of Aoun and the establishment of a compliant regime in Lebanon under President Elias Hrawi cowed any prospect of further serious domestic challenges to Syrian rule in Lebanon. Israel's position in Lebanon was at its weakest since 1978, its army of occupation in the south caught in a small but vicious guerrilla war against the Lebanese resistance. Furthermore, Assad's control of Lebanon was tacitly accepted by Washington, a reward for Assad's decision to join the US-led coalition against Iraq's invasion of Kuwait.

As for Hariri, he had emerged from the war as a major new political force, a powerful Sunni baron whose wealth and enviable array of international contacts, especially in Damascus, meant that it was only a matter of time before his ambition to be prime minister would be realised.

Pax Syriana

After 16 years of war, the once bustling centre of Beirut was reduced to a wasteland of shell-scarred ruins and overgrown streets inhabited by families of destitute squatters and packs of prowling wild dogs. It was a sobering experience to wander through the near-deserted streets of post-war downtown Beirut, split by the infamous Green Line, the front separating the eastern and western halves of the city. Countless bullet holes pitted the sandstone façades of Ottoman-era houses lining streets named after First World War generals such as Foch, Weygand and Allenby, evocative of a bygone era of imperial attention. The gaunt, pock-marked skeletons of these once-graceful buildings looked as though they were suffering from some vile stone-eating leprosy, a terrible contagion that had swept through the entire district, leaving barely a single building untouched. The once sharply defined edges of doorways and window openings, favoured vantage points for gunmen, were ground away and smoothed by years of unrelenting firepower.

Interior walls were daubed with graffiti drawn by bored militiamen, crude childlike depictions of battles with tanks and aeroplanes with party flags prominently displayed. Sandbags, rock hard with age, still filled windows that faced now-dormant enemy lines. The streets had turned into tangled thickets of small trees and bushes. Pools of stagnant sewage nourished clouds of fat mosquitoes and patches of sickly green grass. Piles of bulldozed rubble lined some of the main roads leading to Martyrs' Square, the focal point of the downtown district. Here, idle Syrian soldiers sat in the shade, smoking cigarettes and chatting, their rifles hanging limply from their hands. Tired old men sold tiny plastic cups of Turkish coffee from tall brass pots or plastic thermos flasks. Barefoot urchins peddled postcards depicting a pre-war Martyrs' Square of palm trees, tramcars and crowded roadside cafés.

Although the devastation wrought on central Beirut was the most tangible consequence of the Lebanese war, it paled in comparison to the human cost exacted by 16 years of fighting. Some 144,000 people died from 1975 and more than 184,000 were wounded, including 13,000 who were permanently handicapped, staggering statistics for a country of only about 3.5 million in 1990. Around 90,000 families were displaced from their homes and at least another 17,000 people simply vanished. Over 45,000 homes were either partially or wholly destroyed and 71 towns and villages were left in ruins.[1] Some 800,000 Lebanese were estimated to have emigrated between 1975 and 1990, mainly the middle classes who could afford to leave and establish new lives for themselves in the West.

The electricity, telephone and water networks were severely damaged by war, lack of repairs and outmoded technology. One-third of the electricity generating capacity was not working, explaining the daily roar of portable generators in the streets of Beirut. With half the telephone network out of order, making a call was an exercise in frustration. Eighty per cent of the water table was polluted and half the hotels were not operational.[2] The United Nations estimated that Lebanon had suffered $18 billion in damage and would require $5 billion just to repair the infrastructure.

With the end of the war in October 1990, Hariri focused his initial efforts on planning the reconstruction of central Beirut which he argued could best be achieved through the establishment of a joint venture company of landowners and investors. The company would become the Lebanese Company for Development and Reconstruction, better known by its French acronym Solidere. Rebuilding Beirut would be the fulfilment of a vision he had nurtured for over a decade as manifested by the scale model of the city centre that he liked to keep nearby.

'He was dreaming of Solidere since 1982. This was his real dream,' says Nohad Mashnouq, a close former advisor to Hariri who helped market the scheme to sceptical politicians in 1991.[3]

Although Hariri was impatient to begin, progress was hampered by political infighting and squabbling in the government of Omar Karami, the colourless younger brother of Rashid Karami, a former prime minister who was assassinated in 1987. In early 1992, the Lebanese pound tumbled from LP879 to the dollar to LP2,000 within two months, exacerbating what was already the worst socio-economic crisis since independence. Karami resigned in May when riots broke out in Beirut with rampaging mobs blocking streets with burning tyres.

Damascus had paid little attention initially to Lebanon's economy, leaving general economic and fiscal policy to Karami's government while it concentrated on consolidating Syrian-imposed security around the country. But the poor performance of the Karami government and the ease with which angry Lebanese had taken to the streets of Beirut served as a warning to the Syrians that their control over Lebanon was not as secure as they had believed.

'The Syrians realised that it was not enough to control the political situation. They had to control the economy as well and Rafik Hariri was the only man who could do that,' says Fares Boueiz, who served as foreign minister from 1990 to 1998.[4]

With his Saudi connections and high profile as a major financier of the budding reconstruction programme, Hariri was regarded by many as the only realistic candidate for the premiership. Although he had some powerful allies in Damascus in Abdel-Halim Khaddam, the vice-president, and Hikmat Shehabi, the Syrian Army chief of staff, other members of the Syrian regime regarded Hariri's ties to the West and Saudi Arabia as threats rather than assets. Furthermore, Hariri had to contend with his family, which had serious misgivings about his political ambitions.

'The whole family was totally against politics,' recalls Saad Hariri, Rafik's second son.[5] 'In 1992, when he was trying to take over the premiership, we all tried to convince him not to, but when he decided to take it on we all supported him.'

And why was the family against his move into mainstream politics?

'Look what happened,' Saad says with a grim smile. 'We always felt there was a danger toward him. In that part of the world, politics is not something not to be scared of.'

Hariri would have to wait a few more months, however, as Assad decided to appoint Rashid Solh, a veteran Lebanese politician, as an interim prime minister to oversee the parliamentary elections in summer 1992, the first in 20 years.

The polls were a pathetic affair of last-minute Syrian-brokered alliances and electoral districts gerrymandered to benefit Syria's allies, contradicting aspects of the Taif Accord but establishing a pattern that would continue through the next two elections. The Christians boycotted the elections to protest against Syrian interference; voter turnout was only 30 per cent, the lowest figure since independence. The Syrians wanted an obedient parliament in place before September when the deadline fell for the first phase of the Syrian troop redeployment in line with the Taif Accord. Assad had no intention of staging the redeployment, but he required a pliant parliament in Beirut to stifle any opposition and to protect future Syrian interests. Although the elections reinforced Syria's political grip on Lebanon, another inept economic performance from a

Lebanese government would risk undermining Syria's hegemony and that was something Assad could not afford. Assad was confident and experienced enough to recognize that Hariri was a useful asset for Damascus who could easily be controlled. Hariri would be given wide latitude to pursue his economic policies while security affairs would remain the prerogative of the Syrian and Lebanese intelligence and military.

After months of economic decline, political uncertainty and a series of lacklustre premiers, the Lebanese were electrified at this larger-than-life billionaire businessman and confidant of the Saudi royal family becoming prime minister. Within 24 hours of his appointment in October 1992, the pound rallied from LP2,205 to the dollar to LP2,000.

When Hariri took office, a reporter is said to have asked him if he was not too big for a tiny country like Lebanon.

'So what do we do?' Hariri replied. 'Do we make Hariri smaller or Lebanon bigger?'

Given the level of nationwide destruction, Hariri believed that, if his vision of a revived and prosperous Lebanon was to take shape, he would need a liberal hand in implementing policy. Indeed, the trademark of the Hariri era was the domineering manner in which he ran the country as if it was an extension of his personal business empire. He filled his first cabinet with protégés and former employees, prompting one minister to jokingly dub the government the 'Hariri corporation'. But surrounding himself with people he trusted was his management style – 'the Hariri system' as he had once told Elie Salem.

Other than appointing people close to him to key positions, Hariri sought to circumvent the bureaucratic inertia and inefficiency of some ministries and state institutions by developing a shadow administration of private companies and government agencies closely linked to the premier charged with revitalising the economy and spearheading the reconstruction programme. They included the Council for Development and Reconstruction, which, although created in 1977 to handle national redevelopment, was granted sweeping additional powers in 1992. It became in effect a super ministry, reporting to the prime minister and directing almost every facet of the $18 billion reconstruction programme.

However, the jewel in Hariri's reconstruction crown was Solidere, the property company established to tackle the daunting task of redeveloping the war-shattered central district of Beirut.

Hariri hoped that rebuilding the city centre would be the first crucial step in restoring Beirut's pre-war reputation as the financial and services entrepôt of the Middle East. Solidere's mandate extended over 1.2 million square metres of prime downtown real estate. A further 608,000 square metres were to be reclaimed from the sea to provide open spaces, offices and marinas.

To counter the potentially intractable problems of having one company renovate properties owned by hundreds of different people and institutions, Solidere came up with an innovative plan to involve owners in the project by offering them shares in the company matching the value of their respective properties. A heavily oversubscribed share offering in early 1994 raised $650 million of which Hariri bought $125 million, becoming Solidere's largest shareholder with a 6.5 per cent stake in the company. While Hariri's supporters argued that the prime minister was putting his money where his mouth was, Solidere's many critics complained of a serious conflict of interest. That criticism was compounded by accusations from property owners, including many of Beirut's leading Sunni families, that Solidere had deliberately undervalued their properties. Furthermore, traditionalists bemoaned what they considered the excessive destruction of restorable buildings of historical value. Only 277 original buildings were to be saved. The rest were to be torn down and bulldozed into the sea to form part of the Normandy landfill site. However, Solidere renovated and preserved three districts with aesthetically pleasing if somewhat insipid results. The messy, noisy melting pot that was the old centre of Beirut had disappeared for ever, replaced by isolated pockets of a sterile urban ideal of cobble-stoned streets, art galleries and boutiques where only the wealthy could afford to live and shop, separated by wide patches of barren dusty ground awaiting development.

As the bulldozers removed the ruined vestiges of the twentieth-century city, a much older version of Beirut was gradually revealed. Beneath the billowing clouds of dust and incessant roar of machinery, in pits a few feet deep, teams of archaeologists could be found absorbed in a tiny patch of earth, examining, measuring, scraping, brushing and collecting fragments of Beirut's rich and varied history. The excavations revealed an archaeological goldmine – Hellenistic mosaics, Roman roads, a Roman necropolis, Phoenician burial chambers, part of the original Canaanite city wall, the foundations of a Crusader castle and medieval water and sewage pipes.

However, what should have been embraced as a nationally enriching bonus of the downtown reconstruction project instead turned into a raging controversy, pitting the passion of archaeologists against the mercantile interests of Solidere.

In the mid-1990s, Lebanese newspapers catalogued the apparently wilful destruction by Solidere's bulldozers of dozens of artefacts and even entire sites under excavation, often under the cover of darkness when the archaeologists had gone home. 'A massacre of heritage,' opined Albert Naccache, a Lebanese archaeologist and historian, an accusation echoed by several international experts. For many Lebanese, Solidere's cavalier attitude toward the country's historical legacy was emblematic of the perceived rapacity and fast-buck mentality of the Hariri government.

The apparent disregard for Beirut's pre-Islamic past merely buttressed a belief among some Christians that having a powerful Sunni helm the reconstruction process was resulting in a creeping Islamisation of the city centre, an accusation that would dog Hariri until the end of his life. Lebanon's Phoenician heritage became politicised in the early twentieth century when it was adopted by some Christian thinkers to support the argument that Lebanon was culturally separate from the broader Arab and Muslim world. 'Phoenicianism' was disputed by sceptical Muslim historians who maintained that the seafaring race which inhabited the Levantine coast 4,000 years ago had long since been assimilated into the Arab world.

The accusations that the Hariri government was pushing an Islamisation policy were probably an exaggeration; Hariri described such charges as a 'calumny'. Solidere's blundering manner in regard to the archaeological finds was driven by the profit motive, not an Islamo-ideological desire to spite Christians.

Still, Hariri was an observant Muslim and took his religious duties seriously; he financed the building of several mosques, including the massive Mohammed al-Amine mosque on the edge of Beirut's Martyrs' Square which was just nearing completion when he died. An ostentatiously grandiose sandstone building with minarets tipped in gold and a vast sky-blue dome, the mosque dwarfed the nearby Maronite cathedral of St George's as well as the restored Emir Mansour Assaf mosque. One observer noted, shortly before Hariri's death, that the imposing mosque had 'set back sectarian relations by ten years'. An overstatement, perhaps, but such hyperbole was reflective of the lingering suspicions of some Christians toward Hariri's religious motivations.

Yet Hariri had a keen sensitivity toward Christian fears of being subsumed into a predominantly Islamic society, and was a strong advocate of Lebanon's confessional model. In an interview with the author in 1996, he stated that, given Lebanon's sectarian nature, confessionalism had to remain in place for the foreseeable future.

'I am not for the cancellation of confessionalism unless the Christians ask for it,' he said. 'I don't mean just 51 per cent of them; I mean 75 or 80 per cent. Otherwise, I think it's better to keep it going the way it is.'

Indeed, the charge that Hariri was Islamising Lebanon spoke more of Christian discontent with the post-Taif order, where for the first time since independence a powerful Sunni prime minister was helming the country rather than a Maronite president. Even though the Taif Accord instituted a ruling 'troika' system between the president, prime minister and parliamentary speaker, no one was in any doubt that Hariri was the first among equals. And that inevitably ruffled feathers. Other than Christian concerns at the diminished role of the presidency and hostility toward Pax Syriana, the traditional Sunni elite, the powerful families of Beirut, Sidon and Tripoli, resented the intrusion of this immensely wealthy Saudi-backed newcomer. And the Shiites considered Hariri the vanguard of a strengthened Saudi role in Lebanon, with the vast riches and influence of the kingdom's Wahhabi rulers counterbalancing the demographic advantage of the Lebanese Shiites and their growing political mobilisation.

Yet many Lebanese politicians found themselves torn between opposing Hariri's policies and taking advantage of an alliance with the influential premier.

The 'Hariri experience', wrote Samir Atallah, a columnist with the London-based *Ash-Sharq al-Awsat* in May 1994, is 'unprecedented in Lebanon'.

'This is . . . the first time since independence that everything – from the state of the local currency, to the economy in general, reconstruction, the standard of living, electricity, water and telephones – is linked to the prime ministry, which in turn is linked to Rafik Hariri.'

Between 1992 and 1996, Hariri used his influence to build his own network of loyalists, a new cross-confessional political elite on whom he could count for support to push through his economic and reconstruction programmes. He also expanded his media interests, purchasing shares in Lebanese newspapers, launching Future Television in 1993 and *Al-Mustaqbal* daily in 1998.

Yet even those who derided Hariri's 'bulldozer' tactics could not ignore the fact that the country was making some rapid strides in the early 1990s. Between 1993 and 1995, the GDP growth rate was averaging 8 per cent. The soaring inflation of early 1992 had been brought to heel and the pound was successfully stabilized, appreciating from LP2,000 to LP1,500 to the dollar by the end of the decade.

Hariri used his international connections to attract a raft of grants and soft loans from Arab and international lending agencies. He released high-interest treasury bills and Lebanon's first ever Eurobond issues to stabilise the Lebanese pound and swell the state's coffers. Further revenues came from the Lebanese Diaspora which was estimated to hold between $30 billion and $40 billion. By the mid-1990s, around $1 billion to $1.5 billion per quarter were being repatriated by overseas Lebanese.

Hariri was determined to restore Beirut as the financial and services entrepôt of the Middle East, a crown that had been snatched by the Gulf emirate of Dubai during Lebanon's war years. Beirut once more would become the bridge between East and West, a cosmopolitan hub where wealthy Arabs could escape the heat of the Gulf for the mild temperatures of Lebanon, to conduct business, shop in gleaming malls and holiday in the city's five-star hotels and the resorts scattered along Lebanon's coast and mountains. However, the success of the reconstruction process hinged on one big gamble. Hariri was banking on the Middle East peace process, which began in Madrid in 1991, being concluded by 1996. Lebanon would then be well placed to reap the dividend of a regional peace, allowing the country to repay the enormous debt accumulated through the massive spending spree Hariri oversaw in the early 1990s.

The government's ten-year reconstruction plan, known as Horizon 2000, led to contracts to rehabilitate the telephone network and provide one million new lines, an overhaul of the electricity system and the construction of new power plants, the building of a brand new $486 million airport, the expansion of the coastal roads and the construction of a new Beirut–Damascus highway that would eventually connect the capital with Baghdad. Hariri regularly worked 18 hours a day, beginning at 7.30 a.m. with his closest advisors meeting him, often in his bedroom at Koreitem, to discuss the progress of various projects.

'There would always be a group of us gathered at Koreitem to see him, but he would pick anyone with a map or blueprints or plans of one sort or another to see first. He would close the door and talk for two to three hours. He loved projects,' says Fadi Fawaz, who was one of Hariri's leading development coordinators.[6]

Hariri's tireless energy impressed even his harshest critics.

'He was an exemplary government person in the first degree,' recalls Mohammed Raad, who headed Hizbullah's 'Loyalty to the Resistance' parliamentary bloc, which was a staunch opponent of the premier's economic and social policies.[7] 'We never before found anyone working in the government 18 hours a day. He used to follow all the files, including all the details. There were continuous ideas coming from him. His brain was working continuously. Sometimes, when you talk to someone you get the impression they are not listening. But Hariri was listening all the time.'

But reconstruction came at a price. The internal public debt rose dramatically from $1.5 billion when Hariri became prime minister in 1992 to a staggering $18 billion by the time he left office in 1998. The policy of high interest rates to protect the Lebanese pound was a massive drain on the public purse. The standard of living steadily declined for the majority of Lebanese as the gap between rich and poor widened. Antoine Haddad, a Lebanese researcher, calculated that, according to 1995 figures, 28 per cent of Lebanese, about one million people, lived below the absolute poverty line, measured at $618 per month for a family of five. Of this figure, some 250,000 lived in extreme poverty – $306 a month for a family of five. These bottom-rung families often lived in unsanitary, slum-like conditions in decaying apartment blocks, the rattle of neighbourhood generators compensating for the intermittent electricity supply. Families would pool earnings to buy basic staples such as bread, tea and vegetables.

An average wage for basic white-collar work, such as secretarial or teaching, was between $300 and $500 a month, forcing many people to take on a second job to make a reasonable living. Despite the appreciation of the Lebanese pound, the purchasing power of salary earners dropped by 10 to 15 per cent due to inflation and the exorbitant prices of consumer goods.

The anticipated return of the war emigrants failed to materialise. Instead, another estimated 200,000 Lebanese left the country between 1991 and the end of the decade, most of them university graduates and skilled workers. A graduate engineer or doctor could find a job in Europe or the United States which would pay four or five times what he could receive in Lebanon. Lebanon's rural poor also left the country seeking better opportunities elsewhere, heading for Africa, the Gulf and if they could Europe, the US and Australia.

Rising public discontent peaked in July 1995 when the government announced a 38 per cent increase in petrol prices, prompting a call for a general strike by the country's largest trade union. It was the first serious internal disturbance since the riots which had brought down the Karami government in 1992. With Syrian backing, Hariri ordered a last-minute curfew, the first in 12 years, and authorised the army commander, General Emile Lahoud, to handle public security for the next three months, a move described by the Lebanese media as a 'partial declaration of martial law'.

Although such uncompromising tactics stifled public unrest, the greatest obstacle Hariri faced in pursuing his reconstruction and economic agenda was the opposition from within his own cabinet as well as from his fellow troika colleagues. Within two months of his assuming office, Hariri was embroiled in disputes with Nabih Berri and Elias Hrawi over civil service appointments, with each of them attempting to promote his own allies to key posts. Hariri sought to have the government granted special powers to rule by decree, a move which would have smoothed the passage of his reconstruction policies but at the expense of parliamentary endorsement. To Hariri's intense irritation, Berri rejected the proposal, ensuring that as parliamentary speaker he would have a prominent say in how reconstruction funds were disbursed.

The lack of cooperation from his cabinet colleagues was a continual source of frustration. Driven by his vision of an energised and economically vibrant Lebanon, Hariri could not comprehend why some of his ministers insisted on acting like an opposition rather than members of a cohesive cabinet.

'Rafik was like a bulldozer, a workaholic who never slept,' recalls Mikhael Daher, minister of education and youth in Hariri's first government.[8] 'But he didn't have that governing touch at first. He thought government was like a business where he could push a button and things would happen. But governing is not like that. He didn't realise that being in government means having to compromise.'

He was constantly at loggerheads with his headstrong foreign minister, Fares Boueiz, who was also Hrawi's son-in-law. Hariri saw himself as a de facto foreign minister because of his international influence and contacts.

On one occasion following an Israeli attack against south Lebanon, Boueiz instructed the Lebanese ambassador at the United Nations to lodge a complaint against Israel. The US ambassador in Beirut contacted Boueiz and asked him to withdraw the complaint as it would only 'contribute to the crisis'. Boueiz refused.

That evening, Boueiz heard on the radio that the complaint had been withdrawn. The furious foreign minister called his ambassador in New York and asked what had happened. The ambassador said that Hariri had told him to withdraw the complaint and assumed that Boueiz had been informed. Boueiz instructed the hapless ambassador to return to Beirut to face disciplinary proceedings. Hariri called Boueiz to confirm that the ambassador had been following his orders and that it was not his fault. But Boueiz was undeterred and said he would make an example of the ambassador to publicise the fact that Hariri had overstepped his authority.

'Our relationship from 1992 to 1998 was not good,' Boueiz recalls.[9] 'He was an inexperienced politician. He had no idea about laws and the mechanism of state. He was trying to rule like in Saudi Arabia where the king orders what he wants.'

In May 1994, a spat over a cabinet reshuffle prompted Hariri to go on strike for a week, shutting himself up in his palatial residence in Koreitem and saying he was prepared to resign 'because I miss my children', while his critics accused him of 'sulking' and of being an 'amateur' in politics.

The Lebanese regarded the bickering and unseemly haggling with disgust, even more so when the troika routinely trod the path to Damascus like petulant children to be scolded, have their wrists slapped and be told to behave by the Syrian parent. After one such spat, Abdel-Halim Khaddam told Lebanese officials that Hariri was 'here to stay until 2010', adding that 'We in Syria have had no change [of leadership] since 1970. Continuity leads to stability.'

Saad Hariri recalls his father grumbling one day about his political difficulties in the presence of his friend and justice minister Bahij Tabbara and several other ministers.

'Then Bahij Tabbara told him, "You are the leader of the country. You cannot be depressed. You cannot show people that you are upset." And I think something clicked with him at that moment and he realised that he would have to keep going, and he did.'[10]

Hariri received his long-awaited permission to form a new, more cohesive government in May 1995. The trigger for the government change was yet another dispute with Berri, this time over Hariri's desire to extend Hrawi's presidential mandate for an additional three years. Granting Hrawi an additional term in office would require the amendment of Article 49 of the constitution which decrees that Lebanese presidents can serve only one six-year term. Hariri was pressing for a swift parliamentary vote to amend Article 49. The stated reason at the time for Hariri's support for an additional term for Hrawi was that uncertainty and tensions surrounding a new presidential election could hamper the reconstruction programme. However, the main reason why Hariri was so adamant that Hrawi should remain in office was to prevent General Emile Lahoud, the Lebanese Army commander, becoming the next head of state.

The relationship between Hariri and Lahoud was mired in mutual distrust. Hariri regarded the army commander as a symbol of the rigid security and military ties that bound Lebanon to Syria, the police state mentality being the antithesis of the open, free market enterprise economy that the prime minister was attempting to kindle in Lebanon. Since being appointed army commander in November 1989, and with the backing of the Syrians, Lahoud had assumed control over military affairs and, with Syrian backing, regarded himself as unaccountable to the government.

'The Syrians established a division of labour in Lebanon,' says Walid Jumblatt.[11] 'The army is [their] responsibility. Hariri is the money man. Hrawi is president under [their] orders. The army was a separate institution directly linked to Syrian orders and covered by Lahoud. From that time on, the Syrian infiltration into the army was quite heavy and substantial [as] they built the Lebanese Army their own way.'

The strength of the Lebanese Army was augmented from 20,000 in 1990 to 60,000 by the middle of the decade, drawn mainly from the pool of demobilised militiamen as well as conscripts obliged to serve one-year mandatory national service. The number of Lebanese officers attending military courses in the US and France gradually declined in favour of instruction in Syria, where they were trained on obsolete Soviet equipment. Soldiers attending these courses, even senior officers, were inculcated with stultifying Baathist-style propaganda, extolling the 'brotherly' and strategic relations between the two countries. Senior Lebanese Army officers attending the National Defence College in Damascus found themselves suffering the embarrassment of joining their Syrian counterparts each morning with chants of 'Yaeesh rais Assad. Yaeesh al-Baath' (Long live President Assad. Long live the Baath).[12]

A small handful of army officers opposed the Syrianisation of the Lebanese Army, but they soon found themselves isolated, shunned by fearful friends, their phones and movements monitored, until they resigned or were forced to take early retirement.

The majority of serving soldiers resigned themselves to the new situation, relying on the monthly salary and extensive perks afforded to the military to raise their families and educate their children. Indeed, spending on defence represented the largest slice of the government's annual budget. In 1992, the defence budget was $271 million but by 2001 it had soared to $900 million, which along with another $433 million for the other state security organs represented about 25 per cent of government expenditure that year. The bulk of the defence budget was spent on salaries and benefits for a bloated officer corps, such as vehicles for personal use, unlimited free petrol and free accommodation in one of the army's housing compounds with all bills paid by the government, including land-line and mobile phone charges. Even the children of officers received free education from primary school to university.

The army command was granted a budget for allowances, '*mukhassassat*', which was supposed to be for entertaining, but served as a slush fund. According to a former Lebanese intelligence officer, every year on the anniversary of the Baath party revolution in Syria, as much as

$6 million was distributed from this fund as gifts to Syrian Army officers in Lebanon.[13]

The swollen defence budget was a source of constant frustration for Hariri and his finance minister Fouad Siniora, whose efforts to reduce the figure were stiffly resisted by the army. In September 1994, the army put in a demand with the finance ministry for a fleet of Ford Cherokee four-wheel-drive cars for the use of officers. Siniora was obliged to carry out the transaction but baulked at the army's demand for next year's model.

'They wanted the 1995 model,' Siniora recalls.[14] 'I negotiated a deal with the agent to get them the 1994 model, brand new, but with savings of $5,000 or so on each car. They told me the general [Lahoud] insists on the 1995 model.'

Siniora told two assistants to Lahoud that the army's 'spendthrift' attitude was unacceptable and that he refused to purchase the more expensive 1995 vehicle. He then left his office to give a lecture outside Beirut. He returned to the ministry later that day to find the building stormed by military intelligence officers and surrounded by troops. Hariri was subsequently told by Michel Rahbani, the head of Lebanese military intelligence, and his powerful deputy, Jamil Sayyed, that the incident had been a 'calculated mistake'.

'This [behaviour] was the beginning of a *coup d'état*,' Siniora says. 'That incident was the beginning of the change toward a police state and marked the end of the civilian regime.'

Lahoud considered Hariri politically unreliable and treated the government as little more than a 'municipal council', in the words of a serving minister at the time. It was obvious in political circles that Lahoud was being groomed to assume the presidency. His chief advocate in Syria was Bashar al-Assad, the second son of the Syrian president.

Bashar had been forced to abandon a career in medicine which he was studying for in London when his elder brother Basil and heir apparent to the Syrian presidency was killed in a car crash in 1994. Assad had been grooming Basil for the presidency since the mid-1980s. Now he had to start all over again with Bashar, and he had to work with less promising material. A tall, slim, unassuming man, Bashar lacked his elder brother's steely edge. Where Basil had excelled at sports and was a noted equestrian, Bashar preferred reading, took an interest in computers and information technology and shunned the limelight. Bashar's first public appearance was in the summer of 1994 to inaugurate the first Damascus international conference on information technology organised by the Syrian Information Technology Association which was founded by Basil.

On being recalled to Syria, Bashar was enrolled at the military academy in Homs in the first stage of a crash course to mould him from a shy, 28-year-old ophthalmology student into the leader of 17 million people. Hariri's renewed resignation threat in May 1995 was the first time that Bashar interceded publicly in Lebanese affairs, usually the fiefdom of Abdel-Halim Khaddam, the vice-president.

Hrawi's term was due to expire on November 24 and, as the date drew closer, there was feverish speculation in Lebanon on whether he would serve another two or three years.

In early October, Brigadier General Ghazi Kanaan, the head of Syrian military intelligence in Lebanon, told a gathering of Lebanese politicians attending a party hosted by former premier Omar Karami that Hrawi's term would be extended for a further three years after all. Furthermore, the amendment by parliament of Article 49 would be carried out by a show of hands, not by the customary secret ballot. The London-based *Al-Hayat* newspaper reported that the assembled party goers 'looked as if they had been through a cold shower ... The party broke up early. Presidential hopefuls departed with their wives, one complaining of tiredness, another saying he had a headache.'

The widely publicised incident was later regarded as a trial balloon to gauge the reaction of the United States to extending Hrawi's mandate. The silence of Washington reassured Damascus that Hrawi could be retained for another three years without political cost. The speculation ended on October 11 when Assad in an interview with the Egyptian daily *Al-Ahram* casually declared that 'in general everybody [in the Lebanese leadership] was with the extension'. Assad had made his decision, and the next day 22 MPs filed up to Baabda palace to congratulate Hrawi on winning his extension. Eight days later, 110 of Lebanon's 128 MPs dutifully voted to amend the constitution, with 11 voting against and seven staying away from the session.

Assad was unconvinced that the time was right to allow the Lebanese Army commander to move into Baabda palace. Syria was engaged in hesitant and delicate negotiations with Israel over the return of the Golan Heights captured by the Jewish state in 1967. Assad required continued stability and calm on his western flank while the peace talks lasted. Hrawi had proven a willing and pliable ally since 1989 and had helped ensure that Lebanon's transition from a state of chaos and war to a vassal of Syria had proceeded relatively smoothly.

But most of all, Hrawi's presidential extension was a victory for Hariri and others who shared his distaste for Lahoud, among them Walid Jumblatt. But Hariri was made to pay the price the following year when his government was replaced with a less unified cabinet stuffed with Syrian allies, such as Suleiman Frangieh, grandson of the former president, and Talal Arslan, scion of a leading Druze family and fierce rival of Jumblatt, both of whom were close friends of the late Basil al-Assad and of Bashar.

Hrawi was not alone in having his mandate extended. Lahoud, who was facing obligatory retirement in 1996, was granted an extra two years as army commander, conveniently ensuring that he would leave the military in 1998 at the same time as Hrawi left Baabda palace.

Nohad Mashnouq, a former advisor to Hariri in the 1990s, recalls meeting Lahoud several times during the presidential extension debate at the general's residence at the seafront Bain Militaire army club in west Beirut.

'Lahoud was sure he would be president. It was a real fight,' he says.[15]

But not everyone in Damascus was enthusiastic about Lahoud. Two of the most powerful Sunnis in the regime, Abdel-Halim Khaddam and Hikmat Shehabi, the Syrian Army chief of staff, shared Hariri's reservations over the army commander, arguing that the Lebanese would never accept being ruled by a military man. Although an Alawite, Ghazi Kanaan endorsed the misgivings of his Sunni contemporaries in the regime, recognising Lahoud as a future problem for Syrian relations with Lebanon. According to Walid Jumblatt, Kanaan had opposed Hrawi's extra three-year term, not because he wanted to see the Lebanese Army commander installed in Baabda, but because it set a precedent that could see Lahoud one day granted a presidential extension.

Instead, it was the younger Alawite component of the Syrian regime that tended to favour Lahoud. This group allegedly was centred around Basil al-Assad before his death and included his siblings, Bashar, Maher and Bushra, the headstrong daughter and Assad's eldest and favourite child. Also part of the group was Assef Shawkat, an ambitious military intelligence officer who used his charm and good looks to court and then marry Bushra al-Assad, overcoming the initial objections of the Assad family. Others included Mohammed Nassif, a senior intelligence officer, known affectionately as 'uncle' by the Assad children, and the powerful Makhlouf family headed by Adnan Makhlouf, the then head of the Syrian Republican Guard and brother of Anissa Assad, the president's wife. Adnan Makhlouf's son, Rami, a cousin of the Assad children, would become the most powerful businessman in Syria. Then there were members of the Shaleesh family, related to the Assads, who would later be accused of earning millions of dollars in weapons and oil smuggling to and from Iraq respectively. In 2004, the name of Zualhema Shaleesh, a general in the Republican Guard, would be linked to the rumoured transfer of Iraqi weapons of mass destruction to Syria prior to the US-led invasion of Iraq in 2003.

This powerful Alawite faction saw in Lahoud a figure who could puncture Hariri's aura of Sunni omnipotence, which they regarded as a threatening trait given the Alawites' minority status in Sunni-dominated Syria. Some had argued against granting Hariri the premiership in 1992, accusing him of having deliberately engineered the economic crisis that precipitated the downfall of Omar Karami's government by purchasing dollars in large quantities to lower the value of the Lebanese pound.

The tussle over Hrawi's presidential extension exposed an emerging generational and confessional faultline within the regime, pitting the younger, mainly Alawite, generation against the older, mainly Sunni, contemporaries of Assad. The latter clique comprised Khaddam, Hikmat Shehabi, Ghazi Kanaan, Walid Jumblatt and Rafik Hariri, whose wealth was the glue that bound the group together. Some of the older generation regarded Assad's unspoken agenda of instituting a hereditary republic as an affront not only to their own political ambitions but also to the Baath party's socialist ideology. Abdel-Halim Khaddam recalls that Assad first considered bequeathing the presidency to a member of his family in 1980, his choice then being his younger brother, Rifaat.

'I had a discussion with President Assad for two hours on this matter,' Khaddam says.[16] 'I advised him against it and he was convinced.'

But the idea resurfaced in 1983 after Assad was recovering from nervous exhaustion, which almost cost him not only his life but the presidency when his brother Rifaat took advantage of Assad's ill health to mount an unsuccessful coup. Basil al-Assad began taking on an increased role in the regime, nominating some ministers and senior civil service positions to the irritation of the Baath party politburo. Assad never discussed with his top lieutenants his intention to pass on the presidency, keeping up a pretence until his death in 2000 of a presidential succession based on the Syrian constitution. Khaddam and others had little choice but to grit their teeth and play along.

'After [Assad's] illness [in 1983] this matter was too sensitive to be discussed,' Khaddam says.[17] 'His love for the family was even stronger than his duty as president. The decision was very wrong. This decision was in total contradiction to all laws and regulations in Syria. In the late 1990s, when he was becoming more and more sick, this sentiment grew stronger and stronger.'

The succession issue and its implications in terms of who controlled the levers of power and money in Syria underpinned the schism between the older 'Sunni' faction and its younger 'Alawite' rival, a split that would continue to fester during the 1990s as the latter assumed more authority, eventually threatening the stability of the regime itself.

Hariri was initially reluctant to deal with the sons of Assad, believing, somewhat naively, that maintaining good ties with the Syrian president was sufficient for his needs. He only met Basil al-Assad once, when promoting the Solidere project in Damascus. According to former Hariri aide Nohad Mashnouq, it was an uncomfortable encounter. Hariri dressed in casual clothes for his meeting against Mashnouq's advice, and Basil made plain his opposition to the Solidere scheme. Hariri then went over Basil's head and secured Assad's support for the project.

'The chemistry didn't work between Hariri and this young group. He was too powerful for them. He felt that he was dealing with people the age of his sons,' Mashnouq recalls.[18] The younger Syrian generation, he adds, 'hated Khaddam and Shehabi, which affected Hariri himself. They hated all this old group. They wanted to handle everything themselves. That's why after 2000 [when Bashar became president] the doors to Damascus were closed to Hariri.'

The depth of hostility among the Alawites for Hariri and the older Sunni leaders in Damascus was made clear to Fares Boueiz, the foreign minister, during an incident at the Islamic Conference in Tehran in December 1997. Boueiz's relationship with his prime minister was going through one of its periodic low points because of what he considered unwarranted meddling by Hariri in foreign affairs.[19] Boueiz was in Tehran with Hariri and Hrawi. Assad and a large delegation of military officials were also attending. As Boueiz walked down a corridor past the large salons where delegations were gathered, he heard a voice call behind him, 'You hero! You are the man of courage!' He turned to see Adnan Makhlouf, the head of Syria's Republican Guard, striding towards him, his arms outstretched. Makhlouf grabbed the startled Boueiz, kissed him on both cheeks and congratulated him for standing up to Hariri.

'That son of a bitch is buying up the regime around me,' Makhlouf grumbled, referring to Hariri. 'He's bought Khaddam, Shehabi and his dog Ghazi Kanaan.'

Boueiz, stunned by the outburst from the Syrian general, mumbled that his problems with Hariri were different and walked away.

'These men Makhlouf was talking about were just 50 metres away in the next room. It told me how much the Alawites really hated them,' Boueiz says.

Following the extension of Elias Hrawi's mandate, Raymond Edde, a Lebanese Christian leader living in exile in Paris, succinctly summed up the view of most Lebanese, commenting that 'Lebanon has become a Syrian colony in reality'. Indeed, Assad had voiced Syria's covetous attitude toward its neighbour in a 1976 speech, shortly after his 30,000-strong army had crossed the border into Lebanon for the first time. He repeated the historical claim that 'Syria and Lebanon are one state and one people . . . and have shared interests and a common history'.

Lebanese officials dutifully defended Syria's control of Lebanon, deflecting criticism of the Syrian military presence by mechanically repeating the mantra that it was 'necessary, legal and temporary'. The emptiness of the phrase was hinted at in an interview Hariri gave with Lebanon's English-language *Daily Star* newspaper in 1998 when he stumbled over the correct order of the adjectives and had to be helped out by a cabinet minister.

Between 1991 and 1994, Assad turned Syria's latent irredentism into practice through a series of political and economic agreements with Lebanon that essentially bound the two countries together into something resembling a quasi-confederation. The sweeping Treaty of Brotherhood and Cooperation, signed in May 1991, gave a foretaste of what the Lebanese could expect under Pax Syriana. Article I called for the 'highest degree of cooperation and coordination . . . in all political, security, cultural, scientific and other concerns in pursuit of the interests of the two brotherly countries'.

The treaty set the tempo for a whole raft of further agreements on security and economic issues. The Defence and Security Agreement in September 1991 called for a ban on 'all military, security, political and media activity that might harm the other country'.

Further agreements were signed in 1993 and 1994 covering social and economic cooperation, health, agriculture, cross-border traffic of goods and people, labour, water sharing, tourism and cultural cooperation. The 1994 Labour Agreement legitimised the entry of Syrian workers into Lebanon. Employers readily recruited Syrians because they took round about half the wages of a Lebanese worker. The cash earnings, of which almost all were repatriated to Syria, made a significant contribution to the Syrian economy, with some estimates placing the figure as high as $4 billion a year by the end of the 1990s. Yet the unfettered inflow of Syrian workers was a controversial issue, with critics railing against the loss of millions of dollars from the Lebanese economy. Lebanese labourers complained bitterly that the Syrians were stealing jobs from them and that they could not afford to work at the more competitive rates of the Syrians.

What Lebanon gained in Syrian workers it lost in Lebanese water. The 1994 water-sharing agreement apportioned rights to the Orontes river which rises in the Bekaa, flows into Syria and on into Turkey. Lebanon was allocated 60 million cubic metres a year, or about 22 per cent of the annual flow. The agreement was touted as a success by the Lebanese government, even though in the 1950s Lebanon had proposed to Syria that it receive 40 per cent of the river's waters.

The flurry of agreements and treaties produced a veneer of legitimacy to what was a creeping annexation of Lebanon by Syria. Indeed, in at least one agreement, on tourism, Lebanon and Syria were referred to as the 'twin provinces' (*al-qutrayn al-tawamayn*).

The three members of the troika – Hrawi, Hariri and Berri – handled Syrian hegemony in separate ways. Berri's attitude was 'Syria right or wrong' and as such was an indispensable ally of Damascus. Hrawi was an old-school Lebanese politician, a 'fox', according to one former Lebanese politician, who used the Syrians to help win his own parochial battles but was less than discreet in voicing his views. At a dinner party he hosted in Baabda, which was attended by the American ambassador, Ryan Crocker, the politician recalled Hrawi grumbling that the Syrians 'don't let me breathe'.[20] Hariri was the eternal pragmatist, the compromiser who would do what was necessary to ensure political and diplomatic calm so as not to upset Lebanon's reconstruction and economic revival.

Simon Karam, Lebanon's ambassador to Washington in the early 1990s, found himself a victim of Hariri's appeasing nature. The Syrian authorities distrusted Karam, a soft-spoken lawyer from the Maronite town of Jezzine in south Lebanon who was known to have little sympathy for Pax Syriana. In July 1993 when Israel launched a punishing seven-day air and artillery blitz on south Lebanon, Damascus pressured Beirut to recall Karam from Washington. The pressure became vindictive with Hrawi being given a hand-written intelligence assessment of Karam, accusing his ambassador of plotting against the Syrians, complaining to the Americans that the Lebanese government was 'a Syrian puppet' and even drug smuggling. The document, which was signed by Ali Duba, the head of Syrian military intelligence, is today in Karam's possession.

'Hrawi gave me the letter as a memento,' Karam says, brandishing the yellowing sheet of paper.[21] 'Can you imagine a Syrian president handing to a Lebanese president an intelligence assessment on a Lebanese ambassador?'

As a result of the Syrian pressure, Karam was deliberately sidelined from meetings in Beirut with American diplomats negotiating a ceasefire in south Lebanon. Unwilling to serve as a lame-duck ambassador, Karam resigned. Days later, Hariri dispatched an aide to see Karam.

'Hariri's excuse for my treatment was Syrian pressure and that I shouldn't take it personally,' Karam says. 'Hariri provided cover for my eviction.'

Under Pax Syriana there was little leeway for the more independently minded servant of the state, like Karam, and none for those who refused to accept the new order, such as Samir Geagea, the head of the Lebanese Forces militia.

Unlike most of his militia counterparts who formed the backbone of the post-war political class, Geagea bridled against Syrian domination, resigning twice from ministerial positions and boycotting the 1992 parliamentary elections.

On February 27, 1994, a bomb exploded in a church in Zouk Mikhael, 16 kilometres north of Beirut, killing 11 people and wounding several others. Two weeks later, the government re-activated the death penalty for murder as Lebanese troops surrounded Geagea's home and began arresting members of his Lebanese Forces. Geagea was arrested in June and the Lebanese Forces were banned. Although he was exonerated for the church bombing, Geagea was handed a total of four life sentences for wartime killings, including the assassination of Rashid Karami, the former premier. Geagea was the only militia leader to face trial for crimes committed during the war, even though an amnesty law granted immunity to anyone involved in war-related crimes. Geagea's imprisonment and the banning of the Lebanese Forces effectively crushed the last bastion of anti-Syrian defiance in Lebanon, leaving the disaffected Christian opposition unorganised and scattered.

Keeping tabs on the likes of Geagea and other potential threats was a re-organised Lebanese military intelligence, the most powerful security organ under Pax Syriana which reported directly to its Syrian counterpart.

The hub of the Syrian intelligence network was in Anjar, an Armenian town in the Bekaa valley close to the border with Syria famed for the graceful arches and columns of the eighth-century palace of the Omayyad caliph, Al-Walid Ibn Abdel Malik, an earlier Damascus-based ruler of the Levant. The French mandatory authority picked malarial marshland near the ruins to construct from scratch the modern town of Anjar to house Armenian refugees from the Syrian province of Alexandretta which was ceded by France to Turkey in 1939. From this oddly eastern-European-looking town of squat houses and wide, tree-lined avenues, Ghazi Kanaan, the tough and wily Syrian intelligence chief, flattered, threatened and manipulated Lebanon's fractious politicians, playing them off against each other to ensure that Syria's interests were preserved. His office became a regular port of call for Lebanese politicians travelling to meet Assad or other senior officials in Damascus. Every Saturday, Kanaan would hold an open day to receive MPs, ministers, business figures, governors, mayors, military and security officers, anyone who sought a favour or advice from the most powerful man in Lebanon. Local residents grew accustomed to seeing sleek black limousines sweeping along the pine tree-lined avenues as Lebanon's great and good paid homage to Syria's proconsul.

A mile south of Anjar lay several unremarkable single-storey farm buildings surrounded by flat farmland. The farm, known as the 'onion factory', was Syria's main detention and interrogation centre in Lebanon. Its name struck a chill in the hearts of nearby residents and farm workers who from time to time could hear the screams of detainees carried on the breeze as the interrogators carried out their grim task.

The victim could face several days of interrogation or torture before being released, being coerced into working for Syrian intelligence or in the worst scenario being 'disappeared' – transferred to a prison in Syria.

Yet the most pernicious and consequential impact of Syrian control of Lebanon was the endemic corruption which bled Lebanon of billions of dollars while enriching a small elite of Syrian officials and their Lebanese allies.

Corruption in post-war Lebanon was so widely practised at all levels that it was treated as a fact of daily life, such as paying a government official a small 'fee' to process some documentation. In March 2000, a non-governmental organisation, Kulluna Massoul (We Are All Responsible), released a survey in which 74 per cent of Lebanese felt that 'bribery is necessary to secure a contract from any public institution'. A quarter of those questioned believed that 'all Lebanese politicians are corrupt'.

More egregious forms of corruption by powerful political or business figures were gossiped about and possibly hinted at in the newspapers, but rarely provoked a public outcry let alone led to a criminal case in court unless there was an underlying political motivation. Among the more blatant examples was a law passed in 1995 that required all vehicles to be equipped with a mini fire extinguisher as a safety precaution. That many vehicles were barely roadworthy, lacked lights, possessed faulty brakes and were driven with ruthless abandon by young men or with supreme indifference to other road users by middle-aged housewives apparently was of no consequence to the supporters of the fire extinguisher law. Unusually, the law was enforced with spot checks by Internal Security Forces policemen manning checkpoints along Beirut's streets, with transgressors receiving fines. Yet there was nothing altruistic in the sudden government interest in preventing motorists from burning to death in their vehicles. A cabinet minister had received an import licence for mini fire extinguishers and had used his influence to push through legislation requiring that at least one be carried in every vehicle. After a few months, the enforcement of the law dried up, presumably after the fortunate minister had sold his entire stock of fire extinguishers.

As prime minister, Hariri was widely blamed for cultivating a climate of rampant corruption and cronyism. His policy of appointing former employees into key positions in the government and civil service provided ample ammunition for his enemies. There were repeated allegations of Hariri using his vast fortune to bribe politicians and officials into approving his projects. The most notorious example was the allegation that some 40 MPs in 1991 (before Hariri was prime minister) were bribed with cash sums of $50,000 to $100,000 or interest-free loans of up to a million dollars from Hariri's banks to approve the law establishing Solidere.[22] It remains unclear whether Hariri personally benefited from the corruption of the 1990s, although even his enemies admit that he was not motivated by personal enrichment.

'We can honestly say that Hariri was not corrupt,' says Mohammed Raad of Hizbullah.[23] 'But the sectarian *zuama* [communal and political leaders] that existed around him and the inability to prioritise the reconstruction effort led to high spending and wastage. If we had to give a budget to the Ministry for the Displaced [run by the Druze] then we had to give some to the Council of the South [Shiite] and some to the CDR [Council for Development and Reconstruction] because of sectarianism. The Shiites, the Druze, the Sunnis and the Christians all had to get their share.'

Still, Hariri as prime minister was in a position to exploit reconstruction contracts and state funds to benefit his Syrian patrons and his Lebanese allies. The lack of transparency, nepotism and naked corruption that surrounded the awarding of profitable contracts was part of the Lebanese system of clientelism, the building of patronage networks to enhance one's political position. State-run companies and government ministries and institutions were overstaffed with unsuitable employees whose sole qualities were their allegiances to powerful political patrons. Hariri, however, was unwilling or unable to reverse this traditional way of doing business, and instead preferred to make the system work for him.

Wiam Wahhab, who remains one of Syria's staunchest allies, recalls asking Hariri in the mid-1990s why he continued to allocate vast sums of government funds to the Ministry for the Displaced, then headed by Walid Jumblatt.[24] The ministry was charged with returning war-displaced refugees to their original homes and villages. The government's critics, including Wahhab, complained that Jumblatt used the funds as a source of patronage, dispersing a disproportionate amount to his Druze supporters.

'I kept accusing Hariri about this and he told me that he was buying Jumblatt's silence so that he could continue with his reconstruction project,' Wahhab recalls. 'He believed in bribing people with money. He didn't know how else to deal with a situation.'

If the corruption associated with Hariri tended to fall along lines of bribery and cronyism, the Syrian-controlled system was closer to a mafia-style racketeering operation in which Lebanon was treated as a 'milking cow', in the words of a former minister,[25] a pool of reconstruction cash to be plundered at will.

On the outskirts of the Bekaa town of Zahle is a dishevelled and lifeless industrial estate of pot-holed roads, dilapidated factories and warehouses. In the centre of the estate is a pencil-slim tower about 30 metres tall surmounted by several gleaming white satellite dishes, the largest of which is some 3 metres in diameter. The sight of high-tech communications tucked among the unkempt industrial buildings may appear incongruous, but the satellite dishes are an essential component in an illegal racket that has netted millions of dollars by diverting international telephone traffic from public exchanges owned by the government. Although international telephone calls are supposed to be routed through the government's exchanges, it has been estimated that about half the international traffic is handled by illegal operators. The scam is simple. The owners of illegal exchanges entice foreign operators to place calls to Lebanon through them by offering lower tariffs than the government. In 2002, Jean-Louis Qordahi, the minister of telecommunications, estimated that 30 million call minutes were being diverted each month, which translates into illicit earnings of $262 million a year.

The racket was allowed to continue unmolested by the Lebanese authorities due to its connection to a wealthy Lebanese businessman and his powerful patrons in Syria who all received a cut of the profits.

'The Syrian system was a racket with clear and defined rules,' says Joe Faddoul, a Lebanese financial consultant.[26] 'The Syrians practically took the money out of the government's coffers.'

Often using Lebanese politicians as frontmen, senior figures in Syria and their local allies are alleged to have made immense profits from the Lebanese reconstruction boom in the 1990s, receiving 'protection commissions', securing monopolies in a wide array of sectors and selling goods and services at inflated rates. Almost no sector was immune: construction, oil and gas, electricity, telecommunications. Among the most well known was the awarding of Lebanon's first mobile phone contracts to two companies, Cellis and Libancell, headed by Lebanese closely associated with Abdel-Halim Khaddam and Hikmat Shehabi and their sons. With competitors barred from entering the market, these two companies were allowed to charge exorbitant fees, among the highest in the world at 13 cents per minute compared to 3 to 8 cents elsewhere in the Arab world.

Some $1.8 billion was spent on rehabilitating and constructing ten electricity producing plants to raise the power capacity from an average 900 megawatts to 1,800 megawatts. But the capacity fell short of the target, achieving only 1,400 megawatts with as much as $500 million ending up in 'the pockets of leaders, ministers and entrepreneurs', a minister told Agence France Presse in 2003.

One former minister of electricity and water resources used to levy a 'personal tax' of 20 per cent on fuel purchases, according to Faddoul. His predecessor at the ministry set up a public relations company which charged a 10 per cent commission to companies wanting to sell equipment to the Electricite du Liban, the state-run power utility on which more than $150 million was spent in the early 1990s. The minister split the commission with his Syrian backers.

Customs duties were pocketed at Beirut port, at Beirut International Airport and on the border with Syria. According to Faddoul, Syrian intelligence agents set up an alternative customs office at Beirut port where importers could evade legal customs duties by paying the Syrians a lesser fee to bring in their goods. Syrian military intelligence officers, including Ghazi Kanaan, were alleged to receive kickbacks from hashish growers in the Bekaa valley. During the late 1980s, the turnover from drug cultivation in the Bekaa was estimated at $4 billion, of which Syrian officers reportedly received a substantial cut. A downturn in drug cultivation in the 1990s was reportedly compensated for by the refining of heroin and cocaine in the remoter reaches of Baalbek and Hermel in the northern Bekaa.

Even the world-famous Casino du Liban perched on a bluff overlooking the Mediterranean near Jounieh was plundered on a daily basis by Syrian and Lebanese intelligence agents. Around 3 a.m. every day, after the casino had closed for the night, the agents would haul off around half the evening's takings, reportedly amounting to about $50 million a year.[27] The silence of local politicians was bought by giving them their own personal slot machines. When Habib Lteif, a former manager of the casino, began complaining about the systematic looting, he was threatened and beaten up in his office, prompting him to resign. The impact that the racket had on the casino – as well as the fact that the abuses were widely known – was illustrated by the fluctuation in the share price in the nine-month period that covered Hariri's assassination and Syria's disengagement from Lebanon. In December 2004, shares in the casino were selling at $165 each. Yet despite Hariri's death in February, political turmoil, an economic recession, a downturn in the number of tourists and a sporadic campaign of assassinations and bombings, the share price by September had soared to $300 each. Investors knew that the Syrians were no longer siphoning off the profits, making the casino an attractive venture once more.

Apart from enriching the Syrian elite, the racketeering system helped Syria maintain control over Lebanon by purchasing the loyalty of local clients, either by allowing them direct access to profitable business ventures or by installing them in parliament or the cabinet where they could take advantage of their positions of influence for personal gain. Administrative appointments were sometimes delayed for months while bickering politicians fought each other to promote their own favourite. Millions of dollars in loans and grants from international lenders gathered dust in banks because powerful politicians would block projects that did not benefit them and their patronage networks.

In 2001, a United Nations-sponsored report on corruption in Lebanon claimed that the government was losing $190 million because of the monopoly on the import of oil and its derivatives to five companies directly linked to powerful politicians.

The report estimated that Lebanon was losing approximately $1 billion a year through graft, a 'conservative' figure at that.

Joe Faddoul, after sifting through published accounts of corruption and racketeering that occasionally made the local press, concluded that the Syrian-endorsed racketeering had been netting an estimated $2 billion since 1990 in direct and indirect takings. Therefore, by 2005, Syrian racketeering had cost Lebanon $30 billion, helping explain, according to Faddoul, the country's staggering public debt of nearly $40 billion.[28]

Hariri was not overly troubled by the steadily climbing debt in the early 1990s, predicting that it would be easily repaid if not written off as a consequence of a comprehensive Middle East peace agrement. Not only would peace herald an investment bonanza in Lebanon, but it would also end the festering conflict pitting Hizbullah's guerrilla fighters against Israeli troops in south Lebanon. An Israeli withdrawal from the south would truly mark the end of Lebanon's long, bloody conflict and allow Beirut to re-establish itself as the financial centre of the Middle East. And a Syria at peace with Israel would no longer have a justification for continuing its presence in Lebanon.

'Be patient,' Hariri advised his colleagues.

Yet Hariri's dependence on, and initial faith in, the prospect of an imminent regional peace placed him in direct confrontation with Hizbullah, whose military actions in south Lebanon against Israeli occupation forces threatened to jeopardise Lebanon's revival.

Before 1992, Hariri had avoided any relations with Hizbullah, viewing the organisation as an unsettling creation of Iran. In turn, Hizbullah thought of Hariri as a 'Saudi' and had little inclination to engage with him given the hostility between Tehran and Riyadh in the mid-1980s.

'We knew nothing about him,' recalls Hizbullah's Mohammed Raad.[29] 'It appeared to us that Rafik Hariri had wide relations with the West and this made us cautious. We knew nothing about his childhood, his background, his political life. His appearance was surprising on the Lebanese scene.'

In 1985, King Fahd of Saudi Arabia asked Hariri to make contact with Ayatollah Mohammed Hussein Fadlallah, an eminent Lebanese Shiite cleric whose views echoed those of Hizbullah.[30] Hariri and Fadlallah developed a warm relationship, the latter often visiting Hariri's home in Riyadh when in Saudi Arabia for the annual Haj, or pilgrimage to Mecca. King Fahd told Fadlallah that he wished to help strengthen Sunni–Shiite ties in Lebanon, but he also hoped that the cleric might be able to use his influence to stem some Iran-backed Shiite unrest in Saudi Arabia's eastern province. According to a Lebanese Shiite politician, Fadlallah was offered a Saudi donation of several million dollars via Hariri, but turned it down suspecting it was a bribe or at least that it would be perceived as such by others.[31]

At the time, Nabih Berri was Hariri's principal interlocutor among Lebanese Shiites, and the Amal leader discouraged Hariri from establishing contacts with any other Shiite figure or group. The day after Hariri first met Fadlallah, a rocket-propelled grenade was fired into Fouad Siniora's twenty-first-floor office in a tower block in west Beirut. Hariri saw the incident as a forceful reminder from Berri that the Amal leader was the sole representative of Shiite interests in Lebanon and Hariri would do well to remember it. But by 1992, Hizbullah had become a force that Hariri could no longer ignore. The party was waging an increasingly effective and deadly campaign against Israeli occupation troops in south Lebanon and had won 12 seats in parliament in the 1992 legislative elections.

A few days before he was appointed prime minister in October 1992, Hariri requested and was granted an appointment with Sayyed Hassan Nasrallah, Hizbullah's youthful secretary-general who was elected to the post in February. The two men had a frank conversation, according to Mustafa Nasr, a journalist who served as a go-between.[32] Nasr recalled Nasrallah saying to Hariri, 'You are the resistance that will remove the suffering of the people [in Lebanon] and our party is the resistance that will remove the occupation from our people on the border. If we become allies and agree, our resistance will be your resistance and the country will move on very well. But if we disagree, you will lose both your resistance and my resistance.'

'I am with you 100 per cent,' Hariri replied. He went on to reassure Nasrallah that he was not an 'American agent'.

'I am an Arab nationalist,' he said. 'I help the poor and my convictions and principles are truly Islamic.'

Nonetheless, the contradiction inherent in the policies of the Hariri government and Hizbullah's anti-Israel agenda would prove to be a source of significant tension and deep mistrust.

Hariri was appointed prime minister because he was seen as the one Lebanese who could engineer a revival for Lebanon, attracting essential foreign aid and investment capital to fund the reconstruction process and using his extensive international contacts for the benefit of Beirut and Damascus. But the festering conflict in south Lebanon, which intensified during Hariri's premiership, threatened to undermine the prime minister's vision of turning war-shattered Lebanon into the financial and services centre for the region.

Hariri was a man of compromise, who, as far as Hizbullah was concerned, held dangerous views regarding accommodation with Israel. After all, he was gambling his entire economic and political programme for Lebanon on a successful outcome of the Middle East peace process. What would happen, Hizbullah wondered, if Israel called for a ceasefire in south Lebanon, or even the disarming of Hizbullah, as a condition for a troop withdrawal from the occupation zone? Could Hariri be trusted to reject such offers?

The paradox of resistance and reconstruction became all too obvious just nine months after Hariri took office. A spate of deadly resistance attacks in early July 1993 spurred Israel to mount a massive air and artillery blitz against south Lebanon. The Israeli assault killed some 120 Lebanese civilians, wounded another 500, displaced 300,000 residents, caused damage estimated at $28.8 million and undermined Hariri's public relations campaign to restore investor confidence in Lebanon: he had unveiled the $10 billion Horizon 2000 national reconstruction programme only four months earlier. Hariri bit his lip and dutifully defended the resistance during the week-long escalation in July. But relations plunged into deep crisis six weeks later when Lebanese troops opened fire on a Hizbullah demonstration, killing nine protestors. The shooting caused an uproar, with Hizbullah accusing the government of causing a 'massacre', and resulted in months of bitterness.

But the disagreements between Hariri and Hizbullah were not solely related to the resistance in south Lebanon. Hizbullah's parliamentary bloc represented a vocal and persistent opposition to Hariri's grandiose reconstruction plans. Hizbullah criticised Hariri's economic agenda for its Beirut-centric focus and its apparent neglect of poorer peripheral areas from where the party drew much of its support. While Nabih Berri was able to maintain his support base through access to state funds, Hizbullah won hearts and minds via its own extensive social wing which provided free or discounted medical treatment, education, agricultural assistance, water distribution and subsidised department stores. Hizbullah's lack of dependence on the state's coffers granted it a moral platform from which to rail against the perceived excesses of the Hariri government and attack the endemic corruption of the 1990s.

Relations between Hariri and Hizbullah finally gelled into some form of mutual understanding in April 1996 when Israel embarked upon a second punishing military campaign against south Lebanon. Israeli warplanes targeted the newly renovated infrastructure such as bridges and power plants, the implicit message being that Lebanon had a choice: either reconstruction or resistance.

Hariri played an important diplomatic role by enlisting the support of his friend Jacques Chirac, who was elected president of France in 1995, to form a diplomatic counterweight to an ambitious US initiative that sought to end Hizbullah's resistance campaign in exchange for a cessation of the Israeli offensive. Assad rejected the US proposal for a milder French alternative that set ground rules for the fighting monitored by an international committee. After two weeks, it was obvious that the Israeli offensive was failing to curb Hizbullah and that the Lebanese government would not stop the anti-Israel resistance. Israel called off the offensive after 16 days. A month later Benjamin Netanyahu, the hard-line leader of Israel's Likud party, was elected prime minister of Israel, freezing the Israeli–Syrian track of the peace process for the next three years.

Having reached a modus vivendi with Hizbullah, Hariri faced a more pressing threat in 1998 as General Emile Lahoud prepared to move the short distance from the ministry of defence in Yarze to the concrete and glass presidential palace in the nearby suburb of Baabda.

Lahoud was a popular choice among many Lebanese who saw in the 60-year-old army commander a resolute and principled officer who held politicians in disdain and shunned social events. In a country that celebrates excess and hard partying, the Lebanese media marvelled at Lahoud's frugal and ascetic lifestyle: how he rose every day at 4.30 a.m. and swam a mile before going to work at the ministry of defence just as the sun was rising. Fluent in Arabic, English and French, he was the son of an army general and nephew of one of Lebanon's founding fathers. After nine years, many Lebanese had tired of the dour Hrawi and his submission to the will of Damascus and hoped that the no-nonsense general would loosen Lebanon from Syria's iron grip.

Lahoud also had the support of the Americans who, in the words of one senior diplomat closely involved in Lebanese affairs, regarded the army commander as a 'clean reformer', untainted by the endemic corruption of Lebanese politics, 'as "un-Maronite" a Maronite president' as the Lebanese had seen since the days of Fouad Chehab, another army commander who had served as president from 1958 to 1964.[33]

'Ostensibly committed to economic and fiscal discipline after the ruinous over-spending of Hariri's term . . . Lahoud seemed a breath of fresh air and vigour in the presidency,' the diplomat says.

Yet Lahoud's public image was the result of a carefully crafted public relations campaign that played on Christian desires for a powerful counterweight to the Sunni Hariri, Druze Jumblatt, and Shiites Berri and Nasrallah, coupled with an instinctive respect among Lebanese for the sanctity of the military. It was a campaign that many Lebanese journalists, by mistake or design, helped promote.

'We have some responsibility in this,' admits Sarkis Naoum, the veteran *An Nahar* columnist.[34] 'Some people willingly or unwillingly portrayed Lahoud as firm, strong and clean. For some it was wishful thinking, which included me, some had their arms twisted, and others were working for Lahoud anyway.'

The man behind Lahoud's image-building campaign was Colonel Jamil Sayyed, a Shiite from the Bekaa whose position as deputy chief of military intelligence disguised the extent of the power he wielded. A career officer in the Lebanese Army, Sayyed had become an indispensable ally of the Syrians after narrowly escaping a car bomb explosion in 1983 while serving as chief of military intelligence in the Bekaa. As deputy chief of military intelligence from 1990, Sayyed oversaw the restructuring and merging of the Lebanese intelligence apparatus with that of Syria. A diminutive man with narrow facial features, Sayyed possessed a sharp intelligence which won him the guarded respect of his opponents, among them Hariri and Hrawi.

Although the Syrians told their Lebanese allies that they were biding their time before making a final decision, it was clear that Lahoud was almost a certainty for the job.

Assad, who wanted Hariri to remain as prime minister under Lahoud, realised that the animosity between the two men could complicate Syria's control over Lebanon. However, Bashar al-Assad remained a staunch supporter of Lahoud and his voice was beginning to carry weight within the regime. He began taking over the Lebanon portfolio in early 1998 from Abdel-Halim Khaddam who had run Lebanese affairs since the 1970s. The same year Hikmat Shehabi resigned as chief of staff of the Syrian Army. Bashar also spearheaded an anti-corruption drive in Syria in a bid to raise his domestic profile and boost his popularity. Some of those targeted in his campaign were linked to Hariri, which served to weaken the prime minister's position in Syria. The moves signalled that the old order in Lebanon and Syria was changing, and the patronage networks created by Hariri's wealth were beginning to dissolve. Having neglected to build ties with the younger generation in Damascus and with Shehabi gone and Khaddam stripped of the Lebanon file, Hariri 'found himself cornered', according to former Hariri advisor Nohad Mashnouq.[35]

The erosion of Hariri's influence in Damascus was keenly supported by his Lebanese opponents, among them Suleiman Frangieh, heir to a Maronite political dynasty in north Lebanon, Talal Arslan, Walid Jumblatt's Druze rival, Omar Karami, the ill-fated former premier, and Hizbullah.

'Our team used to tell Bashar that we were not in disagreement about Syria's role in Lebanon but we had a problem with this gang which was harming relations between the two countries,' says Wiam Wahhab, a former journalist and ardent pro-Syrian supporter, referring to Hariri and his Syrian allies. 'Before Bashar arrived, we were depending on the [Lebanese] army [headed by Lahoud] to balance against Hrawi, Hariri, Jumblatt and their friends in Syria, Abdel-Halim Khaddam and Ghazi Kanaan. When Bashar became strong, our team won with the coming of Lahoud.'[36]

On October 5, Assad and Hrawi met in Damascus and afterwards announced that Lahoud would be the next president of Lebanon, even though the army commander had never formally announced his candidacy. Nine days later, 118 of Parliament's 128 MPs gathered to vote unanimously for Lahoud in a light-hearted session that barely lasted 20 minutes. It was the first time since the election of President Bishara

Khoury in 1949 that a candidate received every vote cast. But Walid Jumblatt's bloc of nine MPs stayed away from the vote, reflecting the Druze leader's unhappiness at Lahoud becoming president.

In his inaugural address, Lahoud vowed to adhere to the 'rule of law' and pledged to root out corruption, references that were seen as none-too-subtle swipes at Hariri's autonomy. Lahoud's promised anti-corruption drive mirrored that of Bashar in Syria, further indicating that the future Syrian leader was the muscle behind Lebanon's new president.

Nonetheless, Hariri was expected to lead the next government and, during mandatory consultations between Lahoud and MPs over the identity of the next prime minister, a small majority supported Hariri for the job. But several MPs declined to pick a name, leaving Lahoud the choice of designating whom he wanted. In protest, Hariri announced his resignation, declaring that MPs were obliged under the post-Taif constitution to name their choice of prime minister and could not leave it to the president to decide.

Hariri expected Assad to intervene with Lahoud, which would have strengthened his hand as he and the new president embarked on what was destined to be a fractious and tense relationship. Although Assad favoured Hariri's return to the premiership, he chose against his better judgement not to overrule his son's backing for Lahoud. Bashar required a trusted ally in Lebanon who would preserve Syria's interests there while he established his authority in Damascus. A powerful Sunni prime minister in Beirut would not only challenge Lahoud's authority but could prove a dangerously potent influence with the majority Sunnis in Syria if the Alawite presidency was extended through Bashar succeeding his father.

'Hafez al-Assad was very intelligent and knew well the situation in Lebanon and tried very hard to create a positive atmosphere between Lahoud and Hariri but he failed,' says Ghazi Aridi, a Druze cabinet minister and aide to Walid Jumblatt.[37]

With Hariri out of the running, parliament selected Salim Hoss as the new prime minister. A respected economist and three times premier during some of Lebanon's darkest years in the war, Hoss was the antithesis of Hariri: reserved where Hariri was flamboyant, cautious where Hariri was bold, reticent where Hariri was outgoing. Hariri was dogged by allegations of corruption, but Hoss was a genuinely decent man who enjoyed a clean reputation and was known for his probity. Most importantly, Hoss would not stand in Lahoud's way. Hariri might have been the first among equals in the troika of president, prime minister and parliamentary speaker during the 1990s, but as far as Lahoud was concerned the troika was dead.

The breach

Dennis Ross, the chief American negotiator to the Middle East peace process, strode down a corridor of the Geneva Intercontinental Hotel, deep in thought and silently seething with frustration.[1] The meeting just ended between Presidents Clinton and Assad could not have gone much worse. The eagerly anticipated summit had promised to break the deadlock in the Israeli–Syrian peace track, but, although Assad was offered the best deal yet from the Israelis, the old man simply had not appeared interested in even discussing it. The apparent stumbling point, as it had been throughout the eight years of on-again, off-again peace talks beween the Syrians and Israelis, was the extent of an Israeli withdrawal from the Golan Heights, the strategic volcanic plateau overlooking northern Galilee that was captured from Syria in the June 1967 Arab–Israeli war. Assad was Syrian defence minister in 1967 and it had become an emotional as well as strategic goal to return the Golan to the motherland – all the Golan, every inch that had been taken by Israel east of the border as it stood on June 4, 1967, the eve of the war. All other matters regarding peace – military arrangements, water sharing, diplomatic and cultural normalisation – were open for discussion, but the Golan was non-negotiable.

When peace negotiations resumed in December 1999, ending a four-year freeze, the prognosis was that a deal would be concluded swiftly. So here on this chilly Swiss afternoon in late March 2000, Clinton had met Assad to sell Israeli prime minister Ehud Barak's boldest offer yet – a pull-out from the entire Golan except for a narrow strip of territory along the north-east edge of the Sea of Galilee. To the watching world, the sight of the gaunt and visibly frail 69-year-old Syrian president making the effort to meet Clinton in Geneva signalled that a deal was all but concluded. A breakthrough between Syria and Israel would pave the way for Lebanon to negotiate its own peace deal, allowing for a coordinated, safe and dignified withdrawal of Israeli troops from the bloody quagmire of south Lebanon.

There were few who were awaiting the results of the summit more eagerly than Rafik Hariri. The former premier had been in regular contact with Ross over the past year, repeatedly badgering the US negotiator for information and encouraging him to persist when talks encountered difficulties. The last call Ross received from Hariri before the Geneva summit was two weeks earlier while driving home from his office in Washington.

'He was very optimistic,' Ross recounts. 'He said that everything he was hearing was that Assad wanted a deal done. He was probing me to see if I was coming [to Geneva] with something serious and I said "Yes, I am coming with something serious", and he said he was very confident that it would work out.'

Yet it was not to be. Whether Barak miscalculated by insisting on keeping the ribbon of land east of the Sea of Galilee or whether Assad had changed his mind about the importance of concluding peace with Israel is still unclear. But the Syrian president turned down Barak's offer flat.

Ross entered his hotel room, kicked off his shoes and put on a pair of jeans. If all had gone well, right now he would be briefing the press gathered at the President Wilson Hotel in the centre of Geneva. But they had picked Joe Lockhart, the White House press spokesman, for the unenviable task of putting an upbeat gloss on the summit's failure. As Ross sat down, the phone rang, the first call he had received since the end of the meeting a little earlier. It was Hariri.

'What happened?' Hariri asked, sounding shocked, having just heard the news.

'He didn't want to do it,' Ross told him, referring to Assad.

'Tell me what happened,' Hariri said.

Ross explained Assad's dismissive reaction as Clinton read out Barak's proposal line by line.

'My guess is that it has something to do with succession politics,' Ross said, meaning Assad's intention of bequeathing the presidency to his son, Bashar.

'I just don't believe it,' Hariri said incredulously. 'Look, don't give up.'

'But what do we have to work with?' Ross asked.

'Just don't give up. There's got to be something. I'll find out. It might have something to do with the succession, but it doesn't mean it's over.'

Tellingly, in his memoirs, *The Missing Peace*, Ross misidentifies Hariri as the Lebanese prime minister, although Hariri was still sitting on the opposition benches in March 2000. Lebanon's real prime minister, Salim Hoss, showed no such impatient interest in the results of the talks, and in the days that followed meekly echoed Syria's blaming the failure of the Geneva summit on Israeli intransigence.

In Hariri's calculation, a regional peace was essential for his broader vision of restoring full sovereignty to Lebanon. With the Israelis out of south Lebanon, Syria would be hard pressed to explain why it needed to retain a troop and intelligence presence in the rest of the country. Furthermore, peace in the Middle East would neuter Hizbullah. Lebanon and Syria would have no tolerance for continued anti-Israeli attacks, and the Shiite resistance group's public profile would inevitably decline with the end of hostilities.

'The one thing he was preoccupied with was how he could expand the scope of Lebanese independence,' Ross recalls. 'He was very hopeful that, in the context of an Israeli–Syrian peace deal, Syria would necessarily engage in a relaxation of its control over Lebanon. Clearly, whoever he was talking to had convinced him that the deal was going to be done [in Geneva]. And he was stunned [by the summit's failure]. I can't think of a better way to describe it other than he was stunned.'

The failure to conclude a peace deal between Israel and Syria at Geneva was to have far-reaching strategic implications, setting in motion a chain of events that helped mould the current political landscape in Lebanon and Syria and relations between Israel and the Palestinians.

The first fateful consequence of Geneva was that Barak was obliged to withdraw unilaterally and unconditionally from Lebanon by July if he was to fulfil a pre-electoral promise to be out within a year of assuming office.[2] It was a high-stakes gamble, but one that Barak felt compelled to make. On May 21, however, the Israeli Army's withdrawal plan descended into chaos when several hundred Lebanese who had gathered for a funeral on the edge of Israel's occupation zone suddenly decided to cross the front line and revisit their long-abandoned homes in a near-deserted village. What started as a trickle of returning villagers turned into an unstoppable torrent, forcing a hasty retreat of Israeli forces and the panicked flight of some 6,000 terrified mainly Christian residents of the occupation zone who feared retribution at the hands of Hizbullah.

Three days later, it was all over. It was a truly historic moment in the Arab–Israeli conflict and a triumph for Hizbullah, marking the first time that Israel had been obliged to concede captured territory through the force of Arab arms. Israel, Hizbullah had proved, could be defeated in battle. The Jewish state, said Sayyed Hassan Nasrallah at a victory rally, was 'as weak as a spider's web' and the Palestinians of the Israeli-occupied territories of the West Bank and Gaza Strip could liberate their land as well if they emulated the Hizbullah model. It was a powerful message that resonated deeply with the discontented Palestinians.

The biggest loser of Israel's unilateral withdrawal from south Lebanon was Syria. The tacit assumption of the previous decade was that Assad would guarantee stability along Israel's northern border with Lebanon if Israel returned the Golan Heights to Damascus. The longer Israel procrastinated, the more Israeli Army body bags Hizbullah would fill. But with Israeli troops no longer dying from Hizbullah's bombs and missiles, Israel had less incentive to withdraw from the Golan.

Furthermore, the Israeli troop withdrawal from Lebanon was bound to stoke increased demands from the Lebanese for a similar move by the Syrians. Indeed, a few days before the Geneva summit, Lebanon's *An Nahar* newspaper had published an extraordinary open letter addressed to Bashar written by Gibran Tueni, the paper's general manager and one of Syria's keenest critics in Lebanon.

'I must tell you quite frankly that many Lebanese feel that Syria's behaviour in Lebanon completely contradicts the principles of sovereignty, dignity and independence,' Tueni wrote.

The open letter was loudly decried by the Lebanese political establishment, including by Hariri's *Al-Mustaqbal* newspaper, yet, if such anti-Syrian sentiment was already beginning to stir before the Israelis had even departed Lebanon, surely it would only grow stronger following the liberation of the south.

Assad, however, would not bring his patient cunning and decades of experience to bear on the new challenges facing Syria, for, just 16 days after the last Israeli soldier walked out of Lebanon, the 'Lion of Damascus' was dead.

Assad's death came days before the convening of the Baath party congress, the first in 15 years, at which it was speculated that Bashar would be given a senior position within the party, possibly the vice-presidency, which would have helped formalise his succession. Although Bashar had been groomed for power for six years, it was still unclear whether he was ready to lead the nation of 17 million. However, the machinery of state swung into action to assure a smooth transition. Hours after Assad's death, the Syrian parliament convened and lowered the mandatory age for the presidency from 40 to 34, Bashar's age. On June 11, acting president Abdel-Halim Khaddam, who had never approved Assad's son becoming president, dutifully promoted Bashar to general and appointed him commander of the Syrian armed forces.

'It was all prearranged and orchestrated by Hafez al-Assad that on his death it would move automatically to his son Bashar,' Khaddam recalls.

'Trying to oppose this during that time by me would have led to a serious confrontation in the country and it was not the proper time for this confrontation.'[3]

On June 17, Bashar was elected secretary-general of the Baath party, a position previously held by his father. Three weeks later, 97.3 per cent of voters in a national referendum elected Bashar president and he was inaugurated on July 17.

Bashar's ascendancy to the presidency may have come sooner than perhaps he or his father would have wished, but his position appeared stable. Assad had spent the previous two years building an infrastructure of loyalty around his son. Some of the president's ageing comrades were retired, and middle-ranking army officers were removed and replaced by a younger generation of Bashar loyalists.

Hikmat Shehabi, the Syrian chief of staff and one of the few Sunnis to hold a key security position, retired in 1998. He was replaced by General Ali Arslan, who was a close friend of Assef Shawkat, Bashar's brother-in-law and a rising star in the Syrian security apparatus. In early 2000, Shawkat was appointed deputy head of military intelligence. Shawkat's superior, Ali Duba, whose reputation for illicit dealings was at odds with Bashar's anti-corruption image, was replaced by Hassan Khalil, a member of Syria's negotiating team with Israel and a staunch backer of Bashar as president.

Mohammed Nassif, from a prominent Alawite family and one of Bashar's key supporters, occupied the post of deputy director of the General Security Department, the main civilian intelligence organisation.

Bahjat Suleiman, Bashar's political godfather, was appointed to head the internal security section of the General Security Department. Suleiman had been the first to publicly speak of a role for Bashar in 1994 when the country was still absorbing the impact of Basil's death.

Rifaat al-Assad, Hafez's estranged brother who had lived in exile since mounting an attempted coup in 1983, was stripped of his title as vice-president. The previous October, Bashar had ordered a crackdown on Rifaat's loyalists in the coastal city of Latakia, a warning to his uncle not to interfere in the coming succession.

While Assad undertook measures to bolster his son's domestic position, Hariri used his global influence to help smooth Bashar's reception with world leaders. He persuaded his friend Jacques Chirac, the French president, to meet Bashar in Paris in November 1999, the future Syrian leader's first official encounter with a Western head of state. Days before Bashar's inauguration, a group of four prominent Saudi companies, including Hariri's Oger, announced they were planning to invest as much as $400 million in Syria to fund projects in communications, agriculture, tourism and industry, to 'coincide with the beginning of the rule of Dr Bashar Assad'.

'It was a show of support for Bashar that Saudi companies were interested in Syria,' says Saad Hariri. But within a year, the consortium would have pulled out almost all its investments when, according to Saad, it became clear that the funds were being exploited for the benefit of figures close to the Syrian regime.[4]

'It turned into a disaster,' Saad says with a rueful chuckle. 'We started withdrawing [our investments], us and others, because we saw there was no [financial] benefit.'

Still, in those initial months of Bashar's presidency, Hariri was full of glowing praise for the young Syrian leader, telling CNN that Bashar 'knows Syria very well', was a 'big believer in peace' and 'wants to upgrade the life of the Syrian people'.

Other than Chirac, Hariri pressed Arab leaders including Crown Prince Abdullah of Saudi Arabia, President Mubarak of Egypt and King Abdullah of Jordan to assist the new Syrian leader to find his feet.

'The whole story of Bashar's entry on the international scene was down to Rafik Hariri. He lobbied like hell for him,' says a former advisor to Hariri.[5]

Hariri's hope that Bashar would spearhead a fundamental change in the one-sided relationship between Lebanon and Syria appeared to have some basis, according to Patrick Seale, the British journalist and biographer of Hafez al-Assad.

Seale recalls Bashar telling him in those early months of his presidency that he saw no need for a 'hands-on military control' of Lebanon.

'He told me that he didn't see a reason for Syria to run Lebanon on a daily basis and that, as long as some red lines were observed, such as no separate peace treaty with Israel, then Lebanon could run its own affairs,' Seale recalls.

Bashar's arrival in the presidency represented a new opportunity for both Lebanon and Syria, and Hariri wanted to be there for it. Parliamentary elections in Lebanon were drawing near and Hariri was working hard building political alliances to stage a triumph at the polls which would allow him to overcome Lahoud's objections and return to the premiership.

On becoming president in 1998, Lahoud had launched an anti-corruption drive against Hariri and his allies, purging the civil service of anyone close to the former prime minister. The campaign against Hariri initially was greeted with a certain amount of schadenfreude in Lebanon with lurid accounts of corruption and illicit deals among the tycoon's cronies making for compulsive reading in the media. But public support gradually paled as Lahoud's anti-corruption campaign increasingly appeared to be window dressing for a personal vendetta against Hariri rather than a broad purge of the incompetent and the dishonest. Furthermore, the president's unabashed pro-Syrian sympathies were at variance with his earlier public image of moral certitude and independence. What had happened to the Maronite strong man who was to redress Christian grievances and place Lebanon on an even footing in its relationship with Syria?

The attacks on the former government emanated from an increasingly militarised administration set up by Lahoud, who appointed loyal colleagues from the ministry of defence to key administrative positions. General Michel Suleiman replaced Lahoud as army commander even though he was a junior member of the general staff. His appointment led to the retirement of several older generals whose training and past connections with the West worked against them. Lahoud's aide-de-camp, Brigadier General Mustafa Hamdan, was appointed commander of the Republican Guard. This elite and well-equipped unit was expanded from 1,500 soldiers during Hrawi's mandate to around 4,000.

Jamil Sayyed was promoted from deputy head of military intelligence to run the General Security Department, the Surete Generale, the most powerful of the state's security institutions. Sayyed was Lahoud's inseparable shadow, providing advice on a raft of issues and chaperoning the president on overseas trips and at his meetings with senior Syrian officials. Sayyed's office in the General Security headquarters became an obligatory stop-off for foreign diplomats on their routine diplomatic rounds of Lebanon's most senior officials, knowing that this was where the real power lay in Lebanon.[6]

Critics likened Lahoud's regime to that of Fouad Chehab, a former army commander who served as president from 1958 to 1964 and is remembered for his disdain toward the civilian authorities. But Lahoud's intention, according to Lebanese Army and intelligence officers, was to mirror the structure of the Syrian regime, building a military and intelligence apparatus to shadow, undermine and manipulate the civilian administration run by the government.[7]

The advantage of Lahoud to the Syrians was that the president had no independent source of power and owed his status solely to Syrian patronage. But Lahoud also had his opponents in the Syrian regime, such as Abdel-Halim Khaddam and Ghazi Kanaan, whose ties to Hariri and Jumblatt remained firm despite the gradual changing of the guard in

Damascus as Bashar's influence increased. In early 2000, Kanaan intervened to dampen Lahoud's campaign against Hariri, inviting the former premier and Fouad Siniora to a party in the Bekaa attended by senior Syrian military intelligence officers and pro-Syrian politicians.

'He announced to everyone that "there is no zaim [leader] but Rafik Hariri",' recalls Qassem Qanso, the then secretary-general of the Lebanese branch of the Baath party, who attended the gathering. 'It was a message to Lahoud that, if he tried to break Hariri, Kanaan would break Lahoud.'[8]

In a further attempt to dilute Lahoud's power, Kanaan, with the assistance of Jamil Sayyed, hammered out an electoral law (subsequently dubbed the 'Ghazi Kanaan Law') designed to help Hariri succeed in the parliamentary elections planned for late summer 2000.[9]

As the parliamentary elections drew closer, the embattled Lahoud regime increased its criticism of Hariri, using the state-run Tele Liban television station to air satirical propaganda, caricaturing Hariri as a bloated whale in one and using the theme from *The Godfather* to depict Hariri as a mafia don in another.

Hariri fought back through his own media empire, playing on the failure of the Hoss government to tackle the worsening economic crisis. The debt had reached $22 billion by the summer of 2000. Once more, Hariri was being hailed as the economic 'miracle worker', the saviour who would return to steer Lebanon out of its financial woes.

The elections saw Hariri and his opposition allies smash the government's candidates in all areas except the south and the Bekaa, the traditional Shiite domains. In Beirut, Hariri and his allies captured all but one of the 19 seats available. It was a rout in which even Prime Minister Hoss lost his seat in parliament. Hariri could not be denied the premiership after his electoral triumph, and Damascus calculated that, if his return helped revive the economy, then Syria would benefit as well.

Yet Hariri and his close colleagues knew that they faced a potentially troublesome period ahead having to deal with Lahoud, who was deeply unhappy that his rival had muscled his way back into power. Some friends of Hariri even tried to persuade him not to accept the premiership, calculating that letting the president 'simmer in his economic and administrative troubles' would hasten an early collapse of the regime.

'Hariri accepted because Lebanon had just been liberated from Israeli occupation and he saw an opportunity to revive the financial and economic situation in the country which was always his dream,' says Marwan Hamade. 'But all we did was give Lahoud new blood.'

The relationship with Lahoud was not the only challenge lying in wait for Hariri. His comeback as prime minister coincided with the return of a spectre that had plagued his previous governments and one he hoped had ended with the Israeli troop withdrawal – Hizbullah's guerrilla fighters were back in action in south Lebanon.

In the five months following Israel's flight from the south, Hizbullah units had deployed up to the Blue Line, the UN name for the boundary corresponding to the border behind which Israel was required by the UN to withdraw. Hizbullah men in civilian clothes carrying binoculars and walkie-talkies monitored Israeli troop movements on the other side of the fence from several small observation posts along the Blue Line, while armed fighters in camouflage uniforms and helmets patrolled the remoter sectors. In response to persistent calls from the UN and the international community, the Lebanese government in August dispatched a 1,000-strong force of soldiers and paramilitary police to the former occupation zone, but it did not interfere with Hizbullah's control of the border itself.

The Blue Line runs for 110 kilometres from the chalk cliffs of Ras Naqoura on the Mediterranean coast in the west to the craggy limestone foothills of Mount Hermon in the east. The last 13 kilometres of the boundary follow the edge of the Shebaa Farms, a 25-square-kilometre mountainside at the northern end of the Golan Heights which was occupied by Israeli forces following the 1967 Arab–Israeli war. When Israel pulled out of south Lebanon in May 2000, it retained its military positions in the Shebaa Farms declaring that the area was Syrian, not Lebanese. The Hoss government, prodded by Damascus, insisted that the area was Lebanese and that the Israeli occupation could not be considered ended until the Farms were returned to Lebanon.

Before 2000, few Lebanese had heard of the Shebaa Farms and fewer still knew exactly where it lay, the remote mountain slope only lingering in the memory of people living in adjacent villages. Beirut's inept hand-ling of its territorial claim to the Shebaa Farms persuaded the UN to conclude that the weight of historical and documentary evidence pointed to Syrian ownership. Israel's presence, therefore, was subject to UN Secur-ity Council resolutions regarding the occupation of Syrian territory, not Lebanese.

The debate over the sovereignty of the Shebaa Farms was not merely an arcane territorial dispute. If Israel ignored Lebanon's claim to the Shebaa Farms and maintained its military presence, it could provide a sufficient, albeit contrived, justification for Hizbullah to renew its resistance activ-ities, furnishing Syria with a new point of pressure against the Jewish state. The Israeli troop withdrawal had narrowed Syria's bargaining options in retrieving the Golan from Israeli occupation, and also promised to undermine Syria's control over Lebanon. Since the collapse of the

Geneva summit in March, the US had abandoned the Syria track for a last-minute breakthrough deal between Israel and the Palestinians on which to conclude the Clinton presidency. Syria, with its untested young president, was left to stew. In that context, the remote barren hillside of the Shebaa Farms assumed a strategic importance to Syria. Fomenting a low-scale guerrilla conflict in the Farms, with its attendant risk of igniting a broader conflict, would remind the US and Israel that Syria still had teeth and would not remain passive while its regional assets were stripped away.

The trigger for the new Hizbullah offensive came on September 28 with the outbreak of the Palestinian Al-Aqsa intifada. Seven days later, Hizbullah's fighters struck, snatching three Israeli soldiers across the Blue Line in the Shebaa Farms area in a well-planned and coordinated ambush. That afternoon, the hills and wadis of south Lebanon resounded once more to the crack of artillery shells as Israeli guns pounded the edges of villages opposite the Shebaa Farms while helicopter gunships clattered overhead.

Hizbullah announced that it was willing to swap the three captured soldiers for the 20 Lebanese detainees which Israel had unwisely failed to release when it withdrew from Lebanon five months earlier.

Hizbullah demonstrated that the kidnapping of the three soldiers was not an isolated incident by announcing the kidnapping of an Israeli army colonel in an elaborate sting operation a week later and by staging two roadside bomb attacks in November against Israeli patrols on the edge of the Shebaa Farms, killing one soldier and wounding three others.

The timing of the Shebaa Farms campaign may have served the interests of Syria and Hizbullah but it threatened to complicate Hariri's plans to reverse the economic recession and encourage renewed investment in Lebanon. Hariri already faced difficulties with Lahoud over the composition of the new government. The president had installed his allies at the ministries of telecommunications, electricity and industry, to thwart Hariri's programme of privatising state utilities, the cornerstone of his economic recovery plan. Walid Jumblatt, the prominent Druze leader, attacked the president's meddling and predicted pessimistically that Hariri and Lahoud 'will not even work for one second. There is no harmony between the two men.'

Meanwhile, a fresh challenge to Syrian domination was stirring in the Christian and Druze heartland of Mount Lebanon. Hafez al-Assad's concerns about the effect of the Israeli withdrawal on Syria's status in Lebanon were well founded. The Christians, particularly Cardinal Nasrallah Sfeir, the Maronite patriarch, were growing more vocal in calling for a Syrian troop redeployment as enshrined in the Taif Accord. In

September, a conclave of Maronite bishops delivered an unprecedented attack against Syrian domination, complaining that 'the situation has become intolerable – Lebanon has lost its sovereignty faced with a hegemony imposed on all its institutions'.

Damascus was able to ignore such demands when they were expressed soley by the marginalised Christians, and the Israelis were still occupying the south. But in the autumn of 2000, Walid Jumblatt joined with the Christians in a budding alliance that overturned centuries of enmity between the two neighbouring Mount Lebanon communities and promised to be an influential new anti-Syrian front.

Jumblatt recommended that Syrian forces in Lebanon be 'redeployed' and called for an end to Syria's 'unwarranted interference' in Lebanese affairs. It was the first time since 1990 that a senior non-Christian figure had publicly criticised the Syrian presence, let alone an ally of Syria who had served Damascus well during the Lebanese war. The furious Syrian authorities declared Jumblatt *persona non grata* in Damascus and had their allies in Lebanon issue veiled threats against the Druze leader.[10]

Anti-Syrian unrest grew in early 2001 with students at mainly Christian universities holding sit-ins and demonstrations. In March, Cardinal Sfeir took his message to the United States and Canada on a five-week tour which was closely followed by the Lebanese back home. One sour note of the trip was the refusal of the new American president, George W. Bush, and his administration to meet Sfeir. The White House said it would be inapproriate to grant an audience to the cardinal before having met the Lebanese president and prime minister. The attacks of September 11 were still half a year away and, in these early months of the Bush presidency, policy toward Syria followed the 'constructive engagement' of previous administrations.

More alarming for the Syrian authorities than the alliance between the Christians and Druze was the surfacing of a few Sunni and Shiite figures who added their voices to calls for a more balanced relationship with Syria. Although their numbers were few – a smattering of journalists, feudal chieftains and liberal politicians – it cracked the façade of unspoken Muslim unanimity in support of the Syrian presence. It was often said that the Syrians could only enter Lebanon with the support of the Christians and would only leave if they lost the support of the Muslims. Damascus could not afford to stand by and watch the emergence of a cross-sectarian consensus against its rule in Lebanon.

Some of Syria's more robust allies were activated in a calculated move to stir up the spectre of sectarian unrest. A group of Sunni clerics in north Lebanon organised by Syrian intelligence as the 'Akkar Ulemma' released a statement warning that Christians in the area would be attacked unless Sfeir dropped his anti-Syrian tirade. An anti-Syrian MP had his office firebombed, a letter bomb wounded the niece and sister of a former minister who was close to Jumblatt, and pro-Syrian Muslim extremists issued statements vowing to fight Christians with 'teeth, clubs and kitchen knives'. Syrian and Lebanese intelligence promoted alternative centres of Sunni influence, such as facilitating the re-emergence of the Mourabitoun, a Sunni wartime militia that had fallen foul of Syria in the mid-1980s and had been chased out of Beirut, and orchestrating an aggressive demonstration by Al-Ahbash, a Sufi-inspired Islamist organisation that opposes the Salafi ideology of Al-Qaeda. The Al-Ahbash followers brandished clubs and knives and yelled threats in a carefully choreographed attempt to provide suitably ferocious images for the media.

The campaign of incitement was contrived, transparently so, yet such is the nature of Lebanon that the incidents helped re-kindle the perpetually smouldering embers of sectarianism. That sentiment was evident in the working-class quarters of Ain Roumaineh, a Christian district, and its Shiite neighbour, Shiyah, in southern Beirut where tensions were running high as the country prepared to mark the twenty-sixth anniversary of the outbreak of the civil war on April 13. The opening shots of the conflict were fired in these rundown streets of drab apartment blocks and small stores, and in April 2001 the residents were once more speaking of war.

'I am ready to fight Muslims or Syrians, it doesn't matter. All my friends feel this way,' said 16-year-old Adib to the nodding approval of his grandfather who sipped a cup of coffee outside a small café in Ain Roumaineh. Others spoke darkly of Muslim yearnings to drive all Christians from Lebanon. 'In 1958, they had a plan to make a Muslim nation. They want all the Christians to go. That plan is still there,' said one. Some blamed the tensions on the Syrians while others spoke of rumoured acts of vandalism, such as anti-Christian graffiti, and violence: a priest in the Beirut suburb of Hadath was beaten and stripped of his robes.

A few streets away where the small glass-fronted shrines to Lebanese saints gave way to stencilled logos of the Amal Movement and tattered portraits of Hizbullah 'martyrs', Fahed Salloum, a 25-year-old Shiite, blamed the tensions on Cardinal Sfeir, that 'little virus' who was 'causing trouble between us'.

'I hope Sayyed Hassan [Nasrallah] issues a fatwa against the patriarch. I will be the first martyr. I hope there will be a war so that there will be an Islamic nation,' he said. But his friends scoffed at him and shook their heads. 'There's no problem between us and the Christians. They saw the

Ahbash on the streets with their knives and sticks and they got scared,' said Tariq.

Most of the comments were bluster rather than laden with intent. Yet it exposed just how easily Lebanon's lingering communal tensions could be manipulated and aggravated by third parties.

The Syrians attempted to bolster Lahoud's flagging popularity by releasing in December 45 Lebanese detainees, saying it was in response to a request by the Lebanese president. In mid-June, some 7,000 Syrian soldiers abandoned their positions in Beirut in what was the first significant redeployment since the end of the war. Battered old military trucks painted in garishly bright green ground up the highway from Beirut toward the Bekaa with beaming Syrian soldiers waving rifles and portraits of Bashar. It was stated publicly that the decision for the redeployment had been made by the Lebanese and Syrian presidents several months earlier but had been put on hold because of the anti-Syrian protests in the spring. The implicit message was that only Lahoud could achieve the departure of Syrian troops, while displays of anti-Syrian sentiment would stall the process.

Tensions also were building along Lebanon's southern frontier where Hizbullah's sporadic hit-and-run raids against Israeli forces in the Shebaa Farms not only risked provoking a major Israeli offensive, but also threatened to jeopardise Hariri's globe-trotting campaign to rustle up grants, soft loans and investment funds to revive the economy.[11] In February, Hariri visited Paris, accompanied by his core economic and financial team, to prepare for a donors' conference later that month hosted by Chirac and attended by the World Bank and European Union officials. Hariri reassured the potential donors that there would be no provocations from Lebanon along its southern border with Israel.

'We have a clear agreement with our Syrian brothers in this matter,' he said. 'There will be no provocations on our part.'

The next day, however, Hizbullah fighters attacked an Israeli vehicle with an anti-tank missile, killing a soldier. It was the first assault by Hizbullah since the end of November and appeared to be a deliberate riposte to Hariri's presumption in speaking on behalf of the resistance.

The attack embarrassed Hariri and threatened to stem the anticipated flow of funds that had been secured in Paris. He hurried back to Lebanon and held a flurry of crisis meetings with Bashar, Lahoud, Hizbullah officials and the Iranian ambassador, struggling to win a moratorium on military operations in the Shebaa Farms. Ehud Barak, Israel's outgoing prime minister, was about to be replaced by Ariel Sharon, the godfather of the 1982 invasion of Lebanon. Hariri was worried that the bellicose Sharon would not hesitate in launching devastating attacks against Lebanon. Like a growing number of Lebanese, Hariri resented Lebanon's economic revival being held captive to Syria's strategic interests in regaining the Golan Heights from Israel, which, after all, was the ulterior purpose behind the Shebaa Farms campaign.

In frustration, he released a statement questioning Hizbullah's monopoly of guerrilla operations against Israel. Stung by the criticism, Hizbullah held several urgent meetings with the premier, at the end of which both parties announced they had reached an 'understanding'. No details were given, however, and it remained unclear how Hariri's ambition of rebuilding the economy could be reconciled with Hizbullah's determination to continue waging its war against Israel.

Hariri recognized that the continuation of Hizbullah's armed status was inimical to the future prosperity of Lebanon, but he understood that the party could not be disarmed by force without provoking a new civil war, even if the Syrians were to agree to such a move.

'Hariri took a very pragmatic approach to Hizbullah – as he did toward most issues – and applied a businessman's logic of where the bottom-line interests lay,' says a foreign diplomat closely involved in Lebanon affairs who knew Hariri for over 25 years.[12] 'Hariri saw Hizbullah's continued status as an armed "state-within-a-state" as wholly inconsistent with Lebanon's ability to project an image – and reality – of security and stability essential to secure investment and economic development. Thus, disarming of Hizbullah and integration of Hizbullah into the Lebanese political mainstream were ultimate goals that had to be pursued in Lebanon's long-term interest.'

By the summer of 2001, fears of an imminent violent and sustained confrontation between Hizbullah and Israel had diminished as both sides assimilated the new 'rules of the game' governing the conflict. The Shebaa Farms became the locus of Hizbullah's military action and was tacitly tolerated by the Israeli government as long as the fighting remained confined to the remote unpopulated mountainside.

Hariri's difficulties with Hizbullah, however, paled in comparison to his troubled relationship with Lahoud who, as far as Hariri and his allies were concerned, seemed intent on thwarting the premier's projects and policies.

The struggle for the control of Lebanon was growing more bitter and keenly contested as the fortunes of both sides waxed and waned. Hariri, backed by Ghazi Kanaan and Abdel-Halim Khaddam, had dominated much of the post-war period, only to be checked in 1998 by the growing influence in Damascus of Bashar and his support for Lahoud, who was elected president that year. After two years on the sidelines, the Hariri camp struck back in 2000, taking advantage of the death of Hafez al-Assad to fix the electoral law against Lahoud while Bashar was preoccupied with the presidential succession in Damascus.

But now it was Hariri's turn to be on the defensive as a resurgent Lahoud, enjoying the full backing of Bashar and bolstered by his Lebanese allies in the government, remorselessly chipped away at the prime minister's authority.

In 2002, the Syrians quietly backed a campaign to replace Hariri with Prince Walid bin Talal, a half-Saudi, half-Lebanese business tycoon, described as the world's sixth-richest man. Bin Talal, who was investing heavily in hotel construction in Beirut, publicly backed Lahoud in the president's battles with Hariri, and showed little hesitancy in speaking his mind about how to redress Lebanon's economic ills. At the official opening in July 2002 of his \$140 million Movenpick hotel set in a Beirut cliff overlooking the Mediterranean, bin Talal outlined to an audience stuffed with top Lebanese officials an economic recovery plan for Lebanon, which the media described as a 'policy statement' for a future government headed by bin Talal.

Ghazi Aridi, the information minister and ally of Hariri, quipped the next day that, 'if the government is changed every time a new hotel is built in Lebanon, we will be having 15 or 20 new cabinets lined up for the next few months'. But he admitted that there is a 'crisis of mistrust' between Hariri and Lahoud.

Prior to cabinet sessions, ministers would be handed instructions in sealed envelopes from the presidency telling them how to vote on each proposal tabled for the meeting. When Lahoud chaired the sessions he would often ignore Hariri, refusing to let him speak or cutting him off mid-sentence.[13]

During one heated cabinet debate, Hariri felt compelled to vote against his own proposal after it was rejected by Lahoud. According to a cabinet colleague, Hariri explained his decision, saying 'If I hadn't voted with Lahoud, he would have gone to the Syrians and told them that I'm blocking them and destroying the stability of the regime. You can do that, but I can't.'[14]

Fares Boueiz, the foreign minister in Hariri's governments of the 1990s, recalls meeting Bashar in 2002 and advising the Syrian president that Lahoud's disrespectful treatment of Hariri was a dangerous mistake that would make a 'Sunni martyr' out of the prime minister.[15]

'We as Christians don't want history to write that Emile Lahoud as a Maronite used an external power to attack and threaten a Sunni prime minister,' Boueiz recalls telling Bashar.

Furthermore, he asked, what would happen to the Lebanese economy if Hariri resigned?

'Assad smiled and told me, "Don't be afraid. Hariri will never leave office. We have him nailed to his chair. He will stay because he can't refuse anything from us, whatever we do to him," ' Boueiz says.

While Hariri was locked into his struggle with Lahoud, Syria's relations with the United States were steadily deteriorating, a consequence of Washington's determination to oust Saddam Hussein and Bashar's refusal to cooperate. His father may have recognised the strategic benefits of allying with the US against Iraq in 1990, but the geo-political circumstances had changed 12 years on. Syria and Iraq had embarked on a rapprochement in 1997 ending decades of animosity between the two rival branches of the Baath party which ruled both countries. Syrian trade with Iraq under the 'oil-for-food' programme reached an estimated $1 billion in 2001, double the 2000 figure. Syria was suspected of illegally earning another $1 billion to $1.5 billion a year from smuggled Iraqi oil which was used to satisfy domestic needs, freeing up Syrian crude for export, earning the regime much-needed hard currency.

The Bush administration's broader ambition that Saddam Hussein's removal would trigger the fall of other totalitarian regimes in the region was another pressing reason for Syria to oppose the planned invasion. Furthermore, Bashar appeared to calculate that it would not be to Syria's disadvantage to unfurl and hoist the colours of Arab nationalism, tapping into the seething anti-American sentiment on the Arab 'street' which adamantly opposed the planned invasion of Iraq. Let other Arab nations such as Jordan, Saudi Arabia and Egypt cower behind American tanks; Syria would remain a bastion of Arab resolve and defiance. It was a message with which many ordinary Arabs agreed.

The rhetoric between Damascus and Washington reached unprecedented levels of hostility in the days following the invasion of Iraq in March 2003. The speed with which the Iraqi regime fell stunned and dismayed the Syrian authorities and suggested that Damascus had committed a serious strategic blunder in tying its colours to Saddam Hussein's teetering flagpole.

With American tanks parked in the overthrown dictator's palaces and Washington triumphant, neighbouring Syria suddenly looked particularly vulnerable. US officials took to describing Syria as 'low-hanging fruit', easy to pick off.

At the beginning of May, Colin Powell travelled to Damascus and put on the table before Bashar a list of all the outstanding grievances the US had with Syria. They went through the list one by one, agreeing on some points, disagreeing on others. But one major concession Powell extracted from Bashar was a promise that, by the end of the year, Syrian troops would be redeployed to the Bekaa in compliance with the Taif Accord.

Powell was pleased with the visit, but Hariri was more sceptical. On being told the news by an aide, Hariri asked 'Does this mean they will withdraw the army and the intelligence?'[16]

When the aide said he did not know, Hariri predicted that the Syrians would not withdraw, adding 'If they were serious, they could withdraw next month. Why wait until the end of the year?'

Hariri would have felt justified in his scepticism given that two weeks earlier Damascus had instituted a change of government in Lebanon which had resulted in the most pro-Syrian cabinet line-up since 1989. It included such loyalist stalwarts as Qassem Qanso, the head of the Lebanese branch of the Baath party, and Assad Hardan, the head of the Syrian Social Nationalist party. Although Hariri was retained as premier, he and his allies understood that the composition of the government not only strengthened Damascus's control over Lebanon at a time of heightened international pressure, but it also imposed further restraints on Hariri's ability to push his policies.[17]

Hariri's friends, political colleagues and family urged him to resign. Let the economy collapse. That would remind Lahoud and his Syrian backers of Hariri's value. But Hariri refused to quit. He was locked into the premiership by his need to appease the Syrians and an unflinching optimism that the situation would improve. He blamed his difficulties on Lahoud and the Lebanese–Syrian security framework rather than the Syrian leadership itself. Although the formation of the April 2003 government would later be regarded as a milestone on the road to Hariri's eventual break with Syria, he continued to strive for a healthy relationship with the Syrian regime. He understood that Syria, as a larger, more powerful neighbour, represented an immutable fact of life for Lebanon, with the fate of both countries inextricably linked. Furthermore, abandoning the premiership at this critical juncture would mean throwing away everything he had striven for since 1992.

'He told us to go suck a lemon,' says Saad Hariri. 'He always talked about it with us but I believe he couldn't leave politics because they wouldn't let him. They just wanted to weaken him and weaken him and weaken him. Also . . . he used to look at the bigger picture and saw his suffering as a temporary problem that would pass.'[18]

Five months earlier, Hariri had achieved one of the greatest coups of his premiership in persuading Jacques Chirac to host in Paris a donor conference on behalf of Lebanon, a follow-up to the smaller conference of February 2001. The Paris II conference, grouping 18 of the world's richest and most powerful countries along with eight international lending institutions, raised around $4.3 billion in financial support for Lebanon in exchange for promises of administrative and economic reforms, including privatising state utilities and slashing public spending. Hariri had worked hard to prepare the way for the conference, which was hailed by the Lebanese media as a 'glorious success'. He had received promises from Nabih Berri that legislation concerning privatisation of state utilities would pass unhindered in parliament. Even Chirac had interceded with Bashar and Lahoud during a visit to Lebanon and Syria a month prior to the conference to win assurances that the promised reforms would be implemented smoothly and on time. Therefore, even with an unfavour-able cabinet line-up, how could Hariri step down from the premiership just as the government was about to push ahead with fulfilling the promises of Paris II?

'He thought at the time that the commitments made by Bashar to him and the main donors of Paris II would stand and his main mission would be to implement what was agreed at the conference,' says Marwan Hamade, the economy minister in the new cabinet.[19] 'He understood pro-gressively that the change in cabinet was meant to block the results of Paris II and deprive him of any merit in getting the economy back on its feet.'

Months before the formation of the new government, Syria's military intelligence structure in Lebanon was reshuffled when Major General Rustom Ghazaleh replaced the long-serving Ghazi Kanaan as intelligence chief.

Kanaan's recall was prompted in part by his hostile relationship with Lahoud which had never truly recovered from the Syrian general's tinker-ing with the electoral law of 2000 which had helped Hariri back to the premiership. Kanaan, who was appointed head of the Political Security Department in Damascus, was also regarded as being too close to Hariri, an Alawite 'baron' who had befriended the regime's Sunni 'enemy'.

'In 2000, they hit back at us and Hariri returned to power on a white horse with Walid Jumblatt,' says Wiam Wahhab, the pro-Syrian politician. 'But when Rustom Ghazaleh took over from Kanaan it severed the link between Hariri and his Syrian friends.'[20]

Ghazaleh, until then the head of Syrian military intelligence in Beirut, was a dour, secretive man with a dome-like forehead and thick, dark hair whose chubby frame was squeezed into expensive suits and crisply ironed shirts. He lacked the experience and charisma of his predecessor.

Kanaan had combined cold ruthlessness with a deep understanding and even affection for the Lebanese milieu, but Ghazaleh, says an ambassador in Beirut, was 'clodhopping, brutal and stupid'.[21]

'Ghazi Kanaan was a gentleman, but Ghazaleh was a thug who cruelly humiliated Rafik Hariri. A most disagreeable gangster.'

Describing Kanaan as a gentleman may make more than a few Lebanese wince, but Syria's veteran 'high commissioner' ran Lebanon with the confidence of a senior official in the Syrian regime and a contemporary of Hafez al-Assad, able to adapt his orders as he saw fit and not intimidated by the manipulations of Jamil Sayyed, Lahoud and their allies. Ghazaleh, on the other hand, was a mere factotum, carrying out his orders while 'easily buyable with financial privileges', according to a former Lebanese minister who knew the Syrian officer well.[22]

Nohad Mashnouq, an advisor to Hariri in the 1990s who knew both Kanaan and Ghazaleh, says, 'I don't think he [Ghazaleh] hated Hariri inside, but he could not dare say this. Ghazaleh didn't have the power of Kanaan.'[23]

Under Ghazaleh's watch, the level of corruption, which was already high, increased steadily at the expense of the Lebanese economy.

A glaring example of the Syrian-endorsed racketeering system broke in early 2003 with the collapse of the Al-Madina bank with unexplained losses of over $1 billion. The scandal gripped the Lebanese. It was a rare glimpse into the murky world of corruption and embezzlement involving senior Lebanese and Syrian officials. The Lebanese media were intimidated not to fully investigate the scandal, concentrating instead on the publicity-hungry Rana Koleilat, a humble bank teller who mysteriously rose to become chief aide to a co-owner of the bank. Koleilat apparently was at the heart of much of Al-Madina's illegal activities. Some of the jucier details of the scandal seeped out into the public domain, involving powerful Lebanese and Syrian figures. According to a report in *US News*, a New York-based firm of investigators allegedly discovered that, in a one-month period ending in January 2003, Koleilat used Al-Madina funds to pay $941,000 to Ghazaleh's brothers. Two months later, Koleilat allegedly gave Ghazaleh a $300,000 'donation' from the bank's funds. She is also said to have paid Elias Murr, the then interior minister and son-in-law of Lahoud, $10 million for a villa which was subsequently valued by the Lebanese authorities at $2.5 million.[24]

'Greed', says Saad Hariri, 'was the reason for the Syrians' downfall in Lebanon. Rustom Ghazaleh and this bunch of intelligence officers only cared about filling their pockets, a mafia with political power. The big difference between Hafez al-Assad and Bashar al-Assad is that Hafez used money for political purposes, but Bashar al-Assad uses politics to make money. And this combination is a disaster.'

From April, with the formation of the new government, Hariri found his key economic and reform policies stifled by his own government as the battles in the cabinet worsened. From May to June the government was unable to hold regular meetings due to disagreements over the agenda.

On June 16, two rockets were fired into Hariri's Future TV station in Beirut, burning a television studio but causing no casualties. An unheard-of Islamist group claimed responsibility for what most Lebanese regarded as an ominous warning of Syrian displeasure with Hariri's opposition to Lahoud.

The Council for Development and Reconstruction, which had played the lead role in carrying out the rehabiliation of Lebanon's infrastructure in the 1990s, had its powers limited and was made more accountable to the cabinet rather than the prime minister's office. CDR officials could only watch in frustration as pending reconstruction schemes were put on hold or unfolding projects ground to a halt at a cost of millions of dollars.

'We were given soft loans with grace periods but we were unable to proceed with the projects because Lahoud would block the land expropriations,' says Hisham Nasser, CDR's vice-president from January 2002 to October 2004. 'For three years we were stuck. We had \$3 billion worth of projects. All they had to do was approve \$250 million worth of expropriations. These obstacles by Lahoud set Lebanon back by three years.'[25]

In the summer of 2003, Lebanon was beset with power outages as the cash-strapped electricity utility, Electricite du Liban, lacked funds to pay for fuel oil for the country's power plants. A Lebanese delegation negotiated a deal to buy fuel oil at a preferential rate directly from the Kuwaiti government, a state-to-state arrangement that would cut out the exorbitant fees charged by middlemen. But the transaction was not approved by the cabinet, in part because of the powerful Lebanese and Syrian interests involved in the oil importation racket which stood to lose out if the deal went ahead.[26]

Projects in the Solidere area of central Beirut were frozen, including the construction of the new souk which was set to house the largest concentration of retail and entertainment activity in the city. The government's procrastination in passing a decree to authorise the souk's construction led several prestigious retail companies to locate their outlets at competitor sites.

It was an intensely frustrating period for Hariri, which he would subtly intimate to visiting diplomats.

'He would never say anything against Lahoud to us, nothing quotable, but it was very clear what he meant through the use of raised eyebrows and wry smiles,' says one ambassador.[27]

Although Hariri would try to remain buoyant and optimistic in public, occasionally he let his guard slip to reveal his true feelings toward Lahoud.

'He [Lahoud] does not want to reconcile with me,' he told *As Safir* daily after one particularly tense cabinet session in September. 'I do not want to have a problem with him but he insists on provoking me.' Hariri added that Lahoud was demanding his support for an extension to his presidential term, 'but I have no role in that and he knows very well that the matter is in the hands of another party'.

That other party, Syria, was keeping its options open regarding an additional term for Lahoud, although the overtly pro-Syrian composition of the April 2003 cabinet indicated that that was what Damascus had in mind.

For Damascus, prolonging Lahoud's presidency would provide continuity and stability as Syria's relations with the United States continued to deteriorate. In October, the US Congress approved the long-pending Syria Accountability Act which threatened sanctions against Damascus unless it fulfilled a host of conditions that appeared to suit the security needs of Israel rather than respect the sovereignty of Lebanon. Among the demands were a Syrian withdrawal from Lebanon, ceasing support for terrorist groups, abandoning the development of ballistic missiles and weapons of mass destruction, refraining from violating UN sanctions against Iraq, evicting Hizbullah and Iranian Revolutionary Guards along the border with Israel and replacing them with Lebanese troops, and entering into unconditional peace talks with Israel. Bush waited until May 2004 before authorising a raft of sanctions against Syria, including prohibiting the export of US goods to Syria, excluding humanitarian supplies, and banning Syrian Airways flights to and from the US.

In reaction to the passing of the act, Bashar described the Bush administration as a bunch of 'fanatics' and warmongers. American civilian officials in the Pentagon began to accuse Syria of not doing enough to block militants from entering Iraq. US officials were also pressuring Syria to return an estimated $3 billion in stolen assets allegedly deposited in Syrian and Lebanese banks by the former Iraqi regime, a charge Damascus denied.

On October 8, Cardinal Sfeir, the Maronite patriarch, fired the first public shots in the coming battle over the presidential extension by stating in a speech in Paris that he opposed the amendment of the constitution because it 'should not be manipulated according to whims'. As with

Hrawi's presidential extension in 1995, the constitution would have to be amended once again to allow Lahoud to serve more than a single six-year term. The patriarch made no reference to Lahoud's ambitions for an extended mandate, but the inference was clear.

Days later, Hariri subtly endorsed Sfeir's view, saying 'The patriarch's remarks are great patriarchal remarks.'

But Syrian support for Lahoud remained steadfast. On November 20, Bashar confirmed his solid backing for Lahoud during a summit between the two leaders in Damascus. The Lebanese media reported that Lahoud still represented Syria's closest ally in Lebanon, a 'source of confidence' who would receive the 'backing he needs to confront the looming challenges'.

Two days later, Hariri stayed away from the Independence Day parade in Martyrs' Square customarily attended by the country's top political and military echelons. Hariri's office said he was in Saudi Arabia to perform a pilgrimage to Mecca to mark the end of Ramadan, even though the holy fasting month had several days to go. The failure of a prime minister to attend the annual celebration, or even delegate a representative, was an unprecedented snub and underlined in a very public way just how poisonous the relationship between the prime minister and the president had grown.

The Syrian regime had little sympathy for such theatrics and considered Hariri's disdain of Lahoud as exhibiting a dangerously rebellious streak. At the end of the year, Hariri was summoned to Damascus for a meeting with Bashar and the top Syrian officers connected with Lebanon, Ghazi Kanaan, Rustom Ghazaleh and Mohammed Khallouf, a chief aide to Ghazaleh. For 45 minutes, Hariri was accused of plotting with the US and France against Syria and of deviating from the joint Lebanese–Syrian stand. Specifically, they charged him with secretly meeting a senior US State Department official in Beirut, and of persuading King Abdullah of Jordan to use his influence with Israel to thwart a prisoner swap being negotiated by Germany betweeen Hizbullah and Israel. The meeting was one of the toughest Hariri had to endure in his long career of dealing with the Syrians.

'Hariri considered walking out of the meeting, but he just sat there,' says a close former advisor to Hariri. 'The Syrians were feeling the international pressure. Their whole strategy was based on "We hold Lebanon or else there will be chaos." Suddenly, here was someone who could steer Lebanon safely with international guarantees and without the Syrians.'[28]

At the end of the meeting, Kanaan took Hariri by the arm and led him into his office so that the shaken prime minister could calm down and recover from a nose bleed brought on by high blood pressure. A little later the same morning, Abdel-Halim Khaddam met an agitated Bashar who told him about the heated meeting with Hariri.

'After he told me this, I asked him how could he talk like that to the prime minister of Lebanon,' Khaddam recalls. ' "He is a close ally to Syria. He has served Syria. What would he be feeling now and how would this benefit Syria?" I told him. At this point Bashar al-Assad calmed down and asked me to get in touch with Hariri to invite him back to Damascus.'[29]

Hariri refused to return to the Syrian capital and met Khaddam instead at the vice-president's home in the mountain resort of Bloudan close to the Lebanese border.

'Rafik was clearly angry and showed his frustration. He said he had not expected to be treated in this way and that this treatment would be in his mind until his death. He would never forget it,' Khaddam says.

The Syrian leadership's hostility toward Hariri was stoked by an intensive and pernicious whispering campaign by Lahoud and his allies against the prime minister, according to numerous Lebanese and Syrian political figures. Pro-Syrian Lebanese claimed Hariri was working against Damascus and was a tool of the Americans, and that he was a traitor who sought to disarm Hizbullah. It was a persistent drip-drip of invective and suspicion that steadily eroded Hariri's standing.

'Bashar al-Assad used to receive and meet with Lebanese who were anti-Hariri,' Khaddam says.[30] 'He used to listen to them and take all this information into consideration when making his decisions. Lebanese military intelligence used to send Bashar false reports and studies once or twice a week about Hariri's intentions and his anti-Syrian sentiment.'

The chief architect of the anti-Hariri campaign, according to Khaddam, was Jamil Sayyed, who, with his direct access to Bashar, 'was not only the ruler of Lebanon, he was almost the ruler of Syria'.[31]

There was little Hariri could do to dent the campaign waged against him, even though he persisted in trying to persuade and reassure the Syrian leadership that he was their friend and not a traitor.

'The Lebanese intelligence and the Syrians played an important role in upsetting relations between Hariri and many people and groups, including Hizbullah,' recalls Fouad Siniora. 'Hariri was continually under pressure and attack. He used to get really angry about this. He would say "I cannot reproduce every day that I am a nationalist and good citizen." What did they [his accusers] have to do with nationalism and partriotism? Hariri made many sacrifices in his life and personal wealth. At the end of the day, he used to go crazy.'

Despite the humiliating treatment from Damascus, Hariri continued to defend Syrian interests and utilise his international contacts for Syria's benefit. On one occasion he declared in a press conference that accusations that Syria interfered in Lebanese affairs 'is largely exaggerated to the point of turning matters upside down'.

Yet displays of loyalty to Damascus won Hariri little respite from Damascus. In early 2004, one of Hariri's aides received a telephone call from a friend in Paris who said that a bill similar to the Syria Accountability Act was being circulated in the French parliament by Jacques Chirac's UMP party.[32]

'Your friend Chirac and his party are going for it,' the aide told Hariri. Nonplussed, Hariri said he had no idea that such a bill was being proposed. He put a call through to Chirac. The French president said he too was unaware of the bill. Hariri told him that, if it was allowed to pass, it would be harmful for Lebanon and greatly complicate the Lebanese–Syrian relationship. Chirac promised to look into it, after which the proposed legislation disappeared from view.

'Two weeks later, Hariri received a message from President Assad accusing Hariri of setting up the whole affair so that he could call his friend Chirac and have it cancelled to make the Syrians feel indebted to him,' the aide says. 'It was down to Alawite paranoia because Hariri was a Sunni, a rich, powerful Sunni with five planes who could pick up the phone at 1 p.m. and be with [Prime Minister] Mohammed Mahathir in Malaysia by midnight, the next day in Japan and the third day back in Beirut with pledges of $600 million [for reconstruction] in his back pocket.'

Even in his Koreitem home, Hariri was not immune from the reach of the Lebanese and Syrian intelligence apparatus.

'Hariri believed his house was bugged,' says an Arab diplomat. 'When meeting guests in his office in Koreitem, Hariri would switch on the television and flick between channels to drown out the conversation. If the conversation turned to delicate matters, Hariri and the guest would retreat into the small bathroom attached to his office where they could whisper.'[33]

Other conversations would be held outside in the garden. Occasionally, if Hariri wanted to make a point to his unseen listeners, he would deliberately raise his voice.

Even one of his closest aides turned out to be a double agent for Syrian military intelligence. Ali Hajj, an extravagantly moustachioed officer in the Internal Security Forces (ISF), had been chief of security for Hariri since 1992. He was re-appointed to the post in 2000 when Hariri became prime minister again. But Hariri had grown to distrust Hajj, who enjoyed a close relationship with Rustom Ghazaleh. Hariri tested Hajj's loyalty by feeding him false information on four separate occasions, which he later discovered ended up with Syrian intelligence.[34] Hajj was sacked, but Ghazaleh had him appointed head of the ISF in the Bekaa, a prominent posting that brought him closer to the Syrian intelligence apparatus.

Syria's increasing distrust and resentment of Hariri appeared to correspond to the intensifying international pressure against Damascus, as if the Lebanese prime minister was a punchbag on which Bashar and other regime leaders could vent their frustrations.

In the late spring of 2004, the impasse in US–Syrian relations was kindling some internal discussions about the feasibility of drawing up a UN Security Council resolution against Syria. The Bush administration concluded that, if any UN action was to be taken against Damascus, the US would need weighty allies, namely France, which had a proprietary interest in Lebanon and Syria. The US and France had different but not contradictory priorities in Syria which could combine into a sweeping and powerful Security Council resolution. Terrorism, weapons of mass destruction and Iraq were Washington's principal concerns with Syria. France, however, was more focused on Syria's pervasive hold over Lebanon. Chirac once described Lebanon as his 'second home' and he had taken an unusually intense interest in the fortunes of Lebanon and Syria. Paris was the first Western capital Bashar had visited in an official capacity, and that was in 1998 before he was president. Chirac was the only Western head of state to attend Assad's funeral in June 2000. France had invested much effort in helping bolster Bashar's emergence as a national leader, dispatching a team of technocrats to Syria to provide advice on reform issues and a close advisor to Chirac as ambassador to Damascus.

In October 2002, in an address to the Lebanese parliament, Chirac said that a Syrian troop withdrawal from Lebanon was dependent on a comprehensive settlement of the Middle East peace process, effectively giving French blessing to the status quo. Although Chirac's lenient approach to Syria was in marked contrast to Washington's more bullish attitude, he expected Syria to reciprocate by easing its grip on Lebanon. His 'heart-to-heart' address to the Lebanese parliament in itself was a message to the Syrian leadership that France attached great importance to Lebanon.

But Chirac's patience with Syria began to wane as it grew clearer that Damascus was unwilling to meet France half way. The Lebanese government's failure to implement the promises of Paris II was a source of considerable French irritation with Syria. Chirac had invested his personal prestige in hosting the conference and persuading donor countries and organisations to participate. Yet despite the pledges of cooperation he had received from Bashar and Lahoud, few of the promised reforms had been implemented.

Chirac received another slap in the face in April 2004 when the French Total oil company lost out to a Canadian–British–US consortium in a $700 million contract to develop gasfields in central Syria. According to Syrian and French sources, Bashar had assured Chirac that Total would win the contract. Chirac also wrote a letter to Bashar asking that the negotiations be conducted in a transparent and legitimate manner. The letter went unanswered, however, and the deal went sour when Total rejected an offer by a prominent Syrian businessman to secure the contract for the French company in exchange for a commission. Nine months later, the Syrian government cancelled the contract with the Canadian–British–US consortium and handed it to the state-owned Syrian Petroleum Company. Ibrahim Haddad, Syrian oil minister, said in January 2005 that the decision was made in light of US sanctions against Syria which could hinder the success of the project.

In May, the worsening confrontation between Hariri and Lahoud moved from the cabinet to the ballot box when Lebanon elected new municipal councils. With political heavyweights backing rival lists of candidates, the polls would represent the last chance to assess the popular strength of key figures before the presidential election in November. If the electoral lists Hariri endorsed fared well, it would strengthen his standing against Lahoud's ambition to extend his presidency.

But the results for Hariri were mixed. While the list he backed for the Beirut municipality triumphed, the victory was tarnished by voter apathy and a low turnout, especially in Christian areas. In his home town of Sidon, the Hariri-backed list was soundly defeated by an alliance engineered by Lahoud and the intelligence services that brought together Sunni Islamists, Hizbullah and prominent families.

While the polls were greeted with general indifference in much of Lebanon, the opposite was true in Shiite areas where Hizbullah and the Amal Movement were competing against each other for the first time. In all the previous parliamentary and municipal polls since the end of the war, Hizbullah and Amal had formed joint electoral lists. Although the alliances were at Syria's behest, neither Sayyed Hassan Nasrallah nor Nabih Berri particularly objected. Nasrallah understood that accommodating Syria was the price for protecting the party's resistance priority, while Amal's declining popularity was masked by the alliance with its more organised rival.

The results of the municipal election, in which Hizbullah won landslide victories in its strongholds in the southern suburbs of Beirut and the Bekaa and also did well in the southern border district, its front line against Israel, confirmed what was already suspected – Hizbullah had overtaken Amal as the leading voice of Lebanon's Shiites.

Four days after the final round in the municipal elections, a riot broke out in the Hay as-Sellom district of southern Beirut, a bastion of Hizbullah support, when soldiers fired upon a crowd of Shiite demonstrators participating in a nationwide strike to protest against petrol prices. The riots received the usual chorus of outraged condemnation from Lebanese politicians. But Hariri and Nasrallah suspected that the violence was not spontaneous but an orchestrated bid to embarrass the prime minister and undermine Hizbullah after its success in the municipal elections. Nasrallah pointedly apportioned the blame for the riots to the security services rather than Hariri's government. Hizbullah reportedly managed to film a group of agents provocateurs who moved from one flashpoint to another in Hay as-Sellom, distributing tyres for burning and inciting the crowd to violence. Significantly, Hariri's own newspaper, *Al-Mustaqbal*, carried a carefully worded report in which 'well-informed sources' implicitly accused Amal of trying to discredit Hizbullah.

Surprised at being spared criticism by Hizbullah, Hariri contacted Nasrallah hours after the riots ended to set up an appointment. They met that evening and Hariri asked 'Why didn't you blame me for what happened?' Nasrallah told him 'We know you were not responsible.'[35] The incident was the catalyst for a secret and unexpectedly fruitful new relationship between Hariri and Nasrallah. Despite their long-standing differences and seemingly incompatible agendas, the two men drew closer in the final months of Hariri's life, meeting as often as twice a week in Nasrallah's heavily guarded headquarters in Beirut's southern suburbs. Mustafa Nasr, a journalist and long the intermediary between Hariri and Nasrallah, arranged the late-night gatherings.

'Hariri would call me and ask "Is there any fruit left in the country?" It was his code for me to contact Hizbullah for a meeting that night,' Nasr recalls.[36]

Other than Hariri and Nasrallah, the only other participants were Nasr and Hajj Hussein Khalil, senior advisor to the Hizbullah leader. Hizbullah also handled Hariri's security for his trips from Koreitem to the southern suburbs. Hariri's own bodyguard, Yehya Arab, aka Abu Tarek, stayed in Koreitem along with the rest of his security detail. The late-night meetings with Nasrallah unnerved Nazek Hariri, who feared her husband becoming caught up in an assassination attempt against the Hizbullah leader. When Hariri departed to the southern suburbs, Nazek would mutter 'God protect you, God protect you' and read verses from the Koran.

Hariri, however, relished his conversations with Nasrallah. Despite their differences in the early years of Hariri's premiership and the simmering tensions over the Shebaa Farms, the two men had much in common on a personal level and developed a strong rapport. Both had risen from humble origins to achieve prominence. Both men had suffered the pain of losing a son.[37] The influence they wielded and the regard in which they were held extended far beyond Lebanon's parochial confines. The Shiite cleric and the Sunni tycoon recognised each other as Arab, rather than merely Lebanese, leaders, a distinction that set them apart from most of Lebanon's politicians, whose purview rarely strayed beyond the interests of their clans or sects.

Their conversations were relaxed and peppered with jokes and humorous anecdotes. Demonized by his enemies as a violent fanatic, Nasrallah has the strong sense of humour of south Lebanon Shiites. In private, he is soft-spoken and unassuming and listens carefully to what is being said. He is quick to smile and his eyes twinkle with amusement behind clunky, square-framed spectacles.

Sipping tiny glasses of sweet tea or Turkish coffee and snacking on fresh fruit, their conversations ranged from local issues (Lebanon's relationship with Syria, protecting the resistance, the settlement of Palestinian refugees) to broader regional affairs (the Arab–Israeli conflict, Sunni–Shiite relations and Iraq).

They shared each other's concerns at the potential fragmentation of the Middle East into rival sectarian- or ethnic-based states, agreeing that such an outcome would only benefit the interests of Israel. Nasrallah would voice his suspicions of the Bush administration's intentions toward the Arab world, and Hariri would listen sympathetically.

At the end of each session, which could last until the early hours of the morning, Hariri, accompanied by Mustafa Nasr, would return to Koreitem, often taking a detour through the empty streets of the city centre, gazing at the renovated buildings and cobble-stoned streets or checking on the construction of the huge Mohammed al-Amine mosque he was financing on the edge of Martyrs' Square.

In June, Hariri received some welcome assurances from the Saudis and Egyptians that Bashar would not grant Lahoud a presidential extension, according to several of Hariri's colleagues and advisors.[38] Those reassurances appeared to be endorsed by Bashar himself, who said in an interview with a Kuwaiti newspaper in June that Syria would back any president that was chosen by the Lebanese people.

The US, however, remained sceptical that Bashar would permit the Lebanese to elect a new president independently.[39] It was a suspicion shared by the French. On June 6 during the sixtieth anniversary commemoration of the D-Day landings in Normandy, Bush and Chirac recognised that Lebanon had the potential to form the basis of a transatlantic rapprochement after months of strained relations due to bitter disagreements over the Iraq war.

Buoyed by international promises, Hariri busied himself preparing a list of alternative presidents acceptable to Syria, confident that Lahoud's term would end in November. However, by the middle of August, as Bashar began customary consultations with Lebanese politicians to assess their views of the upcoming presidential elections, there were growing indications that Lahoud might win his presidential extension after all. The debate was not confined to Beirut. Some senior officials in Damascus recognised all too clearly the perils of extending Lahoud's presidential term, chiefly Abdel-Halim Khaddam and Ghazi Kanaan, veteran regime leaders with decades of experience in Lebanese affairs. Khaddam was against the appointment of Lahoud as president from the start and was doubly against granting the Lebanese president an additional three years. But his ability to sway events in Damascus had steadily declined since Bashar had taken office four years earlier.

On August 18, Khaddam met Bashar to say farewell before departing on holiday to France and recalls urging the Syrian president not to extend Lahoud's term. He warned Bashar that 'neither you nor Lebanon can tolerate this extension. All of Lebanon will be against us.'[40] Bashar reassured him that there would be no extension.

Four days later, Cardinal Sfeir warned that granting Lahoud an additional mandate would 'finish off what little is left of the democracy that we boast about once and for all'. His stand was endorsed the following day by a joint statement from Lebanon's most senior Muslim authorities, Sheikh Abdel-Amir Qabalan, president of the Higher Shiite Council, and Sheikh Mohammed Qabbani, the Sunni Mufti. Although the communiqué was read in full on radio stations, the section in which the clerics rejected a constitutional amendment was subsequently cut from the state-run National News Agency report, by 'shadowy hands', according to one newspaper.

Lahoud, seemingly unabashed by his cross-sectarian unpopularity, stated for the first time on August 25 that he was willing to accept a second term 'if asked by a parliamentary majority'.

It was the clearest indication yet that Syria had resolved to extend Lahoud's mandate.

Showdown

5

As Fares Boueiz, the environment minister, drove up to Hariri's sprawling stone villa in the skiing resort of Fakra in the Lebanese mountains on the evening of August 26, he noticed there were no cars parked outside, nor guards at the entrance, and the building appeared to be in darkness.[1] Boueiz, who was staying at his own chalet nearby, had been told that Hariri was spending the night in Fakra having met Bashar in Damascus that morning. Boueiz had heard that the meeting was unusually short and was curious to know what had happened.

He entered the house and found Hariri sitting alone in a vast salon. The premier looked utterly dejected, drained from the events of the last few hours and not altogether happy at having unexpected company. Hariri told him that Bashar had bluntly declared that Lahoud would receive an additional three-year term. According to accounts of the conversation from numerous sources including Hariri's friends and colleagues, the prime minister replied 'But we must discuss this.'[2]

'There is nothing to discuss,' Bashar is said to have responded. 'I am Lahoud and Lahoud is me. If your friend Chirac wants me out of Lebanon, I would sooner break Lebanon on your head and the head of Chirac than break my word.'

Hariri apparently protested, saying he had been a friend of Syria for 20 years. 'You have to listen to me,' he said.

'I have only known you for four years,' Bashar is said to have replied, adding that Hariri had to choose between supporting or opposing Syria and should convey his response to Ghazaleh within 48 hours.

The meeting barely lasted 15 minutes.

'Are you sure? This is their final decision?' Boueiz asked.

'Yes.'

'Did you explain to them how grave this decision will be for Lebanon and Syria?'

Hariri nodded.

Boueiz pressed Hariri again whether he had made clear to Bashar his deep opposition to this decision.

'Fares,' Hariri replied, his eyes damp with tears, 'why do you insist on humiliating me?'

Taken aback, Boueiz apologised. After a moment, he asked, 'What are you going to do?'

'Do you think I have a choice?'

Boueiz urged him to leave at once for Paris. With Hariri out of the country, no cabinet meeting could be held to draw up a law proposal to amend the constitution allowing Lahoud his additional three years.

'It's very easy for you to say this,' Hariri replied. 'But if I did that it would be the final break between me and the Syrians and I can't afford to do that.'

Hariri faced a stark choice. Accepting Bashar's diktat would mean more grinding conflict with Lahoud; resigning to avoid endorsing a presidential extension risked the wrath of Syria.

One of Hariri's assistants asked him what he thought Syria would do should he reject Syria's ultimatum.[3]

'Do you think they could mobilise 100,000 Hizbullah people to march on central Beirut?' Hariri replied.

'Of course.'

'What do you think would happen if someone fired into that crowd?'

'Hizbullah would burn the city,' the assistant said.

Hariri told another advisor that he had been informed by a foreign diplomat that 20 car bombs had been prepared and would be detonated around Beirut if his parliamentary bloc did not support Lahoud's extension.[4] Hariri felt he had no choice. If he did not endorse Lahoud's presidential extension, he risked plunging the country into bloodshed.

'I think he was afraid, mainly physically afraid for himself and the country and to a lesser extent afraid for all the investments he had and for his people who would be arrested and persecuted like they were [during Lahoud's anti-corruption campaign in 1999],' recalls Boueiz.[5]

Bashar apparently also had an ominous message for Walid Jumblatt. Following his meeting with Bashar, Hariri had returned to Beirut, stopping off at Jumblatt's grey-stone mansion in the Clemenceau district of west Beirut. Jumblatt was sitting in the courtyard of his home talking to four political allies when an ashen-faced Hariri stumbled in and recounted what had happened in Damascus.

'Hariri was very angry,' remembers Aridi, one of those present at

Jumblatt's house. 'I think he was expecting to hear this from Assad, but not in the manner or choice of words Assad used.'[6]

Pulling Jumblatt to one side, Hariri told him that the Syrian president had said ' "We will meet Jumblatt again" '.

'He said "Jumblatt has his Druze. Well, we have Druze too, and we will create havoc in Mount Lebanon," ' Hariri told Jumblatt.[7]

After a moment of silence, Jumblatt spoke up.

'Look, I understand your position. Try not to quarrel with the Syrians,' he said. 'I will not accept the renewal of the mandate. But you have freedom of action and you should not quarrel with them.'

After departing Jumblatt's house, Hariri headed straight to Fakra, unable to face his disappointed household in Koreitem.

'He was very sad,' recalls a close aide to Hariri who was with him that evening. 'He told me something that he would repeat to his dying day – "To them we are all ants." '[8]

The next day Hariri informed Rustom Ghazaleh that he would comply with Bashar's demand, saying 'I will not be the tool to break Syria's word in Lebanon.'[9]

Ghazaleh heaped praise on Hariri for his wisdom, hailing him as a 'great statesman' and a 'true nationalist'. Hariri was asked to stay on as prime minister under Lahoud and as a reward for his cooperation was promised that he could form his own government, a ministerial 'dream team' free of any influence from the Syrians.

On August 28, two days after Hariri's fateful meeting with Bashar, the cabinet met with just one item on the agenda. Four ministers in the 30-seat cabinet failed to attend, including Fares Boueiz and Jean Obeid, neither of whom offered an explanation for their absence although both were presidential aspirants known to oppose amending the constitution.

Lahoud began the meeting with a few words on the situation in Iraq and the Palestinian territories and outlined the 'Israeli threats' against Lebanon. Thanking the ministers for their support, he handed the meeting over to Hariri and left the room. A stony-faced Hariri told the ministers that 'the situation in the region requires special measures' and a 'continuity of leadership at this stage'. The bill was approved, although the three ministers in Walid Jumblatt's bloc voted against it.

The meeting broke up after 10 minutes and Hariri immediately flew from Beirut for a short break on his yacht in Sardinia.

The decision to prolong Lahoud's presidency was greeted with uproar by Lebanese politicians. Mikhael Daher, who had declared his candidacy for the presidency, likened the cabinet session which approved the bill to amend the constitution as a 'smuggling operation conducted on a moonless night'. Walid Jumblatt in protest claimed back all the memorabilia of his father, Kamal, from Beiteddine palace, the summer presidential residence, saying that the mementoes of his father, 'the symbol of martyrdom', could not coexist with 'martial bullies'.

The blatant manner in which Syria imposed its will on the Lebanese government was to have far greater consequences than provoking outrage from Lebanese politicians. It was the signal that American advocates of UN action against Syria had been waiting for. A draft resolution was drawn up with unusual alacrity by American and French diplomats and won the approval and support of the British before being submitted to the Security Council. The resolution reflected the interests of Hariri, the French and the US. The 'Hariri' clause called for a 'free and fair electoral process in Lebanon's upcoming presidential election conducted according to Lebanese constitutional rules devised without foreign interference or influence'. France's principal interest, which was shared by the US, was the call for 'all remaining foreign forces to withdraw from Lebanon', in other words the Syrians.

The American component of the resolution demanded the 'extension of the control of the government of Lebanon over all Lebanese territory', meaning principally the border district with Israel under Hizbullah control, and 'the disbanding and disarmament of all Lebanese and non-Lebanese militias', a transparent reference to Hizbullah and armed Palestinian groups. Many supporters of what became UN Security Council Resolution 1559 baulked at this clause, which was principally seen as serving Israeli interests, an irrelevance that would complicate the effort to build nationwide support for the more pertinent goal of unseating Lahoud and disengaging Syria from Lebanon. The clause was a 'catastrophe', according to Chibli Mallat, a Lebanese professor of international law and a democracy campaigner.

'We tried to have this silly clause removed because we could see how 1559 would lead to a schism between the Shiites and the rest,' he says.[10]

The Syrians appeared to have committed a blunder of strategic proportions by extending Lahoud's mandate, a move that exposed them to UN Security Council retribution. The same day Bashar had delivered his ultimatum to Hariri, both Washington and Paris had repeated their calls for a free and fair presidential election in Lebanon. How could the Syrians have flouted the will of the international community in such a flagrant manner?

'Jacques Chirac felt he had been made a fool of by the Syrians after they told him that they would not extend Lahoud's mandate,' says a former

Lebanese minister. 'It really needed a miracle to bring the Americans and French together and the Syrians provided that miracle.'[11]

The possibility of a resolution against Syria gelling between the US and France should have come as no surprise to Damascus. According to Nohad Mashnouq, a former Hariri advisor, Hariri 'knew about 1559 early on'.[12]

'He discussed [the mooted resolution] for sure with Chirac. He sent a letter to Bashar al-Assad, saying "Look out, this is happening. I can help you." But he didn't get any reply from the Syrians,' Mashnouq says.

Ironically, the Syrian leadership blamed Hariri for 1559, believing he persuaded his friend Jacques Chirac to co-sponsor the resolution with the Americans. Hariri's enemies accused him of drafting the resolution along with Marwan Hamade and Ghassan Salameh, a former minister of culture who had left Lebanon in 2003 to work with the UN in Baghdad, on board his yacht in Sardinia, days before the Security Council adopted 1559.

Although many of Hariri's political colleagues and aides deny he helped formulate what became 1559, he did use his influence with Chirac to 'put pressure on Syria not to extend Lahoud's mandate', says Johnny Abdo, former Lebanese ambassador to Paris and long-time friend of Hariri.

'His priority was not disarming Hizbullah nor the total withdrawal of Syrian troops, but stopping the renewal of Lahoud's mandate,' Abdo says. 'He didn't care if there was a rapprochement between the US and France [through agreement on a UN resolution against Syria] so long as it stopped Lahoud.'

Although 1559 included his demand for a free and fair presidential election, Hariri could not publicly support the resolution because of the remaining clauses demanding the disarming of Hizbullah and a full Syrian withdrawal. The latter clause, Hariri understood, represented a humiliation for the Syrians and would only add difficulties to his goal of changing the relationship between the two countries to one of political and economic ties rather than one dominated by security considerations.

Although the Syrian leadership was aware of a potential resolution dangling like a sword of Damocles over its head, Farouq al-Sharaa, the Syrian foreign minister, apparently convinced Bashar that there would be no international repercussions in extending Lahoud's mandate. After all, since 1990 the Americans had essentially turned a blind eye to Syria's hegemony over Lebanon and had not opposed Hrawi's presidential extension in 1995. Why should it be any different in 2004?

Sharaa's misreading of the US mood toward Syria may have stemmed from bad advice he received from some Lebanese allies, including one pro-Syrian cabinet minister who told Sharaa he had met several American officials in Washington and they had dismissed the notion of a UN resolution against Damascus.

'Farouq al-Sharaa told Assad at the time that [they could] go for Lahoud and there will be no repercussions at the UN,' says Ghazi Aridi. 'Some pro-Syrian Lebanese pushed Sharaa in this direction. [They told him] "There is a move from Hariri and Chirac but the Americans are not convinced and the international community is not convinced." '[13]

On the other hand, Syrian and pro-Syrian Lebanese officials maintain that Lahoud's extension was inspired by the perceived inevitability of a UN resolution being tabled against Damascus.

'The Syrians knew through their contacts that a resolution would appear regardless of Lahoud's extension,' says Wiam Wahhab. 'The Syrians knew that with the Americans entering Iraq the region had entered a new phase . . . and that Syria would pay a price. Lahoud was seen as the only one able to resist such pressures along with allies like Hizbullah.'[14]

Months later, Bashar explained in a speech that he had learned that a UN Security Council resolution was being prepared against Syria regardless of Lahoud's extension.

'There is no connection between the resolution and the extension of President Lahoud's term of office,' he said. 'We have discovered in the past few months that there are certain implicit and explicit provisions in Resolution 1559. They were prepared immediately after the war on Iraq.'

In October 2005, Bashar told *Al-Hayat* columnist Jihad al-Khazen that the decision to extend Lahoud's mandate was taken as a defensive measure against the inevitable UN resolution. Lahoud was 'a man of principles and sincerity', Bashar said. 'He was the best choice for fighting the battle with us, as subsequent events proved.'

Plenty would disagree with that last statement. When Bashar allegedly told Hariri that he was Lahoud and Lahoud was he, it set in motion a chain of events that would see Lebanon slipping from Syria's grip in less than nine months.

Nonetheless, Lahoud was 'one of the most efficient protectors of Syrian interests in Lebanon', according to a European diplomat in Beirut, which included the 'mafia links' between the two countries.[15] Syria's hold over Lebanon was not just a politico-ideological goal; it was also a multi-billion-dollar business that risked being jeopardised if a less pliable figure became president.

The Syrians had stated their will over the presidency, but Lahoud's extra term was still subject to the approval of two-thirds of Lebanon's

128-seat parliament to amend Clause 49 of the constitution. The Syrians could be assured of 77 votes from their Lebanese allies, which left them nine short of the required two-thirds. With Walid Jumblatt's parliamentary bloc of 17 MPs expected to vote against the bill, it meant that Hariri's 18 MPs could make or break Lahoud's extra mandate.

Nabih Berri tabled the parliamentary vote for September 3, hoping that Lahoud's mandate extension would become a fait accompli before the UN Security Council adopted the Franco-American-sponsored resolution against Syria. From his yacht in Sardinia, Hariri announced that he would remain loyal to Syria and instructed his parliamentary bloc to vote as they pleased.

Hariri was not the only politician coming under pressure to accept Syria's decision. Mosbah Ahdab, a Sunni opposition MP from Tripoli, announced publicly that he and his wife had received death threats over the telephone. Butros Harb, a Maronite MP from the coastal town of Batroun in north Lebanon, claimed that anonymous automated faxes were being sent to politicians and religious figures opposed to the constitutional amendment containing threats and accusations of 'rape and incest against the clergy'.

Ghattas Khoury, a member of Hariri's parliamentary bloc, also received late-night telephoned death threats.

'They would call me and say "If you think you are smart and vote against the extension you might be killed and your family harmed," ' Khoury says.[16] A day before Khoury met Cardinal Sfeir at the patriarch's summer residence in Diman in north Lebanon, his wife received an anonymous telephone call from someone who said that her husband would not return to Beirut alive.

'She asked me not to go to see the patriarch, but I went anyway and made a public statement in Diman about the threat and said I planned to vote according to my conscience,' he says.

Some MPs were offered inducements of money or position to vote for the amendment. One MP and former minister who had publicly opposed the Lahoud extension voted for the amendment after a ban on his lucrative quarrying activities was overturned a day before parliament met. Another MP, who was having financial problems, was told the banks which had loaned him funds would be pressured into accepting easy terms of repayment if he voted for the amendment. He was also promised a cabinet seat in the next government, a pledge which was honoured two months later.[17]

MPs received phone calls from Jamil Sayyed and Rustom Ghazaleh, who would encourage, cajole and threaten them to gain their cooperation in the parliamentary vote. One minister switched off his mobile phone for several days and instructed his staff to say he was unavailable in order to avoid having to talk to the two security officials.[18]

The Security Council met on Thursday, September 2 and narrowly voted in Resolution 1559, nine votes in favour with six abstentions, the minimum number to adopt the resolution. In a sop to Russia, China and Algeria, the final draft excluded mentioning Syria by name, but there was no mistaking to whom its demands applied.

The resolution provoked a furious backlash from Syrian loyalists in Lebanon who argued, with some justification, that it was an unwarranted interference in Lebanese affairs. There was certainly more than a whiff of hypocrisy in the determination of the US, France and the UN to harry Syria into complying with the resolution. Critics of 1559 pointed out that the US had shown no such enthusiasm in demanding the fulfilment of UN Security Council resolutions aimed at Israel, including those that had dealt with the Jewish state's 22-year occupation of south Lebanon.

Hariri returned to Beirut from Sardinia on Friday, mere hours before the parliamentary session, his left shoulder wrapped in a plaster cast. It was a highly symbolic injury and led to muttered comments about the Syrians having twisted his arm too hard. According to a veteran pro-Syrian Lebanese politician, Hariri made a last-ditch effort to stave off Lahoud's three extra years by offering Rustom Ghazaleh $20 million to tell the Syrian leadership he was unable to arrange the presidential extension. Ghazaleh, however, refused the offer.

'Ghazaleh was in no position to tell the Syrians that the extension was not going to work out. The offer was a sign of Hariri's desperation,' the politician says.[19]

Barely 24 hours after Resolution 1559 was adopted, the Lebanese parliament dutifully approved the constitutional amendment, 96 votes in favour against 29, granting Lahoud another three years in office. With the sole exception of Ghattas Khoury, all Hariri's bloc, including Hariri himself, voted for the motion.

That night, the Beirut sky was lit with exploding fireworks as Lahoud's supporters celebrated. There were no celebrations at Hariri's Koreitem residence, rather a mood of glum resignation as Hariri prepared to form a new government, one that he had been promised would be free of Syrian interference. Hariri sought, and was promised by the Syrians, a broad-based government that would include members of the opposition, such as leading figures in the Qornet Shehwan opposition group which was supported by Cardinal Sfeir.

But it soon became clear that the Syrians were not intending to fulfil their pledge to restrain Lahoud and grant Hariri a free hand in choosing the next government. According to a Hariri aide, a list of 18 ministers was handed to Lahoud in accordance with the constitution. Lahoud passed on the list to the Syrians for their approval.

'It was the same story again,' the aide says. 'The Syrians started to question the names and began naming their own people. The end result was a list of 24 names, many of whom Hariri had not chosen. At that point he said, "Enough. I'm not playing this game any more." '[20]

The Syrians asked Hariri to stay on, however, at least until the publication of the UN's first report on the implementation of Resolution 1559 expected at the beginning of October.

The traumatic events of the previous weeks had left Hariri deeply disillusioned, physically exhausted and mentally strained. Fouad Siniora, who says he knew Hariri 'like I know my fingertips', recalls being in Hariri's office one day in September and asking him a question about the presidential extension 'that was more probing than I should'.

'For 30 seconds he wept on my shoulder,' Siniora says.[21] 'It was as if somebody has an injury and you scratch that injury and it begins to bleed again.'

While Hariri was busy negotiating his ministerial list in September and the government was waging a diplomatic battle against Resolution 1559, the security cameras attached to the neo-classical sandstone façade of the four-storey Italian embassy opposite the parliament building in Beirut were picking up some unusual activity, unusual enough for the embassy to alert Italy's military intelligence service. Days later, on September 22, interior minister Elias Murr revealed that the government had broken an Al-Qaeda-affiliated ring that was on the verge of mounting a series of bomb attacks against Western and government targets in Beirut, including the Italian embassy and the Ukraine consulate.

'We have managed to rid the nation, as well as other Arab and foreign countries, of dangerous terrorist operations that would have targeted innocent people and tarnished Lebanon's reputation,' Murr said.

The announcement of the arrests was greeted with wide scepticism in Lebanon. The revelation came as Syrian forces staged one of their periodic redeployments in Lebanon, whittling the overall number of troops down to about 14,000. The implicit two-fold message behind the arrests, analysts and commentators believed, was that the Syrian military presence was still required to protect Lebanon against Islamist 'terrorists'. It was also a way of Beirut telling Washington that it too faced a threat from Al-Qaeda-style militancy.

But there was a curious postscript to the story. Some of those arrested came from Majdal Anjar, a Sunni town in the Bekaa one kilometre south of Anjar, the Armenian town hosting the headquarters of Syrian military intelligence. Murr apparently contacted US officials regarding the arrests before consulting with Ghazaleh, a serious breach of protocol, which spurred Hariri to later comment to his interior minister 'What you did was very dangerous.'[22] A furious Ghazaleh made his objections known in a heated telephone conversation with Murr during which the two men hurled insults at each other in front of several startled community leaders from Majdal Anjar. Majdal Anjar was in Ghazaleh's backyard. If a cell of Islamist militants was able to plan a bombing campaign within earshot of Ghazaleh's headquarters, it suggested that Syrian military intelligence was either complicit in the operation or incompetent in not having detected it sooner.

Then there were details of the alleged plot that just didn't quite sound right. The Al-Qaeda cell apparently planned to blow up the Italian embassy with 300 kilogrammes of explosives.[23] But the embassy is in the pedestrian-ised Nijmeh Square opposite the parliament building and Café de l'Etoile, where Hariri liked to chat with journalists over coffee. It is one of the most secure areas in all Beirut, with vehicular access restricted, mainly to MPs and government staff. Transporting a 300-kilogramme bomb past the army-manned barriers leading to the square would have been possible only under the cover of the Syrian and Lebanese intelligence apparatus. Some Lebanese military and political officials as well as foreign diplomats sus-pect that there was no planned attack against the Italian embassy, and instead Murr had unwittingly stumbled across the first plot to assassinate Hariri, probably by detonating the explosives as his motorcade departed Nijmeh Square. Evidence remains circumstantial, although it would offer a more compelling reason for Ghazaleh's furious reaction and the subsequent threats and assassination attempt against Murr.[24]

On September 30, Hariri met an angry Chirac in Paris and explained why he had been forced to vote for Lahoud's presidential extension and asked that France not push too hard on Resolution 1559. Hariri later told one of his aides that by the end of the meeting Chirac said he understood the pressures his Lebanese friend was under and promised to ensure that the implementation of Resolution 1559 would not effect Lebanon's stability.

After the meeting, Hariri acknowledged to some reporters that his discussion with Chirac had been 'very frank'.

He said 'One thing is for sure and that is we are passing through a difficult and very sensitive phase and we hope for the better.'

The next morning, Marwan Hamade, the economy minister and Hariri ally, was slower than usual to leave his home in an apartment block on a hill overlooking the seafront corniche in west Beirut. The Druze politician normally left home for his office in parliament at 8 a.m., but on the morning of October 1 he lingered to watch a televised interview with Elie Ferzli, the deputy parliamentary speaker.

At 9.05, Hamade, his driver, Oussama Abdel Samad, and his personal police escort, Sergeant Ghazi Bou Karoum, climbed into his black Mercedes saloon. Abdel Samad drove out of the car park beneath Hamade's building and headed downhill along a narrow street flanked by bamboo thickets to the corniche 400 metres away. As Abdel Samad approached a speed bump, a hundred yards from Hamade's apartment building, he swung the car over to the side of the road so that the left-hand wheels would avoid the bump, lessening the impact – a technique common to Lebanese motorists. Hamade would later say that the manoeuvre probably saved his life, because the Mercedes was at an angle when the car bomb exploded on the other side of the road, just 3 metres away. The blast caused by a 10-kilogramme explosive charge located above the petrol tank of a Mercedes smashed into the back of Hamade's car, setting it and three parked vehicles on fire. Hamade immediately knew it was a bomb and threw open the car door. His foot was broken and he could not stand. He collapsed onto the road just as the fuel tank exploded, turning the car into a fireball.

Mahmoud Arnaout, a Syrian painter and decorator, was getting into his car, having finished his customary stroll along the corniche, when he heard the explosion.[25] He rolled underneath his car for protection and then noticed a smoking body lying beside a burning car further up the road. Arnaout climbed back into his car and drove to the scene to help. Bou Karoum had been killed in the blast and his body was engulfed in flames in the back seat of the burning Mercedes. Abdel Samad was relatively unhurt and he helped Arnaout pull Hamade into the car. Arnaout had no idea who the victim was until Abdel Samad borrowed his mobile phone and mentioned Hamade's name while alerting people to what had happened. Hamade was taken to the American University Hospital a few minutes away.

As news circulated of the attempted assassination, an angry crowd gathered outside the hospital. Among the many well-wishers who flocked to the hospital was Abdel-Halim Khaddam. He braved the hostile throng and publicly embraced Jumblatt, an act that demonstrated Khaddam's deteriorating influence in Damascus.

The assassination attempt against Hamade signalled a new gloves-off attitude that raised the stakes considerably.

'That's it, they have destroyed the new government,' Hariri told an aide on hearing the news.[26] Any chance of forming a national unity government had been obliterated in the blast that nearly killed Hamade.

This was no warning to Hamade. He was supposed to have died in the explosion and was lucky to survive. Other than a fractured foot, he broke all his ribs, suffered serious burns on his hand, required 450 stitches in his head and face and suffered two subdural haemorrhages. He would require months of surgery and therapy before recovering.

Mysterious bombings in Lebanon have a tendency to go unsolved and Hamade's assassination attempt was no different. Following the explosion, investigating officers from the Internal Security Forces reportedly received a phone call from Ghazaleh who told them that the most likely perpetrators were the Israelis and that it was not worth investigating. Ghazaleh added that it was possible that Hamade deliberately engineered the blast 'to bring attention to himself'. It later transpired that a suspect in the bomb attack, Talal Arab, who was arrested on separate security-related charges, had received a pardon from Lahoud in 2000 for an earlier crime. Arab's special treatment was apparently related to his employment in a security firm owned by Majid Hamdan, the brother of General Mustafa Hamdan, the commander of the Presidential Guard and Lahoud's right-hand man. The presidential palace subsequently denied that Arab had received a pardon. Furthermore, a security camera belonging to the International College close to Hamade's apartment building had filmed the bomb-laden car and a man standing beside it before the explosion. The video tape mysteriously disapppeared, however, and a few days later the body of a man said to resemble the filmed figure was found in the Bekaa valley.

'I really had no enquiry into the matter. I had ten minutes with Jean Fahd [a military judge] in hospital,' says Marwan Hamade, who ten months after his ordeal was still walking with a cane and receiving daily physiotherapy.[27] 'We never could see the documents [of the investigation]. [State prosecutor Adnan] Addoum had blocked everything.'

Wearing the Arabic cloak known as an *abaya*, he eases back into the cushions on his sofa. His pale face is enlivened by sharp, intelligent eyes beneath thinning steel-grey hair. On a small coffee table next to Hamade is a framed photograph of himself alongside Hariri and Hariri's sister, Bahiya, in parliament on the morning of February 14, 2005. All three are laughing, unaware that Hariri had less than two hours to live when the photographer clicked the shutter.

In a gruesome epilogue to the bombing, bodyguard Bou Karoum's shredded brain, teeth and tongue were handed to his grieving family in an official envelope from the Internal Security Forces, an act that appeared to be a calculated insult and further enraged the opposition.

In a speech delivered at Bou Karoum's funeral, Jumblatt described Syria's Lebanese allies as 'mercenary trumpeters' and a 'bunch of profiteers'.

Jumblatt read a triple message in the bomb attack: one to the media (Hamade had family ties to *An Nahar*), another to France (Hamade has French nationality), but principally the assassination attempt was a blunt warning to Jumblatt himself, the most prominent and outspoken member of the opposition.

Even as Jumblatt had raced to the hospital to check on the condition of his friend after the bomb attack, Hariri had called from Paris.

'Walid, I have an armoured car waiting for you at the hospital,' he said, referring to one of his armour-plated Mercedes limousines.[28] 'You have to use it now.'

Two weeks later, Hikmat Shehabi, the sidelined and ostracised former Syrian Army chief of staff, departed Syria for the US where he was planning to live, having decided to leave his homeland for good.

'He was on his way to Beirut airport and he told me three times "Take care of yourself. Take care of yourself. Take care of yourself." It meant that I was under a very real threat,' Jumblatt recalls.

Not for the first time. Jumblatt's ability to survive almost 30 years as leader of the Druze was due to his ability to deftly tread a path through the shifting alliances and intrigues that colour the turbulent and often violent politics of Lebanon. He had acquired a well-deserved reputation as someone who seemed to change his views at the slightest whim, his unreliability considered by some as part of the charm of this lanky scarecrow figure with the wild tangle of hair, bulging eyes, dome-like forehead and wry smile. He never seemed to take life – and death – too seriously. He had a playboy reputation during his youth and, when a minister in Hariri's governments in the 1990s, preferred to attend cabinet meetings in jeans, cutting an irreverent figure compared to the often pompous demeanour of other Lebanese officials.

Yet there was steel beneath the image of insouciance. He could be as ruthless and calculating as the most machiavellian of Lebanese zaim in defending what he thought were the interests of the Druze and the Jumblatt family. And despite his reputation for political meandering, he appeared to have embarked on the same perilous confrontation with

Damascus as his father, Kamal, had done nearly 30 years earlier. That previous confrontation had ended with Kamal Jumblatt's death in a hail of bullets.

On a Saturday morning soon after the assassination attempt on Hamade, Jumblatt sat on a cushion-covered stone seat along a wall of a small ante-chamber in his magnificent mansion of honey-coloured stone in the village of Mukhtara deep in the Chouf mountains. Hundreds of Druze men, some of them dressed in traditional black baggy trousers, known as *chelwan*, and white skullcaps, had gathered to meet their feudal chief as they do every Saturday, some bringing specific requests and peti-tions, others merely after a handshake and to show their support. It is a weekly ritual that Jumblatt, ever cognisant of his feudal duties, always observes.

But that day Jumblatt had other, weightier, matters on his mind.

'When we decided to say no to the prolongation of the mandate of Mr Lahoud, the answer back was the car bomb that was supposed to kill Marwan Hamade. [The situation is] quite dangerous,' he said, with a laconic shrug. 'It's impossible to engage in serious dialogue with such people. They don't want any dialogue.'

The window behind Jumblatt looked out over part of his estate with its pine tree-shaded courtyards, steep stone steps, fountains and mountain streams channelled through the gardens. The dense forest rises up behind Mukhtara and thins out below the barren crest of the Barouk mountains, almost 2,000 metres high. Hidden among the trees in the garden is the grave of Jumblatt's father, a flat black marble slab decorated with freshly laid flowers and lined by small candles.

Did he often think of his father's fate during this period of tension? Jumblatt showed some agitation for the first time. He stood and began pacing up and down the room, staring at the floor.

'The circumstances were different,' he said at last. 'We were still in the middle of this dreadful civil war. At that time I decided to forgive. Forgetting is difficult. Forgiveness is possible.'

At the end of the 40-day period of mourning for his father in 1977, Jumblatt went to Damascus to pledge his allegiance to Hafez al-Assad. The Syrian president greeted the young man with the unnervingly ambiguous comment 'How closely you resemble your father.' Jumblatt would prove a loyal and consistent ally of Syria from then on. And even though he was the dominant figure in the Lebanese opposition, his public battle was against Lahoud and the Syrian–Lebanese intelligence apparatus that controlled Lebanon. His personal thoughts on Syria and its leadership he kept to himself.

But a few days earlier, Bashar had delivered a strong speech in Damascus justifying Syria's role in Lebanon and its sacrifices to bring the civil war to an end. 'We took nothing from Lebanon, but we gave blood,' he said.

Bashar described how in 1976 Syria had come to the assistance of Lebanon's Christians 'who were being slaughtered at that time ... in the name of reform of the political regime, and justice, socialism, and progress'.

Although Bashar refrained from mentioning Kamal Jumblatt by name, the allusion to 'justice, socialism and progress' was a transparent reference to Walid's father, the founder and leader of the Progressive Socialist Party (PSP).

Bashar's speech clearly had upset Jumblatt, unsurprisingly given that he believed his father was murdered on the orders of the father of the young Syrian president.

'The father, Hafez al-Assad, was a well-known leader at the end of the twentieth century,' Jumblatt said, still pacing nervously and talking, it seemed, more to himself. 'We cannot deny that, and he played an important role in the region and the Arab–Israeli conflict and building up Syria. But I also claim that my father was a well-known figure in the Arab world and I don't want the memory of my father to be insulted. This is the least that I can ask. I have never challenged the respectability of Hafez al-Assad ... I never mentioned something annoying in the press about him. Never ... But it seems the memory of some people is short, unfortunately.'

The UN released its first report on the implementation of Resolution 1559 on October 1, 30 days after the resolution was passed and the same day that Hamade was nearly killed by the car bomb. Damascus had awaited the UN findings with some anxiety, concerned that it could herald yet another resolution. But the report simply contained a historical overview of Syrian involvement in Lebanon and then a matter-of-fact assessment of Lebanese and Syrian compliance with each of the resolution's demands. Other than a minor redeployment of Syrian troops in September, the report noted that none of the demands had been fulfilled.

The tepid UN assessment granted Syria sufficient breathing space to dispense with Hariri as prime minister. Nabih Berri was employed to deliver the *coup de grâce*. On October 20, Berri told Hariri during a brief meeting that he had two hours to step down or seven cabinet ministers loyal to the speaker and the president would quit.

Hariri returned to Koreitem to write his resignation letter with the help of three colleagues, two of them MPs.[29] Hariri ended the letter with the dramatic phrase 'I trust revered Lebanon and its good people to God Almighty.'

But the other three urged Hariri to cut the sentence.

'Are you sure you want to say that?' one of them asked. 'People will think you are abandoning Lebanon for good.'

'Let them read into it what they want to read into it,' Hariri replied.

Omar Karami, the former prime minister from Tripoli whose disastrous handling of the economy in 1991–1992 had precipitated the arrival of Hariri as premier, was selected to head a new government, a decision that Colin Powell chidingly described as 'inappropriate'.

Hariri's resignation was a cathartic release that shut the door on the bitter events of the previous two months. He may have been forced to leave office, but as far as he was concerned it would be a temporary absence only. Parliamentary elections were scheduled for May 2005 and Hariri was fully intending to repeat on an even larger scale his electoral landslide of 2000. If he was able to forge a cross-sectarian alliance capable of smashing the Syrian-backed candidates, the regime in Damascus would have no choice but to deal with him as a valued equal rather than a despised minion. It was a campaign that required subtlety and dexterity, however. He wanted to make a point with the Syrians, not to confront them. For even at this late stage and despite the humiliations he had suffered in the past two years, Hariri still recognised that Syria was an ineluctable fact of life for Lebanon and that maintaining strong, healthy relations was of crucial importance to Lebanon's stability and future prosperity.

Of course, the assassination attempt against Marwan Hamade was also a powerful and more personal reason for not pressing the Syrians too hard. Following the October 1 car bomb attack, Hariri and Jumblatt began to take greater security precautions, partially reassured by warnings to Damascus from the French and Americans that any further attacks against opposition figures would not be tolerated.

Hariri reassured his worried advisors that the Syrians would not try to kill him, partly because he was not a full-fledged and public member of the opposition, and also because he was simply too big. Hariri was not just another minor local politician unknown outside Lebanon who could be safely dispatched with no repercussions from the international community.

'Chirac thought it was not safe for Hariri to come back to Lebanon. When he returned he was behaving as if nothing had happened. He was overconfident,' Jumblatt says.

Hariri's family and staff, however, remained deeply concerned about his safety. During the three-day Eid al-Fitr holiday marking the end of the holy fasting month of Ramadan, thousands of well-wishers converged on Koreitem to express their support for Hariri. It was a patent display of Hariri's popularity, which, paradoxically, increased the threat against him, even if it was a threat that he chose to ignore.

The noose began to tighten on Hariri. Ali Hajj, Hariri's former head of security, was promoted to director-general of the Internal Security Forces, in early November. One of his first acts was to reduce Hariri's close protection unit from 40 ISF officers to eight. The instructions came from Rustom Ghazaleh but Lahoud provided the justification, saying that, under Lebanese law, a former prime minister was permitted only eight ISF officers for protection. Hariri shrugged it off. He had his own security team and his Mercedes limousines were armour-plated and equipped with state-of-the-art electronic jammers to kill radio signals that could be used to detonate bombs. When his friend Pervez Musharraf, the president of Pakistan, had narrowly survived an assassination attempt in 2003, Hariri had sent him a fleet of his armour-plated cars.

'Hariri was not worried at the time,' a close aide of Hariri says.[30] 'He used to say "You only die when you die." He was a fatalist in the Muslim tradition. I think he became a little reckless because he believed that the Syrians would do nothing to him after they were warned by the Americans and French.'

Despite his initial confidence, Hariri was wary of being seen as a wholehearted opposition figure, although by default that is what he gradually became over the following three months. Although he was in contact via intermediaries with opposition groups like the Christian Qornet Shehwan gathering, he considered them too hostile to Syria and too sympathetic to those awkward, sensitive demands in Resolution 1559 that called for the disarming of Hizbullah and Palestinian groups and the deployment of the Lebanese Army along the southern border with Israel.

'Hariri meant to stay somewhere in between because there were certain matters where he was not in agreement with the opposition. He wasn't going with the opposition all the way. Hariri was in line with Taif not 1559,' says a former minister in Hariri's governments.[31] 'In all honesty, he never thought of doing any harm to the Syrians. Not because he was afraid of them, but because he was a man who believed that it was in the Arab interest to have good relations.'

In December, a multi-sectarian opposition front was born during a conference at the Bristol Hotel in west Beirut. The declaration released at the end of the meeting said that Lebanon had entered a 'very dangerous phase' and called for 'honest and free' parliamentary elections and the resignation of Karami's government because of its 'biased structure and its attitude aimed at further deepening differences between the Lebanese'.

Led by Walid Jumblatt, the 'Bristol Gathering' included a who's who of Christian and Druze opposition parties, including Jumblatt's PSP, secular leftists, Samir Geagea's Lebanese Forces and followers of Michel Aoun. Sunni participants were fewer and the Shiites almost non-existent, underlining that the Christian–Druze alliance still remained the backbone of the anti-Syrian opposition. Hariri stayed away from the Bristol Gathering, but asked Ghattas Khoury to attend in a personal capacity, a move that Khoury says was intended to be deliberately ambiguous.

'We wanted to incorporate the movement of Hariri into the opposition gradually because of the direct threats he and everyone else was receiving,' Khoury says.[32]

Hours after the meeting at the Bristol Hotel broke up, a motorcyclist hurled a stick of dynamite at an office of Jumblatt's PSP in the Wata al-Mosseitbeh district of west Beirut. The explosion caused no injuries or damage but panicked local residents, including the new environment minister Wiam Wahhab who rushed from his house surrounded by bodyguards declaring that somebody was trying to assassinate him.

Khoury attended a second meeting of the Bristol Gathering on December 28 accompanied by Basil Fleihan, the former economy minister and close advisor to Hariri.

Hariri was concious that, if he proceeded too fast in embracing Qornet Shehwan and other Christian groups sympathetic to Resolution 1559, he could lose the support of his Sunni constituency and hamper his attempts to bring on board the Shiites. The Shiites were the one community that was resisting an embrace with the opposition, even tentatively. Hariri had an open and strong alliance with the Druze through Jumblatt. He and the Christian opposition groups were reaching out to each other, albeit with some wariness. The Sunnis were largely behind Hariri as a silent opposition, having yet to move into open defiance of Pax Syriana. That left only the Shiites, Lebanon's largest confession, still standing with the Syrians as a community. At the end of November, Hizbullah lent its considerable weight to a government-organised, pro-Syrian rally dubbed the 'million man march' as a gesture of support for Syria and a rejection of the creeping internationalisation of the Lebanese political scene. The rally, which Omar Karami promised would be massive and overwhelming, attracted only about 100,000 and was clearly a contrived affair in which pro-Syrian parties were drafted along with Syrian workers and Palestinian refugees.

Tellingly, however, Hizbullah took pains to emphasise that it was demonstrating against international interference in Lebanon, not against the Lebanese opposition. On the eve of the rally, Hizbullah dispatched a delegation to Bkirki, the seat of the Maronite patriarch, to reassure Cardinal Sfeir that the party's participation should not be interpreted as a stand against the Christians. During the rally itself, Sheikh Naim Qassem, Hizbullah's deputy secretary-general, told the crowd that 'We will not divide Lebanon between opponents and supporters of Resolution 1559.' And Hizbullah's Al-Manar television station chose to completely ignore the rally's host, ultra pro-Syrian MP Nasser Qandil, whose speech was a deliberately provocative attack on the opposition.

It was that conciliatory, non-confrontational spirit that encouraged Hariri to recognise Sayyed Hassan Nasrallah as his potential Shiite partner. The other choice was Nabih Berri, the head of the Amal Movement. But Hariri finally had given up on Berri, viewing him as irredeemably corrupt and unreliable. Berri was an opportunist and a survivor, not a risk taker. He would remain a dependable ally of Syria for as long as Damascus was calling the shots in Lebanon.

'Rafik had finished with Nabih Berri 100 per cent,' says a close advisor to Hariri.[33]

The late-night meetings between Hariri and Nasrallah had continued uninterrupted since early June. After his resignation in October, Hariri began to steer the discussions toward the necessity of redefining relations between Lebanon and Syria for the benefit of both countries. Hizbullah, Hariri argued, should become his partner in trying to foster a new relationship with Syria, a state-to-state partnership of mutual respect with recognised joint strategic priorities. He revealed to the Hizbullah leader details of the racketeering and corruption that marked Syria's dominion over Lebanon and the corrosive effect it had on the ability of both countries to deal with each other equitably. A relationship based on corruption and governed by the security and intelligence agencies was of no interest to either side, he said. It was time to put relations on a political footing and abandon the mistrust and paranoia of the past.

'I am not with Resolution 1559. I'm with Taif,' Hariri told Nasrallah, according to Mustafa Nasr, the intermediary who sat in on the meetings.[34] 'If the Syrians withdraw to the Bekaa in accordance with Taif and we have a new agreement with the Syrians, then I will take this agreement and make it official in the Arab world, Europe and the United States.'

As for Hizbullah's weapons, Hariri would persuade the international community that the fate of the resistance was a Lebanese issue that could only be settled through internal dialogue not external pressure. As prime minister, Hariri said he would never unleash the army against

Hizbullah. He would never create an 'Algeria in Lebanon', a reference to the bloody conflict in the 1990s between the Algerian government and Islamist militants.[35]

'Hassan Nasrallah became convinced that Hariri was not against the Syrians but had a special point of view that was supportive of the Arab cause and Syria,' Nasr says. 'He understood that Hariri could not deal with the Syrian leadership through the Syrian mukhabarat [intelligence services] because there was no longer any trust between them. Hariri could only deal with the Syrians through a political channel. Nasrallah explained this to President Assad.'

Whether Nasrallah's advice was heeded by Damascus is unclear. But in early January, Walid Muallem, the moderate deputy foreign minister and a former long-serving ambassador to Washington, was charged by the Syrian leadership to begin a round of consultations with the Lebanese government and opposition. The move was interpreted by many as a conciliatory gesture that would lead to a Syrian troop withdrawal to the Bekaa, a quid pro quo in which Damascus would honour its overdue commitment to the Taif Accord rather than a full withdrawal under Resolution 1559.

In early January, the UN appointed Terje Roed Larsen, the recently retired UN Middle East peace envoy, to serve as coordinator for the implementation of Resolution 1559. Larsen, a Norwegian diplomat who was an architect of the Oslo Accords, had been closely involved in Lebanese affairs since early 2000 when he had devised and promoted the Blue Line prior to Israel's troop withdrawal from south Lebanon.

By now it was abundantly clear that Hariri's electoral juggernaut was becoming an unstoppable force that threatened to revolutionise the Lebanese political landscape in the May elections.

Hariri was relentless in building alliances and shoring up his grassroots support, meeting with trade unionists, mayors, political parties and municipal leaders. The election team adopted a white and green flag as Hariri's electoral colours, the white representing peace and the green the future of Lebanon.

All the data received at Hariri's campaign headquarters at Koreitem indicated that he would triumph in the mainly Sunni, Christian and Druze areas of the country, leaving only the Shiite regions of the south and the Bekaa valley in the hands of pro-Syrian candidates.

'Our focus was that most likely there would be a partial Syrian withdrawal to the Bekaa because of the pressures of 1559. Then there would be elections which would give us an upper hand in Beirut, Mount Lebanon and in the north and we would get a majority [in parliament] and form a government even if the Syrians were still in the Bekaa. This was what we thought,' says Ghattas Khoury.

And there seemed to be little the Syrians could do to stop it. According to Abdel-Halim Khaddam, Bashar and Lahoud both recognised that, if Hariri waged his electoral campaign on a national level, building alliances around the country rather than concentrating solely on his own Beirut constituency, the opposition would certainly win a majority in the next parliament.

'That would very much limit the power of Lahoud and Bashar al-Assad over Lebanon,' Khaddam says.[36]

On January 9, Rustom Ghazaleh drove from Anjar to Koreitem for a working lunch with Hariri. The rare meeting – the two men had not seen each other in months – was regarded by the media as a Syrian fence-mending exercise with the troublesome Sunni tycoon. But it was a tense encounter. Ghazaleh proposed a deal in which the election law being drawn up by Suleiman Frangieh, the interior minister, would not be fixed against Hariri but in return Hariri would have to agree to include five or six pro-Syrians on his list of electoral candidates and desist from waging a nationwide electoral campaign. But Hariri refused outright, saying, according to Marwan Hamade, 'Either you believe that we are friends and allies and my bloc will be your friend and ally, or you don't trust us and therefore we will not put Trojan horses into our parliamentary bloc.'[37]

The encounter ended in disagreement, with Ghazaleh storming out of Koreitem and heading back to his headquarters in Anjar. It was the last time the two men would meet. With Ghazaleh's departure, Hariri telephoned the three MPs in his parliamentary bloc who had been imposed on him by the Syrians and bluntly informed them that he was dropping them from his forthcoming electoral list.

It was a fateful moment for Hariri. He had crossed his Rubicon.

Hariri decided that the time was fast approaching to move more formally into the opposition ranks. He agreed with Ghattas Khoury and Basil Fleihan, his two interlocutors with the Christian opposition, to set aside his misgivings about the Qornet Shehwan group and to cooperate openly with the Bristol Gathering.

Hariri explained his electoral strategy to Fares Boueiz, saying that the parliamentary elections would be a 'good field for our battle'.[38]

'I suppose in the next few weeks you are going to barricade yourself in Koreitem and then oppose the Syrians and fight the electoral battle,' Boueiz said.

'Exactly,' Hariri replied. 'I can't do that now but I will in the last month and a half [before the elections]. I won't leave my house but I will move more into the opposition.'

According to Walid Jumblatt and Lebanese military and political sources, in the days that followed Ghazaleh's last visit to Koreitem the Syrian and Lebanese intelligence apparatus hatched a plan to arrest both Hariri and Jumblatt. Hariri was to be charged with being an Israeli agent, while Jumblatt would be accused of ordering the assassination of Rene Mouawad, the former Lebanese president.

In preparing the ground for the arrests, Suleiman Frangieh contacted Nayla Mouawad, Rene's widow and a prominent member of the Qornet Shehwan opposition group, and told her that her husband's murderer had been identified as a member of Jumblatt's PSP. Mouawad understood what was happening and visited Jumblatt to warn him that the authorities were planning his arrest on trumped-up charges.

The arrests were never carried out. Why the Syrians changed their minds is unclear. But given the intense international scrutiny on Lebanon and Syria, it is hard to imagine how the authorities in Beirut could have justified detaining the two men most closely associated with the opposition to the Syrian-backed Lebanese regime.

On January 24, Suleiman Frangieh unveiled the electoral law that would govern the parliamentary elections in May. The qada, or county, was chosen to form the electoral constituency rather than the larger muhafazat, or governorate, or a compromise between the two. The decision suited the Christians, who preferred the smaller constituencies, as they felt it granted them more accurate representation. But in an attempt to weaken Hariri's chances in Beirut where he was running, Frangieh split the city into three electoral districts, which diluted Sunni representation in favour of Shiite, Armenian and Christian candidates. In Sidon, where Hariri's sister, Bahiya, was standing, the predominantly Sunni city was merged for the first time with its mainly Shiite suburbs in a further effort to derail the Hariri vote.

Walid Jumblatt said that the Beirut division was 'without any justification' and was a blatant attempt to hobble the opposition. But it was evident that even tinkering with the electoral law would fail to prevent an opposition victory in an election that was fast turning into a referendum on Syria's presence in Lebanon.

Still, some of his Sunni constituents were growing restless at the incessant attacks on Hariri. One Sunni supporter demanded that Hariri supply them with weapons so that they could form a militia.

'All the other religions are armed. Why can't we be as well?' he asked Hariri.

'Guns?' Hariri replied. 'I don't want you to have guns. I give you education. I'll give you anything. But I don't want anything to do with you if you want guns.'[39]

On February 1, Walid Muallem arrived in Beirut, his second visit inside a month, for a new round of consultations which this time also included members of the opposition. The portly, white-haired career diplomat visited Hariri in Koreitem and during their conversation Hariri asked Muallem when the Syrians had first become aware of a potential Franco-American resolution being prepared against them.[40]

'Last summer, six or seven months ago,' Muallem replied.

'Then why didn't you come and ask me for my help?' Hariri asked.

Since the early 1980s, Hariri had been using his influence to promote and defend the interests of Syria as well as Lebanon to the international community. He had helped the Lebanese resistance attain international recognition and legitimacy in 1996 through the April Understanding, and urged the West to recognise the needs of Damascus. Hariri was 'Syria's unofficial foreign minister . . . much more important than the real foreign minister, Farouq al-Sharaa,' says Walid Jumblatt.[41]

Even at this late stage, Hariri was at a loss to understand the Syrian leadership's inflexible rejection of his offers of assistance. In his conversation with Muallem, Hariri said that Bashar was being deliberately mis-informed by Syrian military intelligence and Farouq al-Sharaa on his intentions.

'I cannot live under a security regime that is specialised in interfering with Hariri and spreading disinformation about Rafik Hariri and writing reports to Bashar Assad,' he said, adding later in the conversation 'Lebanon will never be ruled from Syria. This will no longer happen.'

During the discussion, Muallem admitted to Hariri that 'We and the [security] services here have put you into a corner.' He continued, 'Please do not take things lightly.'[42] According to Fouad Siniora, Muallem agreed at the meeting to attempt a reconciliation between Bashar and Hariri.[43]

Following his meetings with various Lebanese leaders, both loyalists and opposition, Walid Muallem said that 'the Syrian leadership has decided not to interfere in internal Lebanese affairs and is willing to talk to all political forces without any exception'.

But the Bristol Gathering opposition group had the bit between the teeth and following Muallem's departure from Beirut called for the first time for a full withdrawal of Syrian troops from Lebanon. Syria's Lebanese loyalists responded by launching an offensive with a mass of verbal attacks on Hariri, Jumblatt and the opposition that were unprecedented in their ferocity.

One minister, Talal Arslan, scion of a rival Druze clan to the Jumblatts, accused Hariri of financing the opposition against Lahoud, describing him as the 'snake of Koreitem'. Suleiman Frangieh, the interior minister, said Hariri was the 'tutor of the opposition', guiding it against the government from behind the scenes. Omar Karami warned the opposition that 'we will show them what we can do in the next couple of days', while Qassem Qanso, the labour minister and head of the Lebanese branch of the Baath party, called Jumblatt 'a foreign spy', adding 'You will be crucified above the garbage dump of history as a symbol of your ungratefulness, of your back-stabbing' and warning that the Druze leader was 'not out of reach of our militants'. Jumblatt shot back in similar vein, saying that it was 'the dregs of the Baath party' that had assassinated his father, an accusation that spurred the Baath party to file a lawsuit against him.

'Is the country on the brink of a sharp internal split?' asked the Lebanese *As Safir* daily as the hostile rhetoric scaled new heights. The Syrian state-run *Tishreen* newspaper weighed in with a lengthy attack on Hariri's past governments and called the leaders of the opposition 'heroes of corruption'.

The atmosphere was souring by the day and both Hariri and Jumblatt sensed that the loyalist attacks against them were creating an ambience of potential violence. Hariri's feeling of invulnerability was beginning to wane as the political climate turned increasingly poisonous, the attacks on him more malicious and venal.

At the beginning of February, he pulled Jumblatt aside and told him 'You know, it could be me or you in the next two weeks. If they want to create trouble, they will kill either you or me.'

'Clearly he thought something was going to happen,' Walid Jumblatt told the author weeks later.

Hariri, who spoke on the phone with Abdel-Halim Khaddam on a daily basis, met his old Syrian ally for the last time in early February. Khaddam was becoming convinced that his friend was going to be murdered and advised him 'to get on a plane and leave'.

'I repeatedly warned him and told him to resign and leave the country because I knew that the ruler of Syria does not have a logical and balanced mind. He could take any action,' Khaddam recalls. 'But Hariri replied, how could he leave with the elections coming up?'[44]

On February 8, Terje Roed Larsen, the UN envoy, arrived in Beirut to negotiate a mechanism that would allow Resolution 1559 to be implemented with the approval of all sides. In his meetings with the Lebanese leadership, he suggested linking 1559 with Taif as a means of encouraging Syria to begin the process of redeploying troops to the Bekaa.

'My original approach – what I put to the parties – was that, if the withdrawal happens, I don't care if it's called implementing the Taif Agreement or implementing 1559 ... so long as it happens,' Larsen recalls.[45]

Larsen was due to travel straight to Damascus from Beirut to meet Bashar, but he was kept waiting for two days. According to UN officials, Farouq al-Sharaa purposely delayed Larsen's appointment until Thursday, February 10 so that it would collide with a prior engagement with Jacques Chirac in Paris.

In Damascus, Larsen told Bashar that the international community would welcome some significant moves by the Syrian president in Lebanon. Those moves could be symbolic, Larsen added carefully. It was obvious that Damascus could not remove the entire army and military intelligence service overnight. However, he continued, if the president was to withdraw one soldier in particular, then Larsen would reflect that in his upcoming report on the implementation of Resolution 1559.

'What one soldier would that be?' Bashar asked.

'Your man in Anjar,' Larsen replied, referring to Rustom Ghazaleh.

Bashar looked startled and then after a moment replied to the effect that it would be easier to remove the entire Syrian Army from Lebanon than oust Ghazaleh from Anjar.[46]

Sharaa was present at the meeting, along with some of Larsen's UN aides. Larsen asked to speak to Bashar alone for a few minutes and the other attendees left the room. In an awkward postscript to the meeting, Larsen's aides discovered to their consternation that sitting in the office of the director-general of the presidential palace, arms crossed and staring pensively at the floor, was none other than Rustom Ghazaleh. Clearly he was waiting to be briefed on Larsen's discussion with Bashar where he would undoubtedly be told of the UN envoy's suggestion that he be removed.

In his one-to-one discussion with Bashar, Larsen discussed the tensions between Lebanon and Syria, particularly the deteriorating relationship between Hariri and the Syrian leadership which the UN envoy believed 'might lead to a dangerous situation'.

'I met a number of officials on both sides and my impression was, without any qualification or nuance, that there was a rapidly deteriorating situation between the leadership of the two countries that caused [me] concern,' Larsen says. 'I urged both parties immediately to start a dialogue; otherwise it would continue to deteriorate rapidly further. We

[Larsen and Bashar] had a tentative discussion about setting up a meeting between a representative of [Bashar] and Hariri for the following week, the same week that Hariri died.'[47]

Larsen returned to Beirut that evening and had dinner at Koreitem to update Hariri on his talks with Bashar and the possibility of organising a reconciliation meeting.

That same day, the Christian opposition Qornet Shehwan gathering discussed an offer from Marwan Hamade to meet Hariri at Koreitem to form a joint position on the electoral law. Hariri had visited Cardinal Sfeir to reassure the Maronite patriarch that he was not averse to the government's intention to hold the elections on the basis of the qada, the preferred choice of the Christians. That suggested to the Christian opposition that perhaps it would be a good idea to coordinate their stance with Hariri. But there was still some uneasiness. Although Hariri had decided to align himself fully with the established Christian–Druze opposition, he had yet to go public. The Qornet Shehwan decided that they would meet Hariri but not at Koreitem. Instead they settled on the more neutral setting of parliament where the MPs in Qornet Shehwan would meet Hariri on Monday morning.

The parliamentary elections also formed part of the discussion between Hariri and Nasrallah the next day, Friday, February 11, at what would be their last encounter together. Hariri was still refusing to include any pro-Syrians on his electoral list, but Nasrallah successfully persuaded him to accept two candidates, an Armenian and a member of Hizbullah.

'How can I not have a member of the resistance in my Beirut list?' Hariri said.[48] A few weeks earlier, Hariri had used his influence with Jacques Chirac to persuade France not to support adding Hizbullah to the European Union's list of terrorist organisations which EU foreign ministers were planning to discuss in Brussels on February 16. Nasrallah was appreciative of Hariri's intervention and in return agreed to try to broker a secret meeting in Damascus between Hariri and Bashar at which all points of contention would be discussed. Nasrallah's mediation would represent a third track along with the efforts of Walid Muallem and Terje Roed Larsen to achieve a rapprochement between Hariri and Bashar. Even though he was on the verge of publicly announcing his affiliation with the opposition, Hariri had not abandoned the possibility of reconciling with the Syrian leadership, according to his colleagues. After all, if his electoral game plan bore fruit, he would return as prime minister of Lebanon after the May elections and he would once more have to deal with the Syrians.

Nasrallah told Hariri that a senior Hizbullah official would be in Damascus on Monday, February 14 to arrange the reconciliation with Bashar.

The state's pressure on Hariri reached new heights on Saturday, February 12, when four workers from one of his charities, the Beirut Society for Social Development, were arrested by police on charges of providing bribes to families in the form of bottles of olive oil in advance of the parliamentary election. The bottles of olive oil were being distributed by the charity in fulfilment of a pledge during the holy fasting month of Ramadan when Hariri's charities traditionally supplied food packages to needy families. Because the previous Ramadan had fallen before the olive picking season was over, the food packages had contained notes informing the recipients that they would receive the oil as soon as the olives had been pressed and the oil bottled. On hearing the news of the arrests, Hariri intervened personally to have the workers released, describing the incident as 'foolishness'.

Hariri later that day told Adnan Baba, his personal secretary, 'If they [the Syrians] kill me, they will be signing their own death warrant.'[49]

The scandal of the arrested charity workers caused a sensation over the weekend and provoked loud condemnation in Muslim and political circles. Sheikh Mohammed Qabbani, the Sunni Mufti, said the arrests were 'shameful' and demanded the authorities 'stop this game immediately'. When the detained workers were ordered by the police to reveal the names of the families who had been supplied with the olive oil, Qabbani issued a fatwa, a religious decree, saying 'it is forbidden to disclose the names of aid-recipient families'.

Even pro-Syrian politicians appeared embarrassed by such a clumsy attempt to pressure Hariri, with Elie Ferzli, the information minister, saying the arrests were 'unjustifiable'.

Handling the olive oil arrests took up much of Hariri's time over the weekend, although he did receive an unexpected phone call on Sunday morning. It was Rustom Ghazaleh. Sounding agitated, the Syrian general bluntly demanded a large sum of money to be delivered in cash to his headquarters in Anjar, according to a Hariri aide. It was not the first time that Ghazaleh had squeezed money from Hariri. Even though Hariri had decided to no longer deal with the Syrian mukhabarat, he gave in to Ghazaleh's demand, saying that the general would have to wait until the next day because the banks were closed on Sundays. But Ghazaleh insisted on the money being delivered the same day. Hariri made the appropriate arrangements and the money was delivered to Anjar by Abu Tarek, the head of Hariri's security detail. According to Saad Hariri, Abu

Tarek received a tongue-lashing from Ghazaleh, who used 'every single curse in the Arabic dictionary' against his boss. Abu Tarek was so shaken by the tirade that he switched off his phone and drove to his home where he stayed for three hours to calm himself down.[50]

As afternoon turned into evening on Sunday, February 13, Hariri was visited by allies and friends, including Jumblatt and Ghazi Aridi who remained with Hariri until late in the evening.

It was nearly midnight by the time Hariri took the lift to his private quarters on the seventh floor. His wife, Nazek, was in Paris, although he was planning to fly to France on the Friday to celebrate the birthday of his only daughter, Hind, who was staying with her mother. As he undressed for bed, he telephoned his son Saad in Saudi Arabia for his customary late-night chat.[51] He asked after Lara, Saad's wife, and his grandson Hussam, of whom he was especially fond. Saad said that he was flying to Abu Dhabi in the morning. The conversation was limited to general personal matters. Although Saad was curious to hear the latest political developments, he knew better than to ask given that the phone lines were being monitored. After a few minutes, Hariri wound up the call with his customary adieu to his son.

'I love you,' he said, and hung up the phone.

The Beirut Spring

The blast is heard all over Beirut, a shockingly loud thunderclap that reverberates around the city's streets up into the hills to the east, rattling windows, triggering car alarms and bringing anxious Lebanese out onto their balconies. At first, most people gaze skyward, thinking it is a sonic boom from a low-flying Israeli Air Force jet. But the towering column of thick black smoke climbing into the deep-blue sky from the city centre tells a different story.

Amer Shehadi, the bodyguard driving the first Mercedes in the convoy, feels the huge blast slam into the back of his car like a solid wave, lifting the vehicle completely off the ground and propelling it several metres down the road.[1]

'What happened?' yells Mohammed Dia, the bodyguard in the passenger seat.

'We've had it,' Shehadi says.

Carole Farhat is about to enter the St George Annexe facing the St George Hotel when the shockwave hits her. She is hurled some 12 metres to the left and crashes onto the bonnet of a parked car. The blast shatters her left ear drum. A second smaller explosion immediately follows the first and she instinctively screws her eyes shut as a shower of debris falls around her, football-sized chunks of black asphalt and concrete, stones, earth, dust and jagged shards of glass. She opens her eyes again to a world gone dark. Through the dense cloud of dust and smoke, she can just discern the outlines of three bodies lying on the road. It must be an earthquake, she thinks, and begins screaming hysterically.

Ghattas Khoury is in the operating theatre of the American University Hospital (AUH) when the blast occurs less than a mile away. The huge hospital building trembles, dislodging a panel in the false ceiling above the surgery table. Khoury instinctively knows who is the victim. Jumblatt is not in Beirut, and the explosion is so big. It can only be Hariri.

Samer Rida, the newspaper delivery supervisor, and his trainee are standing on the roadside just 20 metres to the right of the bomb when it explodes. Rida doesn't recall hearing the explosion, but he feels a tremendous force yanking him backwards down the steps leading into the St George Yacht Club.

Fady Khoury, the owner of the St George Hotel, is talking on his mobile phone while standing on the steps leading up to the main road when the blast knocks him to his knees. He turns to Yussef Mezher, his chauffeur, who was standing beside him and asks if he is hurt. Yussef replies in a shaken voice that he is okay. Then a second blast topples a stone wall onto Yussef, crushing his pelvis and pinning him to the ground. He screams in pain. Khoury is knocked down by a tin sheet roof which protects him from the collapsed wall. It must be an air raid, thinks Khoury. If there's a third explosion, I'm dead.

Rami Farous, the owner of a mobile phone shop around the corner from the St George Hotel, is sitting in his chair behind the counter when the blast flings him against the wall. The pressure wave squeezes all the air out of his lungs and for a few moments he is unable to breathe. The window fronting the shop shatters and blows inward, showering a customer with hundreds of glass shards. Rami is unhurt. He stumbles out of the shop into a thick fog of dust. He stares at other bewildered and pale-faced people staggering out of neighbouring shops and offices. Hurrying down the road toward the St George, he taps the video button on his mobile phone and begins recording the scene of destruction before him, trembling, blurry images of burning vehicles, thick smoke and dazed survivors, one of them sitting on the road, his clothes stripped from his body by the force of the blast.

Amer Shehadi stumbles out of the Mercedes and stares in astonishment at the inferno behind him, a tortured mass of blazing vehicles and thick, roiling black smoke. Mohammed Dia is also out of the car, but Hassan Ajouz in the back seat is unconscious. Shehadi charges into the flames to look for Hariri. Yet even though Hariri's Mercedes was just 4 metres behind his car in the convoy, he cannot make out which of the burning vehicles belongs to the boss. The heat and smoke force him to back away. He takes a deep breath and heads in again. He sees bodies smothered in flames sitting upright in the burning vehicles, some of them his colleagues. They're dead. There's nothing I can do for them, Shehadi thinks. Abu Tarek, the head of the security team and Hariri's personal bodyguard for more than two decades, was closest to the explosion, sitting in the passenger seat of the fourth vehicle, covering the right flank of Hariri's Mercedes. He was blown to pieces. All they would find of his body is

38 pieces of flesh identified only through DNA testing. Mohammed Darwish, the driver of the fourth vehicle, was cut in half, the upper part of his body thrown dozens of metres. The three bodyguards in the fifth car were killed instantly and left to burn in the blazing vehicle. Shehadi notices that the road is littered with the grim evidence of the explosion's terrible power – severed hands, arms, legs, countless scraps of indeterminate flesh and pools of thick red blood darkening in the heat from the fires. Still he cannot find Hariri and once more the heat and smoke force him to back away. Mohammed Dia hands him the walkie-talkie and he tries to contact his headquarters in Koreitem.

The sound of the explosion brings Abed Arab, deputy to his cousin Abu Tarek in the security team, out of his office and onto the street outside Koreitem where he scans the sky for the vapour trails of Israeli jets. His wife, Rudeina, yells at him from the roof of an apartment block opposite Koreitem where they live. 'It's a big explosion near the Phoenicia,' she shouts, pointing in the direction of the blast.

Arab hurries back into his control room by the main gate.

'Where's the convoy,' he says urgently.

'We don't know,' a colleague answers.

Abed asks for his walkie-talkie and, as it is handed to him, he hears the voice of Amer Shehadi calling his name and saying, 'The convoy's been hit by a bomb.'

Abed keeps the channel open and asks for details as he flags down a passing police car driven by an officer in the Internal Security Forces. Joined by an advisor to Hariri, the three men race through the streets of Hamra toward the St George. The crackle of the walkie-talkie cannot hide the shock in Shehadi's voice.

'Calm down. Take a deep breath and tell me what happened,' Abed tells Shehadi. 'Where's the boss?'

'I don't know. I can't find him,' Shehadi replies.

Ghattas Khoury was wrong. Jumblatt is in Beirut, at his grey-stone mansion in the Clemenceau quarter, barely five minutes' walk from the St George. The blast shakes the building. Jumblatt stares out of a window, thinking initially, like so many other people, that it is a low-flying super-sonic run by an Israeli jet. Then he sees the thick black cloud of smoke rising from the direction of the sea.

'Ghazi,' Jumblatt calls to Ghazi Aridi who is with him in the house, 'try to reach Koreitem. It might be Rafik.' Aridi dials the number but the lines are blocked. Jumblatt dispatches a bodyguard to the scene of the explosion to find out what's going on. Just after the bodyguard leaves, Aridi gets through to Koreitem.

'Where is he?' he asks.

'We don't know,' says the voice on the other end of the line. 'We have no news.'

Ahmad Husari, in charge of the Intensive Care Unit that morning at the American University Hospital, is doing some paperwork in his third-floor office when the building shudders from the tremendous blast, shaking a cloud of dust from the ceiling. Thinking it is an Israeli jet, he waits for the usual second sonic boom, knowing that Israeli warplanes travel in pairs in the skies above Lebanon. But there is no second detonation. A doctor pushes open his office door and tells him there has been an explosion at a branch of the HSBC bank in Hamra, only 600 metres from the hospital. Husari grabs his mobile phone and calls his wife, Lina, who is shopping in Hamra, buying skiing equipment for their son. Lina reassures her husband that she is fine, that there is no explosion in Hamra, and then the phone lines go dead.

Nejib Friji, the UN spokesman who is still standing outside parliament minutes after Hariri's convoy departed for Koreitem, listens in astonishment to the appalling din of thousands of windows shattering onto the pavements of central Beirut. He pulls out his mobile phone and snaps a photograph of a column of yellow dust spiralling into the sky above the sandstone buildings on the northern, seaward, side of Nijmeh Square.

'There's been an explosion somewhere between the sea and Clemenceau,' a guard outside the parliament building tells Friji and Ali Hamade, the *An Nahar* journalist. Jumblatt's town house is in Clemenceau. Both men key in Jumblatt's number on their mobile phones, but the lines are overloaded and no calls go through. Hamade hurries into Café de l'Etoile, where he had been sipping coffee and chatting with Hariri minutes earlier, to use the land line to reach the Druze leader.

'Jumblatt's alive,' Hamade tells Friji moments later. He was not the target.

'Try Hariri,' Friji says.

Carole Farhat feels no pain, even though the heat from the explosion has seared her face and hands. Her leather jacket and jeans are peppered with tiny burns. She is covered in cuts and blood streams from her left ear. Her mobile phone lying on the ground nearby flashes an incoming call. She slides off the car, ripping her jeans on a metal shard. Her hands are trembling too much to answer the phone or even place a call. Through the dust and smoke she hears the sound of gunfire. Are we being attacked? The shooting is the ammunition belonging to Hariri's bodyguards, a total of 750 pistol and machine gun rounds, cooking off in the flames. Terrified, Carole ducks through the shattered entrance of the St George Hotel

Annexe. Ali, the chauffeur for her sister-in-law Marie, is crouching by the entrance. They hug.

'What happened?' Ali asks.

'I don't know,' Carole replies, hiding behind a wall to avoid the gunfire. 'It's the end of the world.'

The two burned corpses sit upright in the front seats of the car, charred beyond recognition, white skull glinting through blackened flesh, twisted and contorted by the heat like some macabre copy of the plaster-cast victims of Pompeii. A fireman, his face blackened by smoke, tugs at the still-steaming door, trying to wrench it free to release the bodies. Two Red Cross workers carrying a body on a stretcher yell at people to get out of the way. The corpse, hidden discreetly beneath a woollen blanket, wobbles like jelly as the medics stumble through the rubble and dirt that litters this usually busy thoroughfare. Firemen's hoses snake across the debris. The water used to douse the burning vehicles mixes with the dust and earth turning the street into mud. Some crumpled vehicles have been blown to the side of the road, like swept leaves, the bodywork stripped to an ash grey by the flames. The engine of one abandoned but undamaged car is still running. Another group of rescue workers and volunteers tear at the door of a car crushed like tinfoil and still pinging from the heat of the fire that transformed the vehicle's occupants into featureless blackened corpses.

Ahmad Husari bursts into the emergency room at the American University Hospital, delivering rapid instructions to the staff to prepare for the imminent arrival of casualties. They agree to do the triage outside the front door of the emergency room to provide immediate assessment of the wounded. The critically injured will be sent to the operating rooms, while the less serious casualties will be dealt with in a separate area. Nurses are called in from all floors of the hospital and elective surgeries are postponed. The hasty preparations remind some of the older doctors of those grim days in the 1980s when treating the victims of bombs and bullets was a daily occurrence. The stretchers are lined up by the entrance and, when all is done, the medical team falls into a tense silence waiting for the first ambulances to arrive.

Samer Rida, the newspaper delivery man, is trapped beneath a pile of rubble from the collapsed ceiling of the entrance to the St George Yacht Club. He is having difficulty breathing and is blinded by blood. Rida's left eye is haemorrhaging and a wooden splinter is buried deep in his right temple behind the right eyeball. He tries to move his legs, but the weight of the rubble is too great. Terrified of being left to die in his shallow grave of dirt and masonry, he wriggles his hands to his face where he scrapes a small hole allowing him to breathe and call for help. Some bystanders lift away the rubble and help him up. Sightless, Rida holds out his hands in front of him to feel his way, listening to the cries of the wounded, panicked shouting and the wailing of sirens. What happened, he asks himself.

The third blast that St George's owner Fady Khoury feared would kill him never comes. He scrambles out from beneath the collapsed tin roof and briefly assesses the ruins of the hotel for potential shelter in case there are more explosions. Yussef is conscious but trapped beneath the fallen masonry. Some people climb down from the main road and help extract him. Khoury notices a man with a broken arm crawling from beneath a pile of rubble beside the hotel. He sees the young man who had delivered *Al-Wasit* newspaper minutes before staggering through the smoke, his arms outstretched. There are two red holes where his eyes should be.

'I can't see,' the young man moans.

Khoury takes his arm. 'Sit here. I'll get help.'

He steps out onto the street. It's an apocalypse, he thinks, as he stares at the burning vehicles, billowing black smoke and the dead and injured lying on the debris-covered road. He sees Suleiman Frangieh, the interior minister, and makes his way toward him.

Frangieh thanks God for Khoury's safety. But Khoury has no time for pleasantries. The St George Annexe is on fire. His people are inside. Smoke coils out of the building where the exterior walls had once been. The façade of flesh-coloured stone panels is almost completely gone. The explosion has not only destroyed much of the outside wall but knocked down all the interior walls as well, like dominoes, stripping the building to a skeleton.

'Put out the fire,' Khoury yells at Frangieh, 'or you will have more dead people.'

Nejib Friji and Ali Hamade in Nijmeh Square cannot reach Hariri's number so the two men walk the short distance to *An Nahar*'s office overlooking Martyrs' Square. Gibran Tueni, the general manager of the newspaper, is grim-faced and shaking. Gazing out of the sixth-floor office window, they can see that the initial cloud of yellow dust has turned into thick black smoke, an ugly contrast to the clear blue sky. The first footage from the scene of the explosion begins playing on the television in Tueni's office. Staring at the television screen, Friji recognises the hearse-like ambulance identified by Hamade only minutes before.

Knocked out by the blast, Rashid Hammoud, the paramedic in the back of the ambulance at the rear of Hariri's motorcade, gradually awakens on the floor of the vehicle. Mohammed Awayni, the driver, and Mazen

Zahabi, the paramedic sitting in the front passenger seat, were also rendered unconscious by the force of the explosion. The ambulance, which for security reasons normally travelled about 50 metres behind the last vehicle in the convoy, has coasted into the inferno, coming to a halt on the lip of the bomb crater. Blood is pouring into Hammoud's eyes from a gash on his head. The back of the vehicle is filled with smoke. Coughing and struggling to breath, Hammoud tries to stand but collapses again. His left leg is broken in the ankle and tibia. It must be a car crash, he thinks, not realising that the convoy has been struck by a bomb. He straps a makeshift splint to his leg and calls out to Zahabi and Awayni. There is no answer and, for a minute more, Hammoud shouts their names. Giving up, he pulls himself up onto his good, right, leg and peers through the narrow access window in the wooden screen separating him from the front cabin. He cannot see his colleagues, but notices that the engine of the ambulance is on fire. He glances fearfully at the two oxygen cylinders beside him in the rear of the ambulance. Panic gives him strength and he lurches to the back door and yanks desperately at the handle. The door is jammed. He looks up and to his astonishment he can see the sky. The entire roof of the ambulance has gone. Hammoud grips the edge of the roof and pulls himself up and through the opening, letting himself slip to the ground outside the vehicle. Amer Shehadi sees Hammoud sitting by the burning ambulance and hauls him clear.

'Have you seen the prime minister?' he asks the shaken Hammoud.

'The prime minister? No,' Hammoud replies, puzzled. Why would he be asking Hariri's whereabouts when they had been in a car crash?

'Is there anyone else in the ambulance?' Shehadi asks.

'Mohammed Awayni and Mazen Zahabi,' Hammoud replies. 'They haven't been burned yet.'

The engine fire is raging and it will only be a matter of seconds before it reaches the ambulance's petrol tank. Shehadi glances through the driver's window. He doesn't notice Awayni who is still out cold, but Zahabi is there, sitting upright but unconscious in the passenger seat. Uncertain if Zahabi is dead or alive, Shehadi moves around the back of the ambulance to reach the passenger door to check. But as he does so the petrol tank of the ambulance suddenly explodes, engulfing the vehicle with burning liquid and forcing Shehadi to back away.

Mohammed Awayni wakes to find his hands grasping the steering wheel of the ambulance. Dazed, he turns his head slowly to the right and sees Zahabi beside him covered in flames. Awayni moves his fingers on the steering wheel and thinks 'I'm alive.' He pushes open the door, falls out of the ambulance and runs towards the nearby Phoenicia Hotel as the vehicle succumbs to the fire.

Abed Arab arrives at the St George and sees Amer Shehadi who tells him that they still have not found the boss. Arab scans the scene before him, the thick black smoke, punctuated every few seconds by explosions as the flames ignite fuel tanks of burning cars. The high-pitched and insistent whine of car alarms fails to drown the crackle of bullets in the flames. His cousin, Abu Tarek, is in there somewhere. Arab notices the body of a large man lying on the road 10 metres away. Is it the boss? Somebody tells him it is Jamal Mansour, one of the bodyguards, who was of a similar shape and size to Hariri.

Amer Shehadi finds Hariri's car. The back of the armoured Mercedes has vanished. Only the crumpled, shattered front half remains, a burned-out shell of twisted metal. Somebody tells him that Hariri is alive and in one of the bomb-blasted buildings facing the St George. Shehadi scrambles over the debris, checking bodies and injured people being treated on the spot by Red Cross medics, but Hariri is not among them. As Shehadi begins to lose hope that the boss is still alive, he is gripped by a terrible blinding pain in the head. Thin trickles of blood seep from his ears and gradually his hearing fades, a result of the concussive effect of the huge explosion. He hitches a ride on an ambulance to hospital. It will be two weeks before he regains his hearing.

Soldiers and paramilitary police form a cordon at either end of the bomb scene, yelling at wide-eyed onlookers to stay back. Windows have shattered for hundreds of yards. Thick piles of glass lie on the street. The side of the towering five-star Phoenicia Hotel facing the St George has had every window blown out. The blast was so powerful that it even warped and splintered the wooden door frames in the hotel's bedrooms. Dozens of tiles lining the walls of the road tunnel near the Phoenicia have popped and buckled from the pressure wave. Dazed employees at a branch of HSBC bank, around the corner from the bombing, step through the shattered façade of the building, many of them dripping blood from glass cuts. Two black limousines, badly damaged but untouched by fire, lie in the middle of the road 30 metres from the crater. One of them is Amer Shehadi's Mercedes, the other a BMW. The indicator light of the BMW is still flashing. The windows are smashed, the bodywork crumpled. A small pool of thick red blood congeals on the road beside the driver's door. On the back window shelf lies a chipped CD: *Tha Last Meal* by Snoop Dogg. The boot of Shehadi's Mercedes was blown open, exposing a shiny metal box with lights, dials and switches, the powerful electronic jammer used to prevent bomb explosions.

There in the heart of the chaos, mud and smoke is the crater, 3 metres deep, some 10 metres wide, with thin tendrils of smoke still writhing from the churned earth. Shattered water pipes jut out from the crater wall like broken teeth. Rescue workers and plain-clothes policemen scramble down the sides of the crater, digging though the dirt for evidence of what could have caused such a massive explosion. More importantly, who was the bomb intended for? A trim-looking man in a dark suit, pale-blue shirt and tie directs rescuers as they sift through the rubble of an adjacent building. He looks like a bodyguard for someone important. Mohammed Azakir, a photographer for Reuters who was among the first to arrive and would later win a press award for the pictures he shot that day, has a terrible look on his face.

'They got Hariri,' he says bluntly.

The anxious silence outside the emergency room of the American University Hospital is broken by the faint wail of the first approaching ambulance. The vehicle lurches to a halt and Ahmad Husari, glancing inside, realises immediately that the first victims are all dead. The bodies are blackened from fire, some of them missing limbs. He orders the ambulance driver to head to the morgue. More ambulances arrive in swift succession, disgorging victims with injuries ranging from lacerations caused by flying glass to severe burns, amputations and deep gashes from metal fragments. Some of the victims are so seriously injured that they die on the operating table before surgery begins. Husari is struck by the fact that most of the victims are wearing suits and ties, very different from the military fatigues worn by the casualties he treated during the war. He hears a rumour that the motorcade carrying Hariri and Basil Fleihan was targeted by the bomb. The rumour is confirmed when he sees an injured Rashid Hammoud, his colleague from the AUH who used to talk with pride about his job on Hariri's medical team, carried into the emergency room on a stretcher. Then somebody tells him that Hariri and Fleihan escaped the bomb unhurt and drove away from the scene in another car. Thank God, he thinks. Husari won a Hariri Foundation scholarship in 1986 to study medicine at Johns Hopkins University in the US and he has known Fleihan since they were both students together at the American University of Beirut. Yet another ambulance pulls up, and out of the back, held up by two medics, steps a horrific, fire-blackened, half-naked scarecrow figure, whose dark suit and striped shirt hang in charred ribbons from his scorched and gashed body. The man's eyes flicker and in a hoarse, rasping voice he calls a woman's name, 'Yasma, Yasma', over and over again. It is astonishing that the man is conscious, let alone alive. The fire has flayed most of the skin from his body and seared the nerve endings so that, mercifully, the man is spared pain. Husari has him stretchered into the emergency room where he is incubated, put on life support and then wheeled into the ICU. He returns to the triage area outside the emergency room and is told that Hariri and Fleihan had not escaped the bomb after all and are, in all likelihood, dead. Husari thinks of the terribly burned man in the ICU who had repeated the name Yasma. Fleihan's wife is called Yasma. He walks back to the ICU and leans over the still-conscious figure.

'Are you Basil Fleihan?' he asks.

Fleihan nods.

'I am Ahmad Husari. Do you remember me?'

Another nod.

'I am here to look after you,' Husari says, but knowing, surely, there is no way Fleihan can survive these terrible burns. He glances at the ring on one of Fleihan's blackened fingers and notices the name 'Yasma' engraved upon it. And he thinks, what am I going to say to his wife?

Abed Arab continues staring at the body lying on the road. Is it the boss or Jamal Mansour, the bodyguard? He calls over two paramedics who place the body in the back of an ambulance. Arab climbs aboard and begins an inch-by-inch examination of the corpse, trying to put a name to the broken body before him. The hair has been burned off and the face is swollen beyond recognition, the eyes reduced to slits, the skin yellowed by the heat of the fire. The shoes have gone, exposing a pair of short dark socks that have been burned into the skin. Arab knew that Hariri tended to wear long socks. It takes him five minutes before he realises who it is. It's the finger-nails that give it away. An image of Hariri in Koreitem flashes into his mind. It was November 1, the boss's birthday. Abu Tarek asked him if he would kiss Hariri's hand as a gesture of respect. Hariri didn't like offering his hand to anyone, but Arab was different. He was family. Hariri had sat on the sofa and raised his hand. Arab took it and kissed it. It was an intensely personal moment. And now here he was sitting in the back of an ambulance before this ruined corpse whose clean, neatly clipped finger-nails were the same as those he had kissed three months earlier.

Jumblatt's bodyguard returns to the house in Clemenceau and says that it seems to have been a bomb attack against Hariri's convoy. Jumblatt and Aridi head to the American University Hospital, a few minutes away. As they arrive, they see Bahaa Hariri, Rafik's eldest son. He looks bewildered and in shock. The three of them enter the hospital together and are told that Hariri might be in the operating theatre. As they make their way to the theatre, a hospital security officer takes Jumblatt aside and says 'It's useless. He died.'

Ghattas Khoury is in the morgue when he is joined by Salim Diab, a former minister and close friend of Hariri. Together, they begin the harrowing task of trying to identify which of the corpses is the former prime minister. A medic indicates one corpse and says it is Hariri, but Khoury and Diab disagree. Hariri bears no resemblance to that burned, broken body. They keep searching.

When the shooting stops, Carole Farhat and Ali help each other back onto the street. The dust is settling and the smoke has cleared enough for her to see the devastation wrought by the blast. To her horror, she sees a man consumed by flames flop out of the window of a burning vehicle and writhe on the dirt. It is the paramedic Mazen Zahabi. He was alive after all. His agonising death will haunt Carole's dreams for months afterwards. She remembers that Marie, her sister-in-law, and other colleagues are on the first floor of the burning St George Annexe.

'Marie, Zahi, Abdo,' Carole yells up at the building. She has worked with Zahi Abu Rujaili and Abdo Farah for 16 years. She feels someone hug her and turns to see her husband, Bechir. He tells Carole to wait for him by the entrance as he looks for Marie in the St George Annexe. Ten minutes later, Bechir reappears along with other rescue workers who had penetrated the annexe from the opposite side. Marie is lying on a stretcher, almost unrecognisable to Carole. Her sister-in-law's face is a bloody mask.

Adnan Baba, Hariri's personal secretary, arrives at the AUH, having run from Koreitem on hearing that Hariri's motorcade has been hit by a bomb. Dr Jaber Sawaya, Hariri's personal physician, sees Baba and calls him over.

'Do you know what he was wearing this morning, Adnan?' he asks.

Baba says he does.

'Then come with me.'

Sawaya leads Baba to his closet and extracts a cloth package. Unwrapping the cloth, the doctor hands Baba a charred scrap of a striped blue and white tie.

'Yes, that's the tie I gave him this morning,' Baba says.

Sawaya shows him a plain white-gold wedding ring and a brown stone pendant given to Hariri by his wife, Nazek, that he used to wear around his neck under his shirt.

Baba nods as he recognises the items.

'Adnan,' Sawaya says softly, 'Mr Hariri is gone.'

Khoury and Diab receive a phone call that Hariri's car has escaped the explosion. They drive to the scene of the bombing, hoping that perhaps Hariri had miraculously survived after all. But they cannot find

Hariri's car amid the destruction. They return to the hospital morgue to re-examine the bodies. Other than Khoury and Diab, standing around a table in the morgue are Adnan Baba, Dr Jaber Sawaya and Abdul-Latif Shamaa, one of Hariri's oldest friends. All of them are weeping. On the slab before them is a torso, all that remains of one of the victims. Baba shakes his head and says that it is not Hariri. Another body, the same one that Khoury and Diab had earlier said was not Hariri, is wheeled into the room and placed on the table. Despite the terrible injuries and disfigurement, 28 years of close friendship allow Baba to recognise Hariri instantly.

'It's him,' he says.

At the hospital, Jumblatt turns to Bahaa, who is still unaware of his father's condition, and says 'Let's go to the house.' Jumblatt drives his car with Bahaa sitting beside him.

'What's happening? Please, in the name of God, tell me what's happening,' Bahaa pleads.

'The news is bad,' Jumblatt replies quietly, unable to bring himself to tell Bahaa that his father is dead.

The young man falls silent.

They arrive in Koreitem and hurry inside. Jumblatt realises that the household still has not learned that Hariri is dead. They fire questions at him, but he cannot say the words they need to hear.

'Well, the news is bad,' he repeats and, after a long pause, shrugs his thin shoulders and says simply, 'Allahu Akhbar', God is greatest.

'I recently asked him if he was ever afraid,' an ashen-faced Fouad Siniora told the author hours later. 'He told me "No, these violent acts belong in Lebanon's past." '

The atmosphere inside Koreitem on the evening of February 14 was grim and tense as the opposition gathered for a crisis meeting. Nine people, including Hariri and seven of his security detail, were known to have died in the explosion. The toll would eventually rise to 23 with more than 220 wounded. The last of the injured to die would be Basil Fleihan. It was a miracle that he had survived at all. AUH staff had surfed the internet to find the hospital best able to deal with his severe burns. They settled on the Percy military hospital in Paris. Ghattas Khoury had made all the arrangements and Fleihan was flown to France that night on Hariri's personal jet accompanied by his friend Ahmad Husari. Fleihan lived for another 64 agonising days before finally succumbing to his injuries.

A crowd had gathered around the upper and lower entrances of the stone mansion in Koreitem. An old woman wearing a headscarf sat on the ground, swaying and keening in a ritualistic display of mourning. The crowd seethed quietly with anger and grief. And then one young man yelled, 'Look into your hearts! We know who did this! Syria!' His expression was one of exhilarated defiance as he gazed at the faces of those around him. It was a pivotal moment. Hariri's death was shattering 15 years of sullen Sunni acquiescence to Syrian rule in Lebanon. Like an aircraft carrier altering course in the ocean, the Sunni community was turning with an inexorable momentum into outright opposition.

Inside the house, the reception areas and hall outside the conference room were filled with members of the opposition, journalists, family friends and diplomats. In one corner, a group of people watched live coverage of the aftermath on the Hariri-owned Future TV channel. The TV presenters were wearing black and there was a black band of mourning across the top left corner of the screen.

A smartly dressed middle-aged woman, tears streaming down her face, saw a Westerner in the reception room and walked up to him. She asked who he was. He told her that he was the Spanish ambassador. She clutched his jacket sleeve and said in broken English 'Please, you must help us. We can't go on like this. We need your help to end all this. We have suffered too long. Please help.' The ambassador nodded sympathetically and said nothing.

The opposition leaders were meeting in the conference room to decide on their statement. The meeting, which was called for by Walid Jumblatt, marked the first time that members of the Christian Qornet Shehwan gathering had formally sat together with Hariri's Future Movement. Several Qornet Shehwan members pondered on the irony that only a day earlier they were refusing to meet Hariri in Koreitem, preferring instead parliament. Now here they all were sitting around the same table and eyeing each other warily. Saad Hariri entered the room and sat at the table, saying nothing. He had flown straight from Abu Dhabi on hearing the news of his father's death, 'the longest flight of my life', he later recalled. Saad had spoken several times during the flight to a 'furious' Jacques Chirac, who had promised to come to Beirut for the funeral.[2]

Most of the participants at the meeting argued for a strong condemnation of the bombing and a denunciation of the Lebanese and Syrian authorities whom they held responsible for Hariri's murder. Hariri had been receiving death threats for months, so how could they possibly release a banal pro forma statement that refrained from pointing a finger of blame?

But whether to name and blame Syria directly for Hariri's death was another matter. A knee-jerk judgement could exacerbate what was already a fraught atmosphere, particularly as there had already been a claim of responsibility for the bomb blast.

At 1.30 p.m., just over 30 minutes after the explosion, the Beirut office of the Arabic Al-Jazeera satellite television station had received a phone call from someone speaking poor Arabic who said that a group called al-Nasr wa al-Jihad fi Bilad al-Sham (Victory and Jihad in Greater Syria) had carried out the assassination.

Al-Jazeera broadcast the statement at 2 p.m. Shortly afterwards, the TV station received another phone call from someone this time speaking fluent Arabic who said that a video tape had been left in a tree facing the United Nations headquarters in the city centre. The Al-Jazeera office is in an adjacent building. The video tape was retrieved, but Al-Jazeera's head office delayed putting it on the air. The station received two more increasingly angry and threatening phone calls before the tape was finally broadcast after 5 p.m.

It portrayed a bearded man in a white turban and black robe reading a statement against a backdrop of a black flag with white writing which read, 'There is no God but Allah. Muhammed is the messenger of Allah. God is greatest.'

He said 'To support our brother mujahidin in the land of the two holy mosques [a description often used by Al-Qaeda to describe Saudi Arabia] and to avenge their righteous martyrs who were killed by security forces of the Saudi regime in the land of the two holy mosques, we resolved, after relying on Almighty God, to carry out fair punishment against the agent of this regime and its cheap tool in Greater Syria, the sinner and maker of illegal money, Rafik Hariri, through the implementation of a resounding martyrdom operation. This confirms our promise to support and wage jihad, and will be the beginning of many martyrdom operations against the infidels, renegades and tyrants in Greater Syria.'

Al-Jazeera later announced that the video statement named the suicide bomber as Ahmad Abu Adas, who turned out to be a 22-year-old Palestinian living in the Tarek al-Jadidi district of west Beirut.

Taysir and Nehad Abu Adas, Ahmad's parents, turned themselves in to the police along with their two daughters shortly after seeing the video statement on Al-Jazeera. Internal Security Force troops raided the Abu Adas apartment and confiscated a computer, tapes and documents. It transpired that Abu Adas had left home on the morning of January 16 and had not been seen since. His parents had reported him missing three days later.

The opposition meeting was under way when the news of Abu Adas's claim of responsibility was aired on television, sparking outrage from some of Hariri's bloc.

'They are accusing fundamentalists. They want it to appear that we killed him,' stormed a Sunni MP.[3]

Bassam Sabaa drafted an initial statement, but Marwan Hamade objected. It was too soft.

'We are not here at a majlis al-azar [council of condolences],' he told the others. 'We are here as a political force and our leader has been assassinated.'[4]

Gibran Tueni warned that Cardinal Sfeir would not support a call for Lahoud's resignation, a comment that caused some momentary tension among the non-Christians in the room who believed that the president was at least guilty by association.

A revised statement was hammered out and the opposition announced it would be read out live on television immediately. A scrum developed at the two doors leading into the room as reporters and onlookers struggled to enter.

The leading members of the opposition sat along one side of the conference table. Jumblatt sat next to Sabaa, unsmiling, his arms crossed and staring at the polished table top before him. Sabaa, who was to read the statement, sat at the centre, his broad brow glistening with perspiration under the glare of television camera lights. He began by describing the 'criminal bombing' as an unprecedented act since the end of the war and said the opposition vowed to 'foil the diabolical scheme' of the assassins. But it was toward the end of the statement that Sabaa came to the substance.

Regarding Hariri's death, the opposition 'holds the Lebanese authority and the Syrian authority, given that it is the de facto authority in Lebanon, responsible for this and other similar crimes in Lebanon'.

'Allahu Akhbar,' yelled a young Hariri supporter who had wormed his way into the room.

It was a forceful declaration after all. The opposition decided to spread the blame between the Lebanese and Syrian governments rather than focus solely on Damascus. But there could be no going back from a such a bold accusation, and suddenly Lebanon was entering uncharted waters. Reading on, Sabaa demanded an international investigation into Hariri's murder, the immediate resignation of the government and the formation of a provisional government, the withdrawal of Syrian forces from Lebanon before the beginning of parliamentary elections, and the holding of a three-day national strike beginning the next day.

The meeting concluded, the opposition members escaped the media mêlé by bustling out of a side door through a kitchen.

'From this morning I have been living my husband's assassination 15 years ago,' Nayla Mouawad, a prominent figure in the Qornet Shehwan gathering, told the author as she paused in the hallway beside the mansion's lower entrance. Her son, Michel, stood attentively beside her. Mouawad, an energetic and attractive woman with a crown of auburn hair, was fired up from the historic events of the day. 'It's about time that the Lebanese people are freed from tutelage . . . We are not afraid any more,' she said. 'You can't stop people expressing their frustration. I think sooner or later the street will grow stronger.'

It would be sooner rather than later. The crowd surrounding Koreitem had grown larger and, in the wake of the televised opposition statement, had lost all inhibitions.

'Syria out, Syria out,' they roared. And the anger was not confined to the vicinity of Koreitem. That night, furious Sunnis took to the streets around the country, brandishing pictures of Hariri and blocking major roads with burning tyres. At the Cola intersection in west Beirut, a crowd tore down a large banner of Hafez al-Assad while others besieged a local Baath party building, breaking the windows with stones and burning a picture of Bashar. In the Bekaa, a truck carrying 20 Syrian labourers was sprayed with machine gun fire, and in one town leaflets signed by the 'The Secret Group – Group of Martyr Rafik Bahieddine Hariri' warned all Syrians in the area that they had until February 20 to leave the country. In Sidon, Hariri's home town, Syrian workers were attacked by a mob chanting 'There is no God but God, and Syria is the enemy of God.'

These were unprecedented, unthinkable scenes, yet perhaps in keeping with the audacity of dispatching someone of Hariri's prominence in such a ruthless and blatant manner. This was no cloak-and-dagger assassination, no phial of poison secreted into the bedtime cocoa or stiletto silently thrust into the back. Whoever killed Hariri wanted to make a very stark and bold point.

'It's the first major peacetime political assassination,' Farid Khazen, a professor of politics at the American University of Beirut who would later be elected to parliament, told the author hours after the bomb blast. 'This is as far as you can go when you target someone of Hariri's stature. This has broken taboos.'

Syria's reaction to Hariri's death was keenly anticipated. While most of the world was wary of apportioning instant blame – even the White House steered clear of accusing Damascus – the Lebanese were in no doubt who was to blame. 'You ask me about party?' responded Saad

Hariri to a reporter's question on who he thought was responsible. 'They are well known,' he said.

Bashar was quoted as saying simply that the assassination was a 'heinous criminal act'. Other Syrian officials, along with the Lebanese government, said that the murder targeted Lebanon's stability and, in Lahoud's phrase, aimed at 'instigating sedition'. The only reaction from Damascus that was heart-felt and contained a genuine sense of shock was that of Abdel-Halim Khaddam.

'With distressing bewilderment, I received the news of the assassination of my brother and friend Abu Bahaa, whom I have known for more than 25 years,' he said, using the phrase 'Father of Bahaa', a familiar term of affection for Hariri. Khaddam went on to describe Hariri as a 'Lebanese patriot who loves his country and the people' who was 'loyal to Syria and this was manifested in everything that concerned Syria'.

Khaddam was the only senior Syrian official who on hearing the news of Hariri's murder drove straight from Damascus to the American University Hospital, braving the enraged crowd gathered outside. He must have had a sense of déjà vu pressing through the throng into the hospital, repeating the same call he had paid to the injured Marwan Hamade just over four months earlier. Khaddam also attended the condolences at Koreitem held over the next three days in which thousands of mourners from the humble to the great filed past the grieving family to shake their hands and murmur their commiserations. Jacques Chirac flew in from Paris on Tuesday and was shown on television comforting a grief-stricken Nazek, tenderly holding her hand as she sobbed beside him on the sofa.

The Hariri family rejected an offer by the government to hold a state funeral, announcing that he would be buried beside the unfinished Mohammed al-Amine mosque in Martyrs' Square. It would be a 'popular' farewell, the family said, one at which Lebanese officials would not be welcome. Jumblatt advised Lebanese officialdom to stay away from the funeral to 'avoid the stones and eggs of the people'.

Beirut ground to a halt the next day as the nation observed the opposition call for a three-day strike. The normally jammed streets were eerily empty and television stations aired readings from the Koran. Schools, shops and businesses closed, with most people choosing to stay at home as the government imposed a security clampdown, cancelling all leave for the military and police and stationing troops at key intersections in the city. Beside the cordoned-off bomb site at the St George, a crowd of mourners gathered, laying flowers on the pavement, praying, reading verses from the Koran and the Bible or simply gazing in teary-eyed awe at the scene of destruction before them. A large portrait of Basil Fleihan pinned to a palm tree near the cordon formed the basis of a small shrine marked by candles and offerings of flowers.

Amid the grief, however, Beirut's Sunnis were making it abundantly clear that they regarded the Hariri family as a political and social dynasty that would continue to endure despite Rafik Hariri's death. Although Hariri's eldest sons were businessmen, not politicians, they understood the duty that fate had thrust upon them.

'My father served Lebanon all his life, and we will keep serving Lebanon also, like him,' said Saad Hariri as he stood beside the crater where his father had died 24 hours earlier.

Indeed, with his death, Hariri had completed the transformation of his family from a humble farming background in a two-room stone hovel among the orange groves of Sidon into the latest, and certainly one of the most powerful, members of that select clique of ruling family dynasties in Lebanon.

And the esteem in which Hariri was held was made impressively clear the next morning, Wednesday, February 16, when the Lebanese bid farewell to 'Mr Lebanon', the man who had come to symbolise the country's post-war rebirth and had dominated the national political scene like no other for more than a decade.

In their tens of thousands they came – rich and poor, old and young, Christian and Muslim – a heaving tide of humanity led by a line of Sunni clerics, a pencil stroke of full-length grey tunics topped by white turbans, their arms interlocked to contain the surging mass gathered behind them. Like a vast amorphous organism compressed and shaped by the narrow confines of Beirut's streets, the crowd of mourners accompanied Hariri on his final six-kilometre journey from Koreitem to the Mohammed al-Amine mosque in Martyrs' Square. Women leaned out of windows overlooking the procession to fling handfuls of rice over the funeral cortège. Jumblatt's Druze had been bussed in from the Chouf mountains, their presence in the throng marked by the profusion of PSP flags, the socialist-style crossed hammers on a red background. Submerged in the frenzied sea of mourners were the limousines carrying the Hariri family to Martyrs' Square and the flower-bedecked ambulances containing the coffins of Hariri and his seven bodyguards. The cavalcade's progress could only be discerned from the young men balancing like surfers on the roofs of the ambulances yelling at people to clear a way, their voices lost amid the wailing sirens, and the chants and cries of the mourners.

A steady stream of people separate from the main procession continued to flow into the square from Muslim areas of west Beirut as well as the Christian districts in the east. The loudspeakers from the Mohammed al-Amine mosque carried Koranic verses against a backdrop of pealing bells from the Armenian Orthodox church on the opposite side of the square.

'This is the first time in 30 or 40 years where I have heard the same slogans emanating from both sides of town,' said Youssef Zein, a prominent Lebanese businessman, as he gazed down at the throng from the over-pass known as 'the ring' at the southern end of Martyrs' Square. 'These aren't the $10 crowd. This is the bourgeoisie,' he added, pointing at the mourners walking from the adjacent Christian neighbourhoods of Ashrafieh and Gemaizeh. 'You never get them out of their homes, but they have come today. They are here for independence and for a dream.'

Indeed, it was a remarkable sight. Glamorous Maronite women, wearing chic black dresses and sporting designer sunglasses, chatted in French and held aloft pictures of Hariri. Next to them stood Muslim women in white headscarves and full-length gowns whose husbands at midday kneeled on the road to pray. Christian students chatted to their Muslim and Druze counterparts; turbanned Shiite clerics stood next to Christian priests.

Hanging on the walls of the towering Mohammed al-Amine mosque were huge portraits of Hariri. In one, his chin rested casually on his fist, a warm, relaxed smile on his face. A full-length picture on the southern wall of the mosque showed him standing with his hands in his pocket, head slightly cocked as he gazed with a seemingly paternalistic eye out over the city centre that he had helped rebuild from the devastation of war.

The coffins were unloaded from the ambulances and conveyed on a stormy sea of upturned palms to the waiting graves. Several young men scaled the cranes surrounding the unfinished mosque, hanging perilously from the sides several metres up to escape the crush below and obtain a better view.

Hariri's coffin, draped in the red and white Lebanese flag with its green cedar emblem, swayed unsteadily on the shoulders of his sons as it inched toward the grave, its progress impeded by the hundreds of hands reaching out for the coffin, as if the intimacy of touching the wooden casket somehow brought Hariri closer to them in these final moments before he disappeared into the ground. As Hariri's shroud-wrapped body was lifted from the coffin and gently lowered into the grave, in accordance with Muslim tradition, a distraught cleric cried out 'The martyr was a dear friend of God . . . Thank God he was able to have such fine sons.' The crowd roared back 'Allahu Akhbar.'

Lebanon had never seen a funeral to match this, and yet it was more than just a funeral. It was also a huge demonstration against Syria's tutelage over Lebanon. Indeed, Hariri's funeral was really the first of the mass anti-Syrian rallies that would shake the political foundations of Lebanon over the next month.

'Syria out, Syria out' and 'Revenge, revenge', chanted the mourners. Many held placards with bold anti-Syrian phrases. One read 'Syrial killer', a pun that would become popular with demonstrators.

If the Syrians and their Lebanese allies hoped that the anti-Syrian sentiment would exhaust itself through the emotional outpouring at Hariri's funeral, they were wrong. On the day of the funeral, wrote Samir Kassir, a columnist for *An Nahar* and a leading democracy campaigner and critic of Syrian rule in Lebanon, 'Beirut was the beating heart of a new Arab nationalism . . . This nationalism is based on the free will of citizens, male and female. And this is what the tyrannical [Syrian] regime should fear more than anything else if it tarries about ending its hegemony over Beirut and Lebanon.'

Hariri's death had unleashed a newfound sense of exhilarated determination among many ordinary Lebanese who had tired of Syria's heavy hand and the Lebanese regime's clumsy subservience. In the days that followed his funeral, Hariri's grave became at once a shrine of heaped flowers and flickering candles for tearful mourners and a nucleus for the revolution building on the streets of Beirut. Panels of bare white hoarding used to seal off the mosque's construction site beside Hariri's grave became sounding boards for a new spirit of rebellion, with multi-lingual graffiti ranging from emotional tributes, 'You will always live in our hearts, O Rafik' to brisk insults, 'Fuck you, Bashar.'

Like a pebble cast into a pond, Hariri's murder initiated ripples that were to spread well beyond Lebanon's borders. It would hasten and further cement the emerging geo-strategic shifts and realignments in the Middle East, spawned by the Bush administration's policies following 9/11 and the invasion of Iraq. For the West, Lebanon would become a new point of pressure against Damascus, a sharpened needle jabbing at Syria's flank to goad the recalcitrant state onto a path acceptable to the United States. Even though the Bush administration declined to publicly blame Damascus for Hariri's murder, Washington's unhappiness with Syria was made clear when Margaret Scobey, the US ambassador to Damascus, was recalled 'for consultations' a day after Hariri's death. That same week, Bush demanded a Syrian troop withdrawal from Lebanon, saying that

Damascus 'is out of step with the progress being made in the greater Middle East'.

A diminishing Syrian influence over Lebanon threatened domino-effect repercussions on Iran's ability to project itself onto the Arab–Israeli conflict via Hizbullah and its Tehran-supported Palestinian allies. Hizbullah was the nexus for Iran's anti-Israel strategy. Its clandestine operations included channelling funds and providing technical know-how and specialised training to cells of Palestinian militants in the Occupied Territories. Hizbullah's Al-Manar television station broadcast an unremitting diet of anti-Israel propaganda and encouragement for the Palestinians while its disciplined, battle-hardened fighters menaced Israel from Lebanon's southern frontier. But after four and a half years of bloodshed, the Palestinian intifada was showing signs of terminal fatigue. Just days before Hariri's murder, Palestinian president Mahmoud Abbas and Israeli prime minister Ariel Sharon had agreed to a ceasefire brokered by the Egyptians. If Syria's position in Lebanon was weakened, Hizbullah's freedom of action – and therefore Iran's – risked being reduced, which in turn would have an impact on the sustainability of the intifada.

If Syria risked an erosion of its position in Lebanon, it also would find itself increasingly isolated by its Arab neighbours, the death of Hariri further reducing Arab patience for the young and seemingly feckless Syrian president. Saudi Arabia, in particular, was incensed at the callous dispatching of its Lebanese protégé, seeing in Hariri's death and the preceding months of humiliation and death threats a deliberate attempt to weaken the kingdom's influence in Lebanon. The Arab world had quietly tolerated Syria's virtual annexation of Lebanon since 1989, choosing to ignore the subjugation of a fellow member of the Arab League over the perpetual fear of displaying anything other than unruffled Arab unity to the public gaze. But after Hariri's murder, no Arab state was going to lift a finger to help Syria prolong its presence in Lebanon. Even Iran, Syria's one dependable (non-Arab) regional ally, was baulking at supporting Damascus's continued hegemony over Lebanon. *Al-Hayat* reported a week after Hariri's death that 'some Iranian officials' consider 'there is no going back on Iranian support of Syria in the face of Israel, but Iran is not ready to support the Syrian presence in Lebanon because Lebanon's sovereignty is important for Iran'.

The strategic picture did not bode well for Syria in the immediate aftermath of Hariri's murder. Yet Syria's Lebanese allies seemed almost oblivious of the political earthquake under way in the Levant and the fate that was to befall them judging from the ham-fisted manner in which they launched their investigation into the assassination. A UN fact-finding mission, led by an Irish policeman, Peter Fitzgerald, reported in March that there was a 'distinct lack of commitment on the part of the Lebanese authorities to investigate the crime effectively'.

The report listed a host of measures undertaken by the Lebanese security services that not only thwarted a proper investigation into the crime scene but appeared to be a barely disguised cover-up. The six vehicles that formed Hariri's destroyed convoy and a black BMW (the car with the Snoop Dogg CD in the rear seat) were removed from the site of the blast on the night of February 14 and taken to a nearby police compound, foiling any chance of an on-site ballistics analysis. Parts of a white Mitsubishi truck, thought to be the vehicle carrying the bomb, were thrown into the crater, photographed by police and labelled as evidence. Broken water pipes flooded the crater within 24 hours because nobody switched the water off, destroying potential evidence. Although the site was sealed off to the public, intelligence and security officers tramped around the scene at will. The Fitzgerald fact-finding report recommended that the UN launch a full investigation of its own into the Hariri assassination, as the Lebanese authorities clearly were incapable or unwilling to do so themselves.

It later transpired that General Mustafa Hamdan, the head of the Presidential Guard and Lahoud's right-hand man, had instructed Ali Hajj, the head of the Internal Security Forces and former chief bodyguard to Hariri, to have the crater filled in immediately so that the road could be opened by 10 a.m. the day after the explosion.[5] Hamdan denied giving the order.

But the procedural mistakes pale in comparison to the negligence and insensitivity shown by the Lebanese authorities toward the victims of the bombing and their families. The body of Zahi Abu Rujaili, Carole Farhat's colleague at the St George Hotel, was recovered from the burned ruin of the St George Annexe the next day. A post-mortem showed that he had survived for approximately 12 hours after the explosion and had died alone in the rubble undiscovered. The body of Farhan al-Issa has never been found. On February 22, a second body was discovered by accident. On March 1, 15 days after the explosion, the remains of Abdel-Hamid Ghalayini, 53, were found buried beneath a thin layer of rubble close to the bomb crater.

Ghalayini's family had been pressing the authorities to find their missing relative since the day of the blast, but were brushed off. When they were finally allowed to inspect the scene for themselves, it took less than five minutes to discover Ghalayini's badly decomposed corpse. Lebanese television stations broadcast extensive footage of the dead man's distraught daughters screaming their fury at the authorities and demanding Lahoud's resignation.

'For weeks they did nothing,' cried Lama Ghalayini, the eldest daughter. 'They kept telling us that cats were finding feet and hands, and today the flies helped find my father. Do we have to count on cats and flies? What is the state doing?'

The television footage of the grieving Ghalayini family was bitingly juxtaposed with scenes of a smiling Lahoud in the presidential palace in the hills above Beirut conversing with his political allies.

'That fatuous image shows just how remote and clumsy Lahoud's image is now,' a European diplomat noted in a conversation with the author at the time.

A day after the explosion, Suleiman Frangieh, the interior minister, said initial indications suggested that the perpetrator 'might have been a suicide [bomber] who blew himself up'.

Adnan Addoum, the staunchly pro-Syrian justice minister, said that investigations were centring on several 'bearded' Australian passport holders who departed Beirut airport the same day as the explosion. He claimed that traces of TNT had been found on two seats used by the suspects on the plane.

In the days that followed the bombing, a heated debate erupted in the media and on the internet as to whether the explosives were planted below ground or on the surface. It was an important point. The Lebanese authorities clearly were pressing the idea of an above-ground blast caused by a suicide bomber, citing the mysterious Abu Adas video confession and the suspect Australians. But those who firmly believed Syria was responsible for the assassination pinned their hopes on a subterranean blast, as digging a hole in the main road outside the St George Hotel would require the collusion of the authorities. An anonymous Lebanese explosives expert circulated by email a photo analysis of the bomb scene to back his argument for an underground explosion. It appeared compelling. The burned remains of Hariri's private ambulance and the fifth car in the motorcade rested on the lip of the crater, suggesting the force of the blast was directed upward, in accordance with a subterranean explosion, rather than laterally, which would suggest a surface blast. The crater itself, the blown manhole covers and the large amounts of earth and chunks of asphalt found hundreds of metres from the epicentre also suggested an underground bomb. But how could one explode a bomb planted below the road given that Hariri's convoy was equipped with three powerful jammers designed to block electronic signals used to detonate bombs? One possibility was if the perpetrator was able to bypass the frequencies covered by the jammers, although that would require advanced technical knowledge and equipment. Another less plausible explanation was for the bombs to be detonated mechanically by a command wire. However, that would entail someone unfurling a cable to a spot several hundred metres from the explosive charge to escape the effects of the blast. Insurgents in Iraq have used wires 300–400 metres long to explode roadside bombs. But those attacks occur in open countryside, not in the heart of a capital city where anyone seen laying hundreds of metres of cable would have attracted attention. And the perpetrator would still need to retain a clear line of sight to the bomb to judge the correct moment to press the button. The street layout around the St George's promontory was not conducive to a line-of-sight detonation. A side-on view of the road is preferable to best judge the moment when the target aligns with the bomb, but obtaining such a view at the St George would have been fatal, as the best side-on locations were either in the hotel itself or in the annexe building opposite.

There was also intense speculation that two bombs were detonated simultaneously, particularly given the insistence of Carole Farhat and Fady Khoury, among the survivors closest to the bomb, that they heard two distinct blasts. The double explosion theory could have explained some of the conflicting evidence, such as the chunks of asphalt found on the roofs of surrounding buildings and the ballistic evidence that the Mitsubishi van was the bomb carrier. In May 2006, the UN commission re-examined the bomb site. In mid-June, the commission reported that it 'was of the view', pending final forensic examinations, that Hariri was killed by one above-ground explosion of at least 1,200 kilogrammes of a TNT and plastic explosives mixture, triggered 'most likely' by an as yet anonymous individual.[6]

Two weeks after the explosion, it emerged that a surveillance camera attached to the front of the HSBC bank branch near the St George had caught the last moments of Hariri's convoy. The time-lapsed images give the footage a jumpy look as cars and trucks race silently along the main road 100 metres from the bank, passing a corner of the St George hotel and out of view. A clock ticks away the time. At 12.56.17, the first vehicle in Hariri's convoy enters the frame. The other cars follow and the ambulance in the rear disappears out of sight behind a corner of the St George Annexe at 12.56.25. A second later, the camera catches a blurry shockwave and then a second of static. The blast knocked the camera from its mooring and as the picture clears it is pointing downward at the road outside the entrance of HSBC, recording ghostly figures staggering out of the front entrance.

It is chilling to watch, but the real significance of the tape is what it shows just two minutes before Hariri's convoy came into view. At 12.54.00, a white Mitsubishi van inches onto the screen, travelling approximately six times slower than other vehicles. The small van is fully laden, a grey sheet covering the contents in the back. It maintains a steady speed, hugging the right-hand side of the road next to the St George Hotel before it passes out of sight at 12.54.37, one minute, forty seconds before Hariri's motorcade heaves into view. The actual explosion occurs just around the corner from the camera's view. But the investigators believe that the truck carried the bomb, and it was probably the same vehicle that Carole Farhat noticed and puzzled over briefly as she crossed the road to the St George Annexe a few seconds before the blast.

It was no coincidence that the bomber chose the vicinity of the St George Hotel to ambush Hariri's motorcade. Of the three routes Hariri could have taken from Nijmeh Square to his home in Koreitem, the shorter two converge to within 600 metres in the vicinity of the St George Hotel. The connecting street is a broad, relatively traffic-free avenue running up a hill from the St George past the Phoenicia Hotel to a junction beside which lies the derelict, 32-storey Murr Tower.

In the assessment of Abed Arab, who replaced his cousin Abu Tarek as the head of the Hariri family's security team, the Mitsubishi van would have been parked somewhere between the St George and the Murr Tower. The driver would have moved into position only after the spotter outside parliament telephoned to confirm Hariri's route as the motorcade departed the square. If Hariri had taken the inland route, the bomber would have intercepted his convoy near the Murr Tower. Furthermore, if the bomber had been unable to manoeuvre into position prior to the arrival of the motorcade on February 14, there would have been two more days for another attempt as the parliamentary debate on the electoral law was scheduled to last until Wednesday.

While the Lebanese investigation plodded along, the opposition, buoyed by the huge outpouring of rage and grief that accompanied Hariri's funeral, as well as international anger, was preparing to take its campaign to the streets.

It called for an 'independence intifada' involving all Lebanese to demonstrate for a Syrian troop withdrawal and the resignation of the Karami government. 'Liberation, Sovereignty, Independence' would become their battle cry and 'Al-Haqiqa' (The Truth) behind Hariri's death their objective.

The first demonstration was held on February 21, exactly one week after Hariri's murder, when some 25,000 people ignored the government's warning that such protests were 'extremely dangerous' and gathered near the St George Hotel. The green and white scarves that had been prepared for Hariri's election campaign had been changed to red and white to symbolise the blood of his 'martyrdom', and were worn by many of the protestors.

A profusion of flags denoted the political, and thus sectarian, allegiances of the demonstrators. Many carried placards in English, among them 'Break the silence' and 'Hey Syria! Who's next?' One middle-aged, smartly dressed woman held up a hand-written placard reading 'Independence is our right. Free Lebanon!'

At 12.55 p.m., the crowd fell silent, a deathly hush as the moment of Hariri's death was marked. It ended with a thunderous rendition of the Lebanese national anthem which echoed from the gaunt, bullet-riddled skeleton of the Holiday Inn hotel, which still bore the scars of the 1975–1990 war. The demonstrators jammed the streets of central Beirut as they made their way to Hariri's grave beside Martyrs' Square. Lebanese Army commandos and riot police lined the route. Hariri's grave was surrounded by a permanent cordon of mourners, Christians praying and making the sign of the cross, Muslims next to them reading from tiny copies of the Koran, all taking a few moments out from the rally. Some protestors clambered up the bullet-holed bronze statue depicting the nationalist 'martyrs' who were hanged by the Ottomans in 1915 to wave Lebanese flags and banners. One of them, dressed as Osama bin Laden with a sign on his chest reading 'Syrian terror', aimed a toy rifle at one of the 'martyrs'.

'This is the beginning of something important,' said a beaming Gibran Tueni, general manager of *An Nahar* newspaper and a courageous and prolific columnist whose opinion pieces for years had been and continued to be relentless hammer blows against Syria's hegemony over Lebanon. His eyes shone with barely suppressed excitement at what was unfolding. 'We asked a few students to attend a sit-in and look how many people showed up. The people are taking the lead, not us.'

Tueni was one of the architects of the independence intifada. From his office on the sixth floor of *An Nahar's* gleaming glass building on the northern edge of Martyrs' Square, he could gaze with some satisfaction at the colourful, flag-waving throng below, putting into action what he had long advocated in his newspaper.

And it was having an effect. Three days after the rally, on February 24, Walid Muallem, Syria's deputy foreign minister, grudgingly announced that Syria would redeploy into the Bekaa valley in accordance with the Taif Agreement. Rumours of a six-point Syrian withdrawal plan were aired in the Arabic media, in which Damascus would pull out all its troops except for 2,000 which would be deployed in the eastern Bekaa. No mention was made of the pervasive intelligence apparatus.

Not good enough, clamoured the UN and the US, both of which demanded a full and unambiguous withdrawal in accordance with Resolution 1559. The Lebanese opposition also was sceptical of Syria's vague commitment to a partial withdrawal.

'This is the sixth Syrian redeployment in five years. How long is it going to take them to leave completely? Another 50 years?' quipped Jumblatt to the author.

In the days that followed, the budding independence intifada hardened as protestors erected tents on a grassy knoll surrounding the statue in Martyrs' Square, the genesis of what would become a tent city, dubbed Camp Freedom, a symbol of the independence intifada. On February 26, thousands of people formed a human chain linking the St George to Hariri's tomb. Two days later, the opposition held the largest rally to date to coincide with a parliamentary debate on the Hariri murder at which opposition MPs had tabled a no-confidence motion. There was one major difference between this rally and the previous one a week earlier at the St George – there was not a party flag in sight. The opposition had decided that the first demonstration had looked like a 'battle of the flags', in the words of Ghattas Khoury. From now on the only flag at the demonstrations would be the national flag and the red and white motif of the 'independence intifada'.

The army set up checkpoints and roadblocks on the main highway leading to the Christian heartland north of Beirut to prevent protestors from reaching the city. But still they came. A surging sea of demonstrators carrying the red and white national flags flowed along the cramped streets of east Beirut until they ran up against a wall of riot police and tough-looking, green-bereted special forces soldiers who had strung coils of barbed wire across the eastern access points into Martyrs' Square. A crowd of several thousand began building up, but, despite some pushing and shoving, it remained a good-natured event. Some protestors sang the national anthem and joked with the soldiers. Others threw rose petals over the soldiers and called out 'The army are our brothers and stand by us and not against us.' Occasionally small groups of protestors would breach the cordon and sprint through, whooping with delight as the cursing soldiers struggled to block the gap. But the crowd eventually grew too much for them. A small group of demonstrators, red and white bandannas tied around their heads, dodged through the line of soldiers and yanked the coils of barbed wire out of the way before the stunned soldiers could respond. The crowd on the other side of the wire roared in triumph and surged through the gap as the troops watched helplessly, clearly unwilling to use force.

'What are they going to do?' asked Fadi Romanos, one of the protestors. 'Kill us all or put us all in jail? We have removed the mask of fear. We are not afraid any more.'

The parliamentary debate on the no-confidence motion was watched by the protestors live on giant television screens erected in Martyrs' Square. One by one, the opposition MPs took to the podium to castigate the government and Lahoud's regime. Omar Karami looked gaunt and tired as his government was bludgeoned with accusations and criticism.

'All the Lebanese want to know their enemy, the enemy of Lebanon who killed the martyr Rafik Hariri, those who took the decision, planned and executed it, those who ignored and prevented the truth from coming out,' said a tearful Bahiya Hariri.

It was too much for Karami. Without informing anyone of his decision, he rose and wearily announced the resignation of the government, adding 'May God preserve Lebanon.'

A moment of stunned silence was broken by the cheers of the opposition MPs and a huge roar of delight from Martyrs' Square which even could be heard in the parliamentary chamber. A visibly startled Nabih Berri glared at Karami from his speaker's seat, and said 'Don't you think that I deserve to be informed of the most important decision in the country?'

It was a remarkable moment. Karami had been expecting to win the confidence vote, as some two-thirds of parliament belonged to the loyalist camp. But the pressure on him had taken its toll. He was being shunned in his home city of Tripoli in the north where his family is traditionally held in high esteem, and was finally defeated by the massive crowd in Martyrs' Square and the withering scorn and biting accusations heaped upon him and his government, which never had much credibility with most Lebanese anyway.

Capitalising on its success in ousting the government, the opposition issued a seven-point list of demands which included the resignations of the seven top security chiefs in the country, among them Jamil Sayyed, Raymond Azar, the head of Military Intelligence, Ali Hajj, the head of the Internal Security Forces, and Mustafa Hamdan, the head of the Presidential Guard.

The collapse of the government proved that the independence intifada had teeth, and it swiftly gained international attention. Organised mass demonstrations against discredited regimes are a rare event anywhere and almost unheard of in the contemporary Arab world. The sight of tens of thousands of Lebanese marching through the streets of Beirut demanding freedom and sovereignty conjured up irresistible images of Ukraine's recent 'Orange Revolution' and Georgia's 'Rose Revolution'. Washington recognised that there was an opportunity to be had in identifying with and supporting the Lebanese street rallies against Syria and its Lebanese 'puppet' regime. The Bush administration dubbed the uprising the 'Cedar Revolution', an unoriginal appellation that sanitised the less palatable Lebanese preference for intifada which, to a Western audience, had uncomfortable associations with Palestinian suicide bombers blowing up pizza restaurants in Tel Aviv. The phrase 'Cedar Revolution', first aired by Paula Dobriansky, US undersecretary for global affairs,[7] displayed little understanding of the sensitivities aroused by Lebanon's national emblem. The cedar was adopted by nationalist Christian militias during the civil war, such as the Phalange party whose symbol is a stylised triangular cedar tree, and the Guardians of the Cedars, an ultra-nationalist group whose leader Etienne Saqr once proclaimed that it was the duty of every Lebanese to kill at least one Palestinian.

Embracing Lebanon's 'Cedar Revolution' not only served as a useful means of maintaining the pressure on Syria, but it also was in accord with Bush's faltering policy of fostering democracy in the Arab world. The invasion of Iraq and the overthrow of Saddam Hussein was supposed to be the catalyst for a democratic revolution in the Middle East, according to the agenda of the Bush administration's neo-cons. It was a laudable, if naive, aspiration that sought to overturn decades of perceiving the Arab world through the lens of realpolitik, tolerating vicious dictatorships and repressive theocracies so long as they remained friendly to the US. A case in point was Iraq, America's friend when it was engaged in its bloody eight-year war against Iran in the 1980s. From now on, Bush argued, America's security interests would be best served through encouraging the democratisation of the Arab world. Yet the programme's half-hearted and clumsy implementation suggested that the Bush administration had underestimated and oversimplified the complexities of the Arab milieu. Even Iraq's role as the paradigm for Arab democracy was undermined by the mismanagement of post-Saddam Iraq. When the Greater Middle East Initiative, Bush's main platform to promote political, economic and social reform in the Arab world, was prematurely leaked in early 2004 it was greeted with contempt and derision in Arab countries for failing to mention that Israel's illegal occupation of Arab land might have a bearing on instability in the Middle East. A diluted version of the initiative was released at the G-8 summit in June, whereupon it promptly sank without trace, scuppered by the suspicion of traditionally anti-American Arab liberals, the hostility of Arab regimes and the preoccupation of the US with the forthcoming presidential election.

But the Bush administration recognised that Lebanon's independence intifada could provide a necessary shot of adrenalin into the moribund Arab democracy initiative. Unlike most Arab countries, Lebanon had a genuine, if flawed, democratic tradition upon which to build. The world, Bush said, 'is speaking with one voice when it comes to making sure that democracy has a chance to flourish in Lebanon'.

The hyperbole even ensnared the ever-mercurial Walid Jumblatt, who in a reversal of his traditional hostility toward US policy in the Arab world began a dialogue with Paul Wolfowitz, who as deputy secretary of defence was one of the leading proponents of using American military muscle to democratise the Arab world. Ironically, just 18 months earlier, the US State Department had stripped Jumblatt of his diplomatic visa after he publicly called Wolfowitz a 'virus' that should be destroyed, and lamented the fact that the American official had escaped injury in a rocket attack on his hotel during a visit to Baghdad.

While American officials hailed the independence intifada as an expression of a freedom-seeking people, Lebanese leaders spoke of the uprising as having unified the nation.

'February 28 was a celebration of national unity, democracy and free will,' wrote Gibran Tueni in *An Nahar*. 'The Lebanese unity is stronger than all forms of tutelage, weapons, terror and occupation. Lebanese unity is the strongest weapon. It is stronger than the Taif Agreement, UN Resolution 1559 and all the Arab and international decisions.'

While the independence intifada was a truly historical event, it was not the demonstration of national unity that its organisers claimed, more a convergence of confessional interests united by opposition to Syrian hegemony over Lebanon. Although the Sunnis had turned out for Hariri's funeral, the bulk of the subsequent rallies were composed of Christians and Druze, the backbone of the opposition. Crucially, however, the independence intifada was missing a key component of Lebanese society – the Shiites.

Many Shiites had little fondness for Syria as they more than most Lebanese paid the daily economic price of Syrian hegemony over Lebanon. The estimated 1 million Syrian labourers provided competition for jobs, and Shiite farmers in the rural south and the Bekaa were also forced to compete in a market flooded with Syrian agricultural imports, which bred deep resentment. Few Shiites would shed tears if the independence intifada forced Syria to disengage from Lebanon. But those

Shiites who supported Hizbullah and Amal – the vast majority of the community – suspected that the end of Syrian influence would mean the advent of American influence. As far as they were concerned, the 'Syria out' chants of the independence intifada should not be replaced by 'America in'.

In the immediate wake of Hariri's assassination, Hizbullah adopted a low profile. Nasrallah visited Koreitem to pay condolences to Hariri's family, and the party issued appeals for calm and dialogue between the loyalist and opposition camps. Hizbullah was biding its time to see how the political struggle would play out. Hariri's death and the independence intifada posed a serious dilemma for Hizbullah. If Damascus was forced to withdraw from Lebanon, the party would lose the political cover it had enjoyed since the end of the Lebanese war, which risked jeopardising its autonomy in south Lebanon. Hizbullah perceived the crisis as a struggle for the future of Lebanon epitomised by the poles of Resolution 1559 and the Taif Accord. For Hizbullah, fulfilling 1559 entailed abandoning the anti-Israel axis of Lebanon, Syria and Iran and falling under the political influence of the West. The Taif Accord was the Arab alternative, allowing for close ties with Syria, and leaving the option open for Hizbullah to retain its military wing.

'Resolution 1559 contradicts the main principles of the Lebanese,' Mahmoud Haj Ali, a member of Hizbullah's political Council, told the author in March. 'The need now is to hold onto Taif and reject 1559 because 1559 wants Lebanon to move from one bank [anti-Israel, anti-America] to another bank [pro-America, pro-Israel].'

Hizbullah was not alone in feeling the pressure. In early March, Syrian officials began touring leading Arab states looking for a diplomatic solution to the crisis. Bashar was given a frosty reception in Saudi Arabia where the royal family was still seething over Hariri's killing. According to a Lebanese source with close ties to the Saudi royal family, Crown Prince Abdullah asked Bashar why Syria had murdered Hariri, to which the Syrian president replied that if Syrian hands were responsible 'it's probably one of those intelligence pockets that we have'. Whether the Saudis believed that or not is unclear, but they 'advised' Bashar that he should withdraw fully and immediately from Lebanon; that meant all troops and intelligence agents. When Bashar said that it was 'not entirely up to me' and that it would take several months to withdraw, Abdullah told him he had to leave within weeks or risk upsetting Syrian–Saudi relations.

On March 5, the day after his tense meeting with Abdullah, Bashar delivered a speech to the Syrian parliament which was broadcast live on television and watched by a crowd in Martyrs' Square on giant TV screens. Lebanese protestors booed loudly every time the Syrian MPs interrupted their president with applause. When Bashar chuckled at a couple of points in the speech, the Lebanese mocked him, chanting 'Ha ha, Syria.'

Although Bashar played down the extent of the anti-Syrian sentiment in Lebanon, Abdullah's 'advice' apparently had been heeded. He announced that, in line with Taif and 1559, 'we will withdraw our forces that we have stationed in Lebanon fully to the Bekaa area and then to the Syrian–Lebanese border area'.

Lahoud and Bashar met in Damascus two days later to provide a formal stamp to the initial phase of the withdrawal, which began the same day. At Dahr al-Baidar, the lofty, snow-streaked mountain pass on the main road between Beirut and the Bekaa, an aged Syrian truck ground to a halt in a cloud of thick black diesel smoke, having inched painfully up a steep side road. A soldier jumped out and wedged a rock beneath one of the back tyres to prevent the vehicle rolling back down the hill, while another soldier lifted the bonnet to inspect the smoking engine. It was not an auspicious start to the redeployment.

There was little sense of activity in the Syrian camps spread along the gentle grassy slopes behind the Bekaa towns of Chtaura and Zahle. Soldiers played football or lounged in the sun while sentries stood guard at the entrances decorated with the Syrian national colours and faded pictures of Hafez al-Assad. Hidden behind earth berms were several T-55 tanks covered in canvas sheets. Fuel bowsers and water trucks painted in green and brown camouflage were parked in the sprawling encampments.

Outside the Syrian military intelligence headquarters in Anjar, soldiers lolled around the swing gate at the entrance to the compound consisting of small square houses originally built by the French to house Armenian refugees in 1939. Among the ruins of the eighth-century town built by the Islamic Omayyad dynasty, several ancient stone dwellings were used as billets by plain-clothes Syrian intelligence agents. Signs of their habitation lay scattered around one corner of the site, empty cans, plastic water bottles and laundry hanging to dry in the warm spring sunshine. Two intelligence officers, unshaven and dressed in black leather jackets, light cotton trousers and sandals – the ubiquitous uniform of the Syrian mukhabarat – squatted over an open fire brewing tea, their rifles leaning against a wall. Their presence struck a bizarre and incongruous contrast to the graceful columns and arches of the nearby palace of the Omayyad caliph Al-Walid Ibn Abdel Malik.

Even as Syrian troops packed their bags and began the process of moving out, some 30,000 Lebanese gathered for another rally in central Beirut, marching from Martyrs' Square to the St George Hotel. But the independence intifada was about to have competition. After nearly a month of sitting on the fence, Sayyed Hassan Nasrallah announced on March 6 that the loyalist camp would hold a rally in two days' time which would be a demonstration of support and gratitude to Syria for 'all the sacrifices' it had made for Lebanese 'unity and integrity'.

The crowd that gathered in central Beirut on March 8 packed the car park in front of the glass UN building and spilled out into surrounding streets, beneath over-passes and up avenues and walkways like a creeping lava flow of humanity. The Lebanese government estimated the turnout at 1.5 million, but the media estimated that 500,000 showed up. The majority of the crowd consisted of Shiites, but some Christians also attended, members of pro-Syrian parties. There were also several thousand Syrians, most of whom had been bussed across the border from Syria the night before.

'We are here for President Assad and our Lebanese brothers,' said one beaming Syrian who was holding a sign reading in English 'no to foreign interference' upside down.

The size of the demonstration was due in no small measure to the organisational skills of Hizbullah. Many people had walked up from the southern suburbs of Beirut, Hizbullah's stronghold. Women pushed prams or carried babies in their arms. The throng was so tightly packed in Riad al-Solh that it was difficult to move. The roads leading into Beirut from the south were jammed with minibuses and cars carrying Hizbullah supporters up from the towns and villages of south Lebanon. As with the opposition rallies, Hizbullah instructed that all party flags be left at home. Only the Lebanese flag was to be carried by the crowd. The speech was classic Nasrallah. He appeared on a small balcony smothered in red and white Lebanese flags rather than the customary yellow party emblem and launched into a long oration that combined fiery rhetoric with flashes of humour and glints of conciliation. Apologising for the 'insults' heaped on Syria by some of his fellow countrymen, Nasrallah said 'You are present in the souls, in the hearts, in the minds, in the past, in the present and future, and no one can drive out Syria from Lebanon or Lebanon's mind, or Lebanon's heart or Lebanon's future.'

The crowd booed when he mentioned the name of Jacques Chirac. It booed louder and longer when Nasrallah mentioned George W. Bush.

'Lebanon will remain the country of Arabism, the country of nationalism, the country of resistance. Lebanon is the nation itself,' he roared.

It was powerful rhetoric. Nasrallah's speech and the huge loyalist rally cast a pall over the optimism and defiance generated by the anti-Syrian independence intifada. Critics of Hizbullah and proponents of the anti-Syria campaign mocked the loyalist demonstration for its press-ganging of a sizeable section of the Shiite community as well as the blatant attempt to boost numbers by ferrying Syrians into Beirut and dragooning Palestinian refugees. But nobody could disguise the stark fact that Lebanon was a country divided, not united, over the broader issue of international influence on Lebanon, be it Syria or the West. That the division fell along sectarian lines – generally the Shiites versus the rest – only exacerbated the tension and sense of unease.

Hizbullah promised that further 'farewell' rallies would be held for Syria in the coming days. The opposition received another blow two days later when Lahoud, emboldened by the Hizbullah rally, re-appointed the hapless Karami as prime minister, a move that Gibran Tueni described as the 'utmost insult'. Karami called for a government of national unity, saying the alternative was 'chaos', but the opposition refused to deal with him.

Hizbullah organised a second massive rally in the southern town of Nabatieh, the heart of the party's territory, which drew some 200,000. But instead of being cowed by the strength of the loyalist rallies, the organisers of the independence intifada picked up the gauntlet and called for a huge demonstration on March 14. For the first time, the Sunnis turned out en masse to side with the Christians and Druze in what was the largest demonstration in Lebanese history, with a turnout of around 1 million people, about a quarter of Lebanon's population. The March 14 rally was the climax of the month-long independence intifada and was deliberately intended to convey a message to the Shiites that, as far as other communities were concerned, the bulk of Lebanese wanted the Syrians gone and a new independent government installed.

The army once again set up roadblocks along major roads leading to the capital and insisted on body-searching protestors to delay their arrival in Martyrs' Square. But it made little difference. The whole of central Beirut turned into a sea of red and white flags, the extent of which could only be fully appreciated by the helicopter-borne television cameras filming the scene high above.

Hizbullah wisely decided to abandon its plans for other protests, recognising that even its formidable skills in mustering the faithful could not outdo the extraordinary scale of the March 14 demonstration.

After the setback of the Hizbullah-organised loyalist rally, the tide seemed to be turning in favour of the opposition once more. Two days earlier, Terje Roed Larsen, the UN envoy, had secured a pledge from the Syrian authorities that its troops and intelligence apparatus would be out of Lebanon by the end of April.

While the announcement that the Syrians were actually planning to leave in weeks was widely welcomed by the opposition, the sheen of victory was tarnished by the spectre of renewed violence in the shape of several late-night bomb attacks in Christian districts. The first blast on March 19 in the Jdeidet suburb of Beirut was heard over the eastern half of the city, a gentle reverberation that rattled windows and was recognised instantly as a bomb explosion by the war-hardened Lebanese. Eleven people were wounded in the blast which devastated several warehouses and factories. There were three more bomb attacks over the next two weeks, mainly late at night and in sparsely populated locations. They were clearly intended to terrorise rather than inflict heavy casualties. And in that they succeeded. The restaurants, cafés and shops lining the pedestrianised streets of downtown Beirut stayed empty as people remained at home. Security guards manning checkpoints at car park entrances to shopping malls became a permanent fixture. Small bands of vigilantes set up their own checkpoints in some east Beirut districts, monitoring traffic throughout the night and stopping and questioning strangers. Crude hand-drawn posters appeared on walls, jokily asking that their cars be spared a bomb. Inevitably, as the attacks continued, some Christians began muttering darkly about why the Muslim areas were not being targeted as well.

In early April, the US and France submitted a draft resolution to the UN Security Council for an international investigation into the Hariri assassination. It met with some robust opposition from the representatives of the Lebanese government and its sympathisers on the council, mainly Algeria, which successfully reduced the commission's mandate from six months to three. Resolution 1595, which was passed unanimously on April 7, called for the creation of an international investigation commission to be based in Lebanon which would begin work as soon as possible.

Meanwhile, as the deadline for the final phase of the Syrian troop withdrawal neared, the last military positions in the Bekaa were dismantled and bulldozed. Tanks on the backs of lengthy transporters trundled along the highway cutting across the Bekaa towards the Masnaa border crossing accompanied by green military buses festooned with Syrian flags and portraits of Bashar. Other trucks over-loaded with equipment lashed down by tarpaulin and ropes swayed precariously toward the border. A Syrian Army officer, a television camera on his shoulder, stood beside the main road before the Lebanese customs building at Masnaa filming each truck as it passed by, capturing for posterity what many Syrians regard as a humiliating retreat.

'I am sorry to leave like this because the Syrian and Lebanese people are brothers,' the officer said. 'We would have liked to stay.'

His was not an opinion shared by many Lebanese. In the cluster of Sunni towns and villages around Masnaa, the final Syrian pull-out was conducted under the watchful eye of Hariri, whose beaming countenance gazed down from hundreds of posters plastered over walls, shop fronts, telegraph poles, advertising hoardings and the rear windows of cars and trucks. What would he have made of these inglorious final moments of Syria's military control over Lebanon? Hariri had always wanted to be Syria's friend and ally, and was even willing to accept a limited Syrian troop presence in eastern Lebanon. Yet his murder had transformed him into the figurehead of the anti-Syrian struggle and the catalyst that had led to this rather dismal last withdrawal.

It is hard to extract any glory or dignity from a military retreat, but the Lebanese and Syrian army commands attempted to gloss over the humiliation by staging a farewell ceremony on April 26 at a military base in Rayak in the Bekaa. That morning, the road between the border and Rayak was lined with Syrian soldiers spaced every 50 metres, clutching rocket-propelled grenade launchers or rifles with fixed bayonets. They were supposed to be guard of honour for the visiting Syrian generals, yet all they looked was faintly comical in their wide-brimmed tin helmets. Rustom Ghazaleh had vacated his headquarters in Anjar the day before and spent the night in Damascus, less than an hour's drive away. But he returned to Lebanon the next day for what must have been a profoundly embarrassing experience. Wearing a dark-grey suit, white shirt and dark glasses against the brilliant spring sunshine, Ghazaleh sat in the grandstand, stony-faced, looking slightly out of place among the paunchy and perspiring Syrian generals in their brown wool uniforms dripping in gold braid and rows of coloured ribbons. He studiously ignored the photographers who jostled before him for the rare opportunity of capturing his picture. What was Ghazaleh thinking as these final minutes of Syria's military domination of Lebanon ticked by? How quickly the whole enterprise had collapsed. The passing of Resolution 1559 may have signalled the beginning of the end of Syria's tutelage over Lebanon, but not even the most optimistic supporter of the resolution could have predicted that it would take only seven months for Syria to pull out of Lebanon. And where were those Lebanese officials who a few months earlier had so ardently defended

Syria as a legitimate presence in Lebanon and so fervently attacked 1559 as an unwarranted interference in Lebanese affairs? Certainly, they were not to be seen in Rayak that spring morning. Most of the zaims had already turned their backs on their erstwhile Syrian patrons, playing to the new mood of independence, adjusting to the post-Pax Syriana realities in Lebanon to ensure their own political survival. Lebanese officialdom stayed away, but Syria's enemies, in the form of Western military attachés, including those from the US and France, were there, wearing crisp, starched uniforms and sitting quietly next to Lebanese and Syrian generals.

Some of Syria's crack troops were bussed in from across the border for this last hurrah. Tall and lean, the red-bereted paratroopers were a cut above the poor, ill-educated conscripts that most Lebanese were familiar with seeing at Syrian Army checkpoints. The soldiers jog-marched down a narrow pine tree-lined avenue to the parade with their rifles clutched to their chests, small portraits of Bashar, his brother Basil and their father Hafez al-Assad fixed above their right breast pockets.

Lined up beside a company of Lebanese soldiers, the Syrian para-troopers pledged to sacrifice their souls and their blood for Bashar, punching the air with their fists as they chanted.

'By withdrawing all its forces from Lebanese territory, Syria has imple-mented all its commitments to 1559,' Syrian General Ali Habib said in an address to the troops. 'This farewell celebration is proof that the relations between Syria and Lebanon are very special and will continue to increase more and more.'

'Brothers in arms, farewell.'

'Farewell,' the soldiers roared back.

And then it was all over.

The Syrian troops climbed back on board their lorries, smiling and waving V-for-Victory signs as they made the final journey home.

Lebanese troops had already deployed at the Syrian military intelli-gence headquarters. At the 'onion factory', the notorious mukhabarat interrogation centre, several soldiers sat in a courtyard, relaxing in the sunshine. Syrian military motifs had been painted out on the walls of the farm buildings, although the departing intelligence agents spray-canned one wall with slogans and quotations from the Koran.

One slogan read 'The Arab nation won't die.'

In the following days, the UN team charged with verifying the Syrian troop withdrawal visited former Syrian positions to make sure there were no soldiers lurking behind. It was evident that the troops had left, but what was impossible to verify was whether the Syrians had dismantled their intelligence system in Lebanon. Few Lebanese doubted Damascus would continue to exert a potentially malevolent influence in Lebanon through its elaborate and extensive networks of agents and informers. The troops might have gone, but the civilian–military apparatus that was created to ensure control over Lebanon remained largely in place with Lahoud still president and much of the military, security and judicial administrations essentially intact. The only significant changes were to the top security positions. Jamil Sayyed, head of the General Security directorate, and Ali Hajj, the head of the Internal Security Forces, announced their resignations on the eve of the final Syrian troop withdrawal. Raymond Azar, the head of military intelligence, who in early April took a month's leave of absence, flew to France with his family four days before he was due to return to work on an open-ended 1 million Lebanese lira ($660) a day assignment authorised by the outgoing pro-Syrian defence minister Abdel-Rahim Mrad. The new defence minister, Elias Murr, rescinded the assignment days later and then in early May Azar was dismissed along with Ghassan Toufeili, the head of signals intelligence responsible for wiretapping, Edward Mansour, the head of State Security, and Adnan Addoum, the justice minister. The only senior security official to retain his position was Mustafa Hamdan, the head of the Presidential Guard and Lahoud's chief aide.

Despite concerns of a lingering Syrian mukhabarat presence, the sacking of the once all-powerful security chiefs and the departure of the Syrian Army from Lebanon was 'a huge achievement', according to Samir Kassir, the *An Nahar* columnist and democracy campaigner.

'Even if there is undercover mukhabarat, they can't detain people, they can't torture people, they can't kidnap people. They could do some sabotage but nothing more,' he told the author following the Syrian withdrawal.

It was not just the hidden hand of Syria in Lebanon that caused some anxiety, but also the small military encampments manned by pro-Syrian Palestinian groups that could be found tucked among the rugged hills and mountains along Lebanon's remote eastern frontier with Syria. The Palestinian bases, many of them over 30 years old, had existed under the protection of the Syrian military. With that umbrella having been lifted, there was a growing clamour in Lebanon to have the bases shut down and the fighters returned either to Syria or to the refugee camps in Lebanon. There might be profound disagreements in Lebanon over whether or not to dismantle Hizbullah's military wing, but few Lebanese were willing to tolerate the presence of armed Palestinian groups. The Palestinians, however, had no intention of abandoning their positions with the rapidity of their former Syrian Army protectors.

The largest of the Palestinian bases in the eastern Bekaa, consisting of huts and tents scattered over a mountain plateau about 1,000 metres above the Bekaa valley floor, was operated by the Popular Front for the Liberation of Palestine – General Command (PFLP-GC), a small radical group headquartered in Damascus. The base could only be reached by a precipitous winding stone track which led to a swing gate blocking the entrance. Wind-tattered and sun-faded Palestinian flags snapped in the icy wind beside a tiny hut. Inside, Abu Abdullah, the *nom de guerre* of an officer, and six of his comrades sat on beds made from cinder blocks covered with thin mattresses and grey blankets. An AK-47 rifle hung from the roof with two magazines bound together with yellow tape. An old military radio set connected to car batteries sat on the table next to a small red portable television.

'We have many posts in the Bekaa but we are not going to leave any of them because the Palestinian issue has not been resolved,' Abu Abdullah said.

Residents of the Christian village of Qussaya in the valley below claimed that the PFLP-GC were using the numerous tracks that crisscrossed the border to bring in weapons and equipment. But Abu Abdullah claimed the position was for administrative purposes only. 'We don't carry weapons and we don't wear military uniforms,' he said.

The Palestinian commander was polite but reticent and clearly unused to uninvited guests. A day after the author dropped by, the Palestinian gunmen fired their weapons over the heads of the visiting team of UN inspectors who beat a hasty retreat back down the mountainside. The shooting incident stirred further calls for the Palestinians to be brought under control. But the Lebanese government was unwilling to be sidetracked from its sole task of ensuring that the parliamentary elections were held on time. Omar Karami had resigned for a second time in April after conceding his inability to form a government. Najib Mikati, a Sunni businessman from Tripoli, was appointed prime minister and he unveiled his cabinet four days later.

For the opposition, now dubbed the 'March 14 coalition' after the million man rally on that date, the next step following the Syrian troop withdrawal was to overturn the pro-Syrian majority in parliament, which would lead to the formation of a more representative government. Some of the young opposition activists had developed a taste for the visceral politics of the street and mulled over the prospect of translating what they had begun into a broader movement to involve the younger generation in mainstream politics.

In Lebanese parliamentary elections, the airing of political platforms and earnest debate over key policy issues is generally overshadowed by fervid speculation over which candidate is going to be included on whose electoral list. The principal criterion adopted by political bosses in choosing candidates for their lists is how many votes they each can bring with them. Consequently, the heads of large families or established businessmen tend to be selected over young idealists or women, unless they come from one of Lebanon's political dynasties. These elections would prove no different and, as the electoral horse-trading began in earnest in early May, it became clear that there was little room for those youthful champions of the independence intifada who sought to trade street activism for a seat in parliament.

The sight of the familiar former warlords, powerful businessmen and scions of Lebanon's political families bickering and bartering to ensure political survival left many Lebanese jaded, disillusioned and bitter.

'It's a betrayal of all those demonstrations which represented a moment of true popular anger with the system,' Karim Makdissi, a young professor of politics at the American University of Beirut, told the author. 'It could have gone in a different positive direction but it was taken over by the political sharks who used that idealism to serve their own purposes.'

Among those old faces competing for a share of power was Michel Aoun who ended 14 years of self-imposed exile in France by returning to Beirut one week after the final Syrian withdrawal.[8] The fiery-tempered general had barely touched down at Beirut airport before he was courting controversy, however, angering the March 14 coalition by suggesting that Syria withdrew its troops because of his lobbying efforts in Washington rather than Hariri's death.

Walid Jumblatt snapped back that 'Hariri's blood' was responsible for the Syrian withdrawal, not the 'returning tsunami' of Aoun. Downplaying the effect of Hariri's murder in propelling the extraordinary events of the previous three months was regarded by the Hariri and Jumblatt blocs as tantamount to sacrilege, and signalled that the irascible Aoun was charting his own political course independent of the March 14 coalition.

The one new face who would play a key role in the elections was Saad Hariri, Rafik's second son. In mid-April, at the end of the traditional 40-day mourning period, the Hariri family announced Saad as Rafik's political heir, the eldest son, Bahaa, having chosen to remain in business.

'I was the unlucky one,' Saad later joked to the author.

Tall and well built with slicked-back dark hair, thick moustache and goatee beard, the 35-year-old Saad bore a striking physical resemblance to his slain father, which undoubtedly resonated with the public. His mild-mannered, almost shy, persona, soft voice and quiet, self-deprecating wit could have been mistaken for insecurity, but Saad was no neophyte. He may have been new to the cut and thrust of Lebanese politics, but he was an accomplished businessman, having helmed Oger for over a decade. Sharing his father's workaholic reputation, Saad had built a personal fortune that ranked him at 548 in *Forbes Magazine*'s annual list of billionaires, with an estimated fortune of $1.2 billion. He had inherited his father's penchant for globe-trotting and was on good terms with numerous world leaders. Hariri used to tell friends that, of all his children, 'Saad is the one that is most like me'.

But even with these credentials, Saad was unable to prevent the broad opposition coalition from gradually unravelling along sectarian lines as parochial political interests overrode the more altruistic goal of creating a 'new' Lebanon. Indeed, on the eve of the elections the new Lebanon was looking very much like the old, with the creation of electoral alliances that were bizarre even by Lebanese standards. The list Saad Hariri headed in Beirut included some uncomfortable bedfellows. Among them were Solange Gemayel, the widow of former president-elect Bashir Gemayel who had helped engineer Israel's 1982 invasion, and a member of Hizbullah, an organisation which was born to resist that same Israeli invasion.

In mainly Shiite south Lebanon and the Bekaa, Hizbullah forged an alliance with the rival Amal Movement. It had been assumed that, with Syria gone, Hizbullah and Amal would have fought it out for dominance of the Shiite community at the first available opportunity. Yet both groups recognised that their mutual needs were greater than their differences. By allying with Amal, Hizbullah was strengthening its domestic position against pressure to disband its military wing, turning the fate of its weapons into a sectarian issue. From now on, calls to disarm Hizbullah would mean disarming the Shiites. In turn, Nabih Berri needed Hizbullah's assistance to bolster his own political position now that his Syrian benefactors had gone.

Then there was the irony of the Hariri and Jumblatt blocs, sponsors of the anti-Syrian March 14 demonstration, hammering out electoral agreements with Hizbullah and Amal, the driving forces behind the pro-Syrian March 8 rally.

Perhaps the strangest electoral alliance building was by Michel Aoun. Once the most persistent and harshest critic of Syrian influence in Lebanon,

Aoun felt squeezed out by his erstwhile opposition allies in the March 14 coalition, so instead he suddenly began cutting deals with some of Syria's traditionally most loyal supporters. It was an unconventional but astute move. The collapse of Damascus's hegemony over Lebanon had to a large extent erased and rendered meaningless the previous political division pitting pro-Syrian loyalists against the anti-Syrian opposition, a confrontation that had blurred the country's established confessional faultlines. Syria's dominion over Lebanon had allowed it to curb, control and manipulate Lebanese sectarianism to suit its own interests. Consequently, the departure of that constraining factor was leading to fresh political realignments based on the spontaneous and unchecked resurgence of confessionalism.

The splintering of the political landscape along confessional lines was as evident as it was predictable. The broad-based Muslim alliance of Hizbullah, Amal, Hariri's Future Movement and Jumblatt's Democratic Gathering bloc, combined with pressure from France and the US, ensured that the electoral law of 2000 (the one drawn up by Ghazi Kanaan to spite Lahoud) would remain in place for the 2005 polls, overcoming the strong objection of the Christians. Indeed, the Christians were growing disillusioned, resentful and worried that their political renaissance after a decade and a half of marginalisation under Syrian rule was about to be undone by the bulldozing tactics of the Sunni–Druze–Shiite alliance. That sectarian polarisation even resulted in an unlikely wave of Christian support for Lahoud, whose removal from Baabda palace was energetically pursued by Jumblatt and Hariri. The fate of the presidency remained a prerogative of the Maronites, and, although Lahoud lacked credibility in the Christian community, the Maronites had no intention of standing aside so that he could be unseated by the Sunnis and the Druze.

The tensions between the Sunnis and Christians were manifest in the first round of voting in Beirut. In west Beirut, huge banners featuring a beaming Saad Hariri were suspended above streets carrying the Hariri campaign slogan, 'Maak' (With you). Many posters portrayed Saad superimposed on a picture of his father. One read 'He who fathers children lives on.' Paramilitary police in blue camouflage uniforms guarded crowded polling stations while cars plastered in campaign posters and pictures of candidates tore up and down the unusually traffic-free streets. Saad called for a large turnout, saying 'Each ballot is a bullet fired at Rafik Hariri's assassins.'

But in the mainly Christian eastern half of the city, voter turnout was low, with many residents heeding a boycott by Aoun supporters in protest at the electoral law.

Christian discontent failed to stop Saad Hariri from sweeping Beirut. A week later, the Shiite–Hizbullah–Amal alliance secured all the available seats in south Lebanon. But the third round in Mount Lebanon caused a major upset when the frustrated Christians sided overwhelmingly with Michel Aoun against the March 14 coalition. Aoun was an avowed secularist, but as far as the Christians were concerned they had found in the 70-year-old general their first popular and effective leader since the end of the war in 1990.

Aoun's temporary home was a heavily guarded villa lent by a supporter set among the hills and pine trees of an exclusive suburb overlooking Beirut. A green canvas screen erected around the perimeter of the property provided privacy, while coils of razor wire, searchlights, closed circuit television cameras and armed bodyguards provided security. From here, the general had mounted an intensive and slick election campaign, adopting the colour orange and the Greek letter omega (the symbol of resistance in electrical terms) as his motifs. He was the only political leader to actively promote an electoral platform, a 43-page manifesto printed in English, Arabic and French outlining a comprehensive political, economic and administrative reform programme.

Aoun was in his element when bathed in the light of television cameras and surrounded by supporters and journalists. He commanded attention and conveyed an image of resolve, dependability and honesty. His critics accused him of being a martinet and a 'little Napoleon' with naked presidential ambitions. And there was something of the Napoleon about this short, egotistical army general. But away from the media limelight, he could be reticent and unassuming, uncomfortable among strangers and in unfamiliar surroundings. Invited to a dinner at the American embassy, an ill-at-ease Aoun barely said a word, leaving some of the foreign guests wondering what his supporters saw in him.

When the author met Aoun at his villa for an interview in mid-June after his Mount Lebanon election triumph, it was a somewhat timid but polite grandfatherly figure who shuffled into the salon smiling shyly. With his thinning hair, sagging jowels and paunch, Aoun looked as if he would be more comfortable pruning roses in the garden or bouncing his grandchildren on his knee than aspiring to the presidency. But there was steel in his words as he accused Saad Hariri of vote buying on a massive scale in north Lebanon, the venue for the final round of the elections which was turning into a showdown between the Sunnis represented by the Future Movement and the Maronites represented by Aoun's Free Patriotic Movement.[9] He remained resolutely unapologetic for allying himself with some of Syria's staunchest allies.

'I don't care if Syria supports me,' he said in French-accented English. 'They respect me because I am an honest adversary. They don't respect those who claimed to be their allies for 15 years but right now are insulting them like animals. Since 1988, I said the Syrians have to withdraw from Lebanon and then we will become good friends. What I said in 1988 I say in 2005.'

But Aoun's critics accused the general of being a turncoat, selling out on his former comrades in the anti-Syrian opposition in exchange for an unimpeded return to Lebanon after 14 years in exile and a future shot at the presidency.

If some members of the March 14 coalition were disappointed and angered at Aoun's perceived defection from their ranks, there was outright alarm at reports in the media claiming that Syrian military intelligence officers were back in Lebanon, holding secret meetings to forge electoral alliances among their old Lebanese friends.

Mohammed Khallouf, the former head of Syrian intelligence in north Lebanon, was reported to have met Jamil Sayyed and Suleiman Frangieh for lunch, which led to a reshuffling of candidates for the northern polls and an alliance between Aoun and Frangieh, whose powerbase was in the northern town of Zghorta.

Rustom Ghazaleh, Jumblatt charged in a television interview, had been spotted eating lunch at a restaurant in the Bekaa and had scuppered an electoral deal between Hariri's Future Movement and a local Christian politician. Other senior military intelligence officers were sighted in the Chouf, one of them asking questions about Jumblatt's security arrangements.

The news reports suggested that sinister forces were at work in Lebanon. And the grim evidence of that menace could be found on the morning of June 2 in the crumpled, smouldering remains of the Alfa Romeo in Beirut's Christian district of Ashrafieh. Samir Kassir couldn't have known what hit him when the bomb placed under his seat exploded as he started his car to go to his office at *An Nahar*. An eloquent and incisive critic of Syrian hegemony over Lebanon and an ardent democracy campaigner, the 45-year-old journalist's writings in *An Nahar* had earned him some powerful enemies.

A stunned crowd clustered around the vehicle until they were pushed back by soldiers stretching yellow tape across the road to seal off the crime scene.

'Samir was very optimistic,' said a tearful Malek Mrowe, a Lebanese businessman and friend of Kassir who had dined with him just the night before. 'He said "Now the Syrians have gone we can say whatever we want. Lebanon will be the democratic model for the region." '

Had Kassir's optimism blinded him to the threats that still lurked unseen in Lebanon's darker corners? What was it he had told the author barely a month earlier about the lingering Syrian intelligence presence?

'Even if there is undercover mukhabarat, they can't detain people, they can't torture people, they can't kidnap people. They could do some sabotage but nothing more.' Those words had a chill echo now as Kassir's gutted body was extracted from the twisted remains of his car.

Against the backdrop of Kassir's murder, the last round of elections was held on June 19. It was a thoroughly bad-tempered and rampantly sectarian affair, in which the Christian axis of Suleiman Frangieh and Michel Aoun stood no chance against the alliance of Sunnis and Hariri's Christian allies in the Muslim-dominated northern constituency. Omar Karami, who had refused to stand in the elections, attacked Saad Hariri for vote-buying and accused Lebanon's Sunni Mufti, Sheikh Mohammed Qabbani, of instructing Sunni sheikhs in Tripoli to politicise their sermons on behalf of the March 14 coalition. Frangieh, who lost his parliamentary seat in the polls, declared that Saad Hariri 'has used the ugliest and most provocative confessional tactics', pitting Muslims against Christians, as a result of which 'the north of Lebanon is divided along sectarian lines'.

As Safir newspaper opined the next morning that 'no one knows how to overcome the sectarian tension that characterised the elections across Lebanon'.

Saad Hariri had been gunning for a majority of more than two-thirds of the 128-seat parliament, necessary to begin the untested and complicated constitutional process of unseating Lahoud. Lahoud's removal was considered a prerequisite for a thorough purge of state institutions of all lingering traces of Syrian control. But the success of Michel Aoun in the third leg of voting had left the March 14 coalition 13 seats short, thus sparing Lahoud an early retirement. With Lahoud entrenched in Baabda palace for the foreseeable future, Saad Hariri ruled himself out of the premiership race. How could he sit around the same table with the man who he believed was at least partially responsible for his father's murder? Lahoud was not the only leading figure of the former pro-Syrian regime to safeguard his position. Even Nabih Berri, that most wily and opportunistic political survivor, was back as parliamentary speaker, buoyed by the support of Hizbullah, his powerful new ally.

Still, although Hariri was denied the clean sweep he was seeking and despite the heightened sectarianism accompanying the polls, the elections had resulted in the most representative parliament since the end of the war in 1990.

The day after the northern round of voting, Saad Hariri held a press conference in the underground ballroom at Koreitem in which he promised to pursue the 'project of Rafik Hariri' of coexistence, social and economic development and administrative reform.

Rafik Hariri gazed down at his son and political heir from more than a dozen large portraits hanging on the walls or mounted on stands as Saad read from a prepared speech. All Lebanese, he said, knew who had obstructed his father's goal of bringing 'prosperity to Lebanon and dignity to the Lebanese'.

'They crippled Rafik Hariri's project deliberately, but the Lebanese will not accept from now on any policy that will stop the economical, social and developmental progress,' Saad read in his soft, at times barely audible, voice. 'We assert today that elections are behind us. We only see the future of Lebanon, its freedom, sovereignty, independence, democratic system, economic prosperity and social solidarity.'

But those same sinister forces that murdered Samir Kassir were still at work in Lebanon, seemingly intent on ensuring there would be no easy transition from Syrian domination to full sovereignty.

The morning after Saad's upbeat press conference, George Hawi, a former leader of the Lebanese Communist party, was killed when a bomb exploded beneath his dark-blue Mercedes moments after he left his home in west Beirut.

Hawi's death appeared to confirm what was first suspected with Kassir's death – an assassination campaign was being waged against opponents of Syria's enduring influence in Lebanon. The violence, which had begun with the bomb attack against Marwan Hamade the previous October, peaked with the brutal slaying of Rafik Hariri and continued with the killings of Kassir and Hawi, was still to cast a dark shadow over Lebanon.

A new Lebanon?

As the storm clouds of winter scudded across the Mediterranean, lashing Lebanon's coastline with sheets of icy rain, the ghosts of the independence intifada continued to linger in Martyrs' Square. By the end of the year, the grass had yet to grow back on the mound beside the martyrs' monument where the tents of Camp Freedom had stood in the spring sunshine. The graffiti that once choked the white marble walls surrounding the bronze statue of the martyrs had been scrubbed off, yet it was still possible to discern the faint traces of scrawled anti-Syrian insults, nationalist slogans and maudlin eulogies for the slain Hariri. Mourners and the curious continued to trickle past Hariri's flower-smothered grave 100 metres from the martyrs' monument. A giant digital clock ticked the number of days since February 14 in glowing red numerals. 'The Dream' read an inscription in Arabic gold letters on a wooden archway leading to the grave.

The shadow of Rafik Hariri continued to loom large over a Lebanon that began 2006 deeply divided, split by a resurgent sectarianism generated by the argument over Hizbullah's weapons, threatened by the emergence of a militant brand of Sunni Islam that had taken hold in the poorer areas of the north, and torn by competing visions over the future direction of the country. The traditional Christian–Muslim faultline in Lebanon was being superseded by an inter-Muslim struggle between Shiites and Sunnis, reflecting the broader cleavages rending the Middle East. Lebanon seemed fated to be a pawn in a broader struggle for control of the Middle East, pitting the strengthening axis of Iran, Syria and Hizbullah against the influence of the West, chiefly the United States, Britain and France.

'Lebanon will be engulfed again in a huge power game that will last quite a long time. This is the tragic destiny of Lebanon.' Such was the bleak prognosis of Walid Jumblatt, who by December had become a virtual prisoner in his castle in the Chouf mountains to avoid the same fate that had befallen Hariri, Samir Kassir, George Hawi and others.[1] For the campaign of assassinations and bomb attacks that began with the attempt against Marwan Hamade in October 2004 had continued to claim victims, a remorseless vendetta, it seemed, against some of the leading voices of the independence intifada.

The killings gave an added sense of urgency to the United Nations International Independent Investigation Commission (UNIIIC) charged with investigating Hariri's murder which began work in mid-June. The commission initially was headed by Detlev Mehlis, a German prosecutor who led a team of more than 100 investigators, technicians, translators and security personnel. Mehlis was picked to head the investigation because of his 25 years' experience in handling trans-national terrorism cases, notably the La Belle disco bombing in Berlin in 1986. The commission was granted a three-month mandate by the UN Security Council with the possibility of an additional three months if needed. Mehlis, a soft-spoken and methodical investigator, was fully aware of the formidable task ahead of him, commenting in May that 'I hope one can uncover the crime in three months; otherwise it will take 10 years.'

He could expect the full assistance of the new government which was formed at the end of July and headed by Fouad Siniora, Hariri's long-serving right-hand man for financial affairs. The new consensus government included for the first time a member of Hizbullah, recognition by the Party of God that with Syria gone it would have to defend its interests by participating more fully in Lebanese political life.

But these were not easy months for Siniora's government or those who had spearheaded the effort to remove Syria from Lebanon. In August, Gibran Tueni, the battling columnist and general manager of *An Nahar* who had been elected to parliament in May, revealed that the UN commission had handed to the Lebanese government a 'hit list' of prominent anti-Syrian Lebanese it had compiled through its interrogations of witnesses and suspects.

'There is an assassination list and my name tops it,' Tueni said in France where he, along with several other Lebanese, had sought refuge. The precautions were well founded. Elias Murr's prediction in October 2004 to Marwan Hamade that he would be the target of an assassination attempt came true in July when a car bomb exploded beside his motorcade as it passed through a wealthy east Beirut suburb. Murr, who was travelling in an armour-plated Porsche four-wheel drive, survived the blast, suffering facial wounds and a broken hand. He subsequently blamed the bomb attack on Rustom Ghazaleh, revealing for the first time in a talk show on Lebanese television that the Syrian general had threatened him following the discovery of the Italian embassy bomb plot.

Lahoud, who was becoming an increasingly isolated figure as he clung onto Baabda palace, released a statement in reaction to his son-in-law's revelations, lavishing praise on 'sister' Syria and earning the headline in the *Beirut Al-Balad* daily 'Lahoud removes the shrapnel of his son-in-law's bombshell.'

Random bombings in Christian areas continued from July to September. A small bomb planted beneath a parked car in a narrow alleyway exploded one Friday evening just 50 metres from Rue Monot in east Beirut, one of the city's busiest nightspots. Another bomb targeted the Kuwaiti information office, killing one person. The Kuwaiti media had been particularly critical of Syria, especially *Al-Siyassa* newspaper whose near-daily 'scoops' against the Syrian regime were widely read for entertainment value if not accuracy.

At the end of September, May Chidiac, an anchor for a political news programme on Lebanon's LBC television channel, was critically wounded when a bomb exploded beneath the seat of her parked car hours after her Sunday morning talk show was aired. She survived, but lost her left arm and leg in the explosion.

The bomb attacks evidently were part of a calculated attempt to undermine political stability and thwart Lebanon's economic recovery. Yet who were these ruthlessly efficient hit men stalking the country, dispatching their victims with such effortless, cold-blooded precision? One rumour posited that they were former Christian militiamen from the Damascus-allied Syrian Social Nationalist Party (SSNP) who prepared their car bombs in an underground car park in the Jeanne d'Arc district of Hamra in west Beirut, an area traditionally under the control of the SSNP. If Syria was responsible for the attacks, as most Lebanese firmly believed, there was no shortage of willing perpetrators to carry them out. Syrian military intelligence over the years had built up numerous small groups and networks that they could draw upon to foment trouble. Some of these groups existed within broader political organisations such as the SSNP and Baath party; others operated as small mercenary gangs supplied with cash, vehicles and weapons from local offices of Syrian military intelligence.

Although the Lebanese authorities appeared unable to catch the killers, despite technical assistance from European and US law enforcement agencies, they did discover several arms caches, which not only suggested that the acts of violence were a pre-planned and systematic campaign of terror, but also tellingly pointed to the involvement of individuals and groups associated with Lahoud and the Syrian regime. In late July, police arrested Sheikh Ahmad Abdel-Aal, a security officer with the pro-Syrian

Ahbash Islamist group, and his brother Mahmoud after a weapons cache was discovered in the latter's home south-east of Beirut. The religiously moderate Ahbash had been promoted in Lebanon in the 1990s by Syrian intelligence to undercut fundamentalist Sunni Islamic groups, in particular the Jamaa Islamiyya, the Lebanese branch of the Muslim Brotherhood which fought a bloody insurrection in Syria in the late 1970s and early 1980s.

Also in July, a police raid uncovered a stockpile of new and unused weapons in the Beirut home of an employee of Majid Hamdan, brother of Mustafa Hamdan, commander of the Presidential Guard and right-hand man of Lahoud. Majid Hamdan owned a security company in partnership with Ralph Lahoud, the president's son, which among its operations was responsible for security in the area of the St George Hotel – the scene of Hariri's murder. The Hamdan employee claimed to be a member of the Mourabitoun, the Sunni militia which had been chased out of Beirut by pro-Syrian militias in the mid-1980s only to return in 2001 at the instigation of the Lebanese and Syrian intelligences services in a vain attempt to counterbalance Hariri's influence over the Sunni community. Mustafa Hamdan also had connections with the Mourabitoun, being a nephew of the group's former leader Ibrahim Koleilat and having fought with the militia in the opening stages of the Lebanese war in the 1970s.

The activities of the Hamdan and Abdel-Aal brothers were also attracting the interest of the UN commission. Operating from an isolated and heavily protected hotel set in the forested Monteverde suburb of east Beirut, Mehlis ordered the first arrests at the end of August. Investigators accompanied by Lebanese paramilitary police stormed the houses of several senior former security officials in a pre-dawn raid that included temporarily cutting the power in the city. Among those arrested were Jamil Sayyed, Raymond Azar, the former head of military intelligence, and Ali Hajj, the former head of the Internal Security Forces. All three had been fired from their posts in May. Mustafa Hamdan turned himself in for further questioning after being summoned by the police. He was the first senior security official to have been questioned by the commission and named formally as a 'suspect' a month before the arrests.

'We think . . . they were to some extent part of the planning that led to the assassination,' Mehlis said, adding that the four men were only 'part of the picture . . . We do think more people were involved.'

The arrests of the former security barons electrified the Lebanese. Just one year ago they had been the most powerful men in Lebanon, commanders of the top security and intelligence services, who served as loyal guardians of Syria's dominion over Lebanon. Now languishing in their solitary underground cells, they had ample time to brood on where it had all gone wrong. If they were brought to trial and convicted they could face the gallows or a firing squad.

The investigation into Hariri's murder was clearly tilting toward the involvement of the Lebanese and Syrian intelligence services, including security officers considered close to Lahoud. The intriguing connections between the arrests of the security chiefs, the discoveries of the arms dumps, Lahoud, Hamdan and the Syrian regime continued to sustain calls for the president's resignation.

Yet Lahoud appeared resolutely blasé at his unpopularity. He enraged the March 14 coalition by describing his arrested aide Hamdan as a 'most honest, loyal and dedicated' army officer. Lahoud then ignored the advice of friends and foes alike not to attend the annual UN General Assembly meeting in New York in September. Instead, he departed for New York at the head of an 80-member delegation stuffed with family members and officers from the Presidential Guard. While Saad Hariri was fêted by world leaders in New York and Fouad Siniora discussed preparations for a donors' conference for Lebanon tentatively scheduled for November, Lahoud remained ensconced in his five-star hotel, shunned from diplomatic receptions, including a banquet hosted by President Bush for visiting heads of state.

The Syrian regime continued to deny involvement in Hariri's murder, arguing, correctly, that the assassination had rebounded on Syria more than anyone else. The UN commission had requested interviews with up to 15 Syrians, including military intelligence officers previously responsible for security in Lebanon, but the Syrian regime was less than forthcoming in cooperating with the investigation. It insisted that its sovereignty be preserved and cast doubt on the impartiality of a commission whose very existence was due to US and French muscle in the Security Council.

'Syria is still dealing with the issue as though it is a suspect,' wrote Sahar Baasiri in *An Nahar* at the end of August. 'What does it mean that Syrian officials repeat that discovering the truth is in Syria's interest while it behaves in return in a manner that actually harms its interest? Why is Syria delaying the work of the committee?'

On October 20, Mehlis released his first interim report, which concluded that there was 'converging evidence pointing at both Lebanese and Syrian involvement in this terrorist act'.

'Given the infiltration of Lebanese institutions and society by the Syrian and Lebanese intelligence services working in tandem, it would be difficult to envisage a scenario whereby such a complex assassination plot could have been carried out without their knowledge,' the report said.

But it added that the investigation was not complete and recommended that it continue 'for some time to come'.

An unedited version of the report which found its way into the hands of journalists, the author included, carried the names of several senior Lebanese and Syrian officials allegedly involved in the Hariri assassination plot. They were Maher al-Assad, Bashar's younger brother, Assef Shawkat, the president's brother-in-law and at the time the deputy head of military intelligence, Hassan Khalil, the then head of Syrian military intelligence, Bahjat Suleiman, the then head of the internal affairs section of the General Security Directorate, and Jamil Sayyed.[2]

The report was critical of Syria's lack of cooperation with the UN commission, saying that, although it had cooperated to a 'limited degree', some Syrian officials interviewed had 'tried to mislead the investigation by giving false or inaccurate statements', among them Farouq al-Sharaa.

The report went beyond merely updating the Security Council on progress so far. By judiciously including enough damning information to point a clear finger at Syria – and suggesting that he had much more that remained unpublished – Mehlis apparently hoped to provide sufficient ammunition for the Security Council to pass a resolution obliging Damascus to be more cooperative. If so, it worked. Resolution 1636 adopted by the Security Council on October 31 demanded that Syria detain any Syrian national whom the commission suspected of involvement in Hariri's assassination and warned of 'further action' if Damascus continued to procrastinate, an implicit threat of sanctions.

But Damascus denounced the Mehlis report as lacking 'credibility, seriousness and professionalism' and, other than announcing the creation of its own commission of inquiry into the Hariri assassination on the eve of Resolution 1636 being adopted, showed little sign of yielding to the intensifying pressure. In a speech to Damascus University on November 10, Bashar was defiantly belligerent, accusing Lebanon of being a 'route, a manufacturer and financier for ... conspiracies [against Syria]' and describing Fouad Siniora as a 'slave' of his American masters. In an address redolent with Arab nationalist rhetoric, he savaged the March 14 coalition, calling them 'blood traders' who had 'made a stock market of Hariri's blood; and this stock market is yielding money and positions'.

The ferocity of Bashar's comments on Lebanon spurred Gibran Tueni to opine that it was tantamount to a 'declaration of war on Lebanon'. Certainly, it illustrated the depth of distrust and antipathy between Beirut and Damascus, the poisoned legacy of Syria's long and humiliating dominance of its neighbour. Attempts at a rapprochement had faltered even before Fouad Siniora had composed his government. Tentative discussions to demarcate the joint border between Lebanon and Syria had led nowhere. A deal for Syria to supply natural gas to Lebanese electricity plants went unfulfilled. Even Hizbullah's new addition to the cabinet, Mohammed Fneish, the energy minister, was unable to persuade Damascus to honour the arrangement, although his party remained supportive of Syria.

In July, Syria effectively closed its border to goods vehicles departing Lebanon, which left hundreds of truck drivers stranded bumper to bumper along a remote 10-kilometre stretch of highway snaking through the mountains between the Lebanese and Syrian border posts. Syria said the delays, which were costing Lebanon some $300,000 a day in lost business, were due to increased checks to prevent weapons and explosives being smuggled into Syria, part of a nationwide security crackdown. But most Lebanese believed that the Syrians were acting out of spite.

More alarming, however, were the reports from September of weapons being smuggled into Lebanon via the remote mountain trails along the border with Syria by pro-Syrian Palestinian militants belonging to the Fatah Intifada organisation. The reports provoked an outcry and spurred renewed calls for the closure of the small Palestinian military outposts in the eastern Bekaa and international warnings for Syria to cease destabilising Lebanon. But if weapons were being smuggled into Lebanon, it was not by Fatah Intifada's grizzled veterans.

The handful of isolated Fatah Intifada positions set in remote, rock-studded wadis along the border were more like secluded retirement homes for wrinkled veterans of the Palestinian Revolution. Dressed in an eclectic mix of olive green or camouflaged fatigues with tracksuits, sweaters and sandals, they whiled away their final days reminiscing about past glories, smoking cigarettes and sipping endless tiny glasses of hot sweet tea.

A more likely culprit was the Popular Front for the Liberation of Palestine – General Command, a tougher and better-armed outfit than Fatah Intifada who hunkered down when the Lebanese Army surrounded their positions in October. At the entrance to a PFLP-GC base in a shallow valley near the village of Sultan Yacoub, Lebanese soldiers wrapped in thick camouflage jackets and wool hats against the chill breeze manned a checkpoint and milled around armoured personnel carriers. A dirt track meandered across the valley floor leading to the Palestinian base, which consisted of a few foxholes covered in camouflage netting and narrow tunnels sunk into the sides of the valley. Near a swing gate leading into the base, the Palestinians had rigged up an improvised explosive device made from a half-buried tank shell connected to a black cable which snaked across the track and up into the rocky hillside.

'Go away. This area is forbidden,' yelled a Palestinian fighter emerging from a rock outcrop above the track, waving a rifle above his head.

After the bomb attack against May Chidiac in late September there was a lull in violence, and for a moment it seemed that the menacingly proficient killings might have ended. That illusion, however, was shattered one sunny December morning on a narrow lane cut into the side of a steep valley above the dried-up bed of the Beirut river. Gibran Tueni didn't stand a chance. It was the most professional assassination since Hariri's killing ten months earlier. The estimated 40-kilogramme shaped charge bomb hidden in a Renault Rapide blasted Tueni's armour-plated four-wheeler through a concrete balustrade, sending the burning wreck tumbling 100 metres down the side of the valley. The explosion set light to the grass on the side of the valley and smashed windows for hundreds of metres in a nearby industrial estate, lightly injuring at least ten people. Other than Tueni, two people were killed, one of them his driver.

The proficiency of the assassination was chilling. Tueni had returned to Lebanon only the night before from Paris where, like so many prominent Lebanese critics of Syria, he had been spending much of his time because of death threats. His assassins must have been tracking him from the moment he touched down at Beirut airport on Sunday night, following him to his home in the mountain village of Beit Meri on a ridge overlooking Beirut. A security camera recorded footage of the bomb-laden Renault driving down the road shortly before 9 a.m. the next morning and parking beside a BMW. Two men got out of the car and climbed into the BMW and drove off at high speed. The road was used by local residents as a short cut to avoid the rush-hour traffic on the nearby main road leading into the eastern half of the city. The assassins must have known that Tueni regularly took the short cut. It was a well-chosen site. From the other side of the narrow valley, the bomber would have had a clear view of the road and Tueni's vehicle as it approached, just two minutes after the car bomb was parked, triggering the remote control at the exact moment the two vehicles were aligned. Shaped charge explosives channel the blast in a single direction and are designed to punch through the sides of armoured vehicles. Tueni, who was sitting in the passenger seat, took the full brunt of the blast and was torn to shreds.

'I had a discussion with Tueni about me returning to Beirut, and he said "Don't even think about it," ' says Saad Hariri, who had been living between Jeddah in Saudi Arabia and Paris since July. 'He was adamant that I not return and I was adamant that he should not return. And look what happened.'[3]

The bullheaded, uncompromising Tueni had returned to Beirut anyway, telling a friend on the flight from Paris that he felt encouraged by the calm. The temporary cessation in bomb attacks in Lebanon had lulled him into a false sense of confidence.

Two days later after his murder, tens of thousands of mourners converged on central Beirut, standing vigil beside the glass *An Nahar* building and cramming the cobble-stoned streets outside the St George Greek Orthodox cathedral where Tueni's funeral was held. In the parliament building opposite the cathedral, a special session was held prior to the funeral for MPs to pay tribute to their slain colleague. Tueni's empty chair was draped in a Lebanese flag with a red rose placed on his desk. Covering five floors of the *An Nahar* building was a vast portrait of Tueni, the red and white scarf of the independence intifada that he had so actively helped promote wrapped around his neck, his hand raised in greeting. Tueni's dark 1930s-matinee-idol looks beamed over the crowd of mourners gathered below.

Following the flag-draped coffin as the funeral procession wound through central Beirut to the Greek Orthodox cemetery in Ashrafieh was a gaunt and frail-looking Ghassan Tueni, the publisher of *An Nahar* and former ambassador at the UN who had helped Hariri's humanitarian aid ship sail under the UN flag from Cyprus to Israeli-occupied Sidon so many years earlier. Tueni senior was no stranger to family tragedy, having at the age of 80 buried his first wife, his only daughter and two sons. Now the father would inherit his son's position at *An Nahar* and weeks later his political role as well, being selected unopposed to represent the Ashrafieh district of Beirut.

Saad Hariri also knew what it entailed to inherit a political legacy. He was the leader of the largest political bloc in the Lebanese parliament, the Future Tide movement, and was regarded by many as a prime minister-in-waiting, the capable Fouad Siniora filling in until his father's nemesis Emile Lahoud had stepped down or been evicted from Baabda palace. But Saad was a political leader living in self-imposed exile, forcibly separated from his constituents by the assassins lying in wait in Lebanon.

'Me not going to Lebanon isn't about being scared,' he says in his soft, slightly hesitant voice, 'but about not giving them a present of the pleasure of killing me because we have not achieved what we wanted to achieve.'[4]

Saad was dressed casually and slouched in a soft armchair in the opulent purple and gold splendour of the Royal Suite on the fifth floor of the Plaza Athenee, one of Paris's most luxurious hotels. He was surrounded by some of his father's close advisors and staff, and the suite had been transformed into a mini Koreitem overseas.

He had arrived two days earlier to hold talks with President Chirac amid an attempt by Saudi Arabia and Egypt to promote a Syrian document to reduce tension between Beirut and Damascus and relax Western pressure on Syria.

The Lebanese government showed little enthusiasm for the initiative, which was said to include muzzling inflammatory rhetoric in the media and establishing a committee to forewarn the Lebanese and Syrian authorities about potential security breaches. Walid Jumblatt described the plan as a 'booby-trapped attempt by the Syrian regime to return to Lebanon' while Fouad Siniora said that 'top priority should be given to Syria's cooperation with the UN investigation'.

The Lebanese could expect little more than lip-service support from the two Arab powerhouses when it came to Lebanon's difficulties with Syria. Both Saudi Arabia and Egypt are wedded to the creed of non-confrontation and viewed the crisis from the perspective of their own interests. If Syria's Baathist regime buckled under the pressure, it could trigger a revival of the long-suppressed Syrian branch of the Muslim Brotherhood, an unwelcome prospect for Egyptian president Hosni Mubarak whose home-grown Muslim brothers had fared strongly in the parliamentary elections in November and December. Furthermore, the failure of Syria's experiment with a 'hereditary republic' could doom Mubarak's own ambition to bestow the presidency upon his son, Gamal. Similarly, Saudi Arabia was worried that Bashar's collapse could herald Iraq-style turmoil, which would further destabilise the Middle East and possibly strengthen Al-Qaeda's brand of militant Islam which had sworn to overthrow the Saudi monarchy.

Consequently, the Saudi–Egyptian initiative stoked a growing sense of unease among many Lebanese who suspected that their interests would be sacrificed as part of some broader deal concocted by the international community to ensure regional stability. Saad's visit to Paris was in part to seek reassurance from Chirac that there was no deal being prepared at the expense of the UN investigation into his father's death. That reassurance from Chirac was given, and confirmed by Condoleezza Rice, the US secretary of state, who insisted that Washington rejected 'any deals or compromises that would undermine the UNIIIC investigation, or relieve Syria of its obligations'.

'Politics is a very difficult life,' Saad says a day after meeting Chirac. 'I am going through a learning process, a crash course on politics in Lebanon. It was difficult to follow after my father. I tried to think about what he would have done. I think of it as a replay of a boxing match. You know the results but you have to go through the 12 rounds. You have to go through some tough punches and maybe get some broken bones but at the end of the day you will get the belt.'

Hariri had never intended that his children should follow him into politics, disdaining the monopolisation of Lebanese politics by a handful of family dynasties. The horror of Hariri's murder and the outpouring of public grief, however, had compelled the family to anoint a successor. Saad was the only eligible choice after his elder brother Bahaa decided to remain in business. But in January 2006, it seemed to be a legacy that weighed heavily on the young man's shoulders.

'I was a businessman,' Saad says, his knee jogging nervously up and down as he speaks. 'I had all my freedoms. I could travel wherever I want, do what I want, walk alone. Now I have to have security. I have to live a life where I'm afraid about my family and their safety. My son Hussam was watching the TV and saw there was an explosion in Lebanon and he ran to his mother and said "Where's baba?" and she said, "He's in Paris." And Hussam said "Thank God he's not in Lebanon." And he's only six years old.'

It had been a discouraging winter for the Lebanese government and the March 14 coalition. Following the release in October of the first report of the UN commission investigating Hariri's murder and the adoption of Resolution 1636, Syria began to fight back. It won a valuable propaganda coup in November when Hussam Hussam, a key witness in the first UN commission report, publicly recanted his testimony to the investigators, saying he had been coerced by Saad Hariri and other March 14 coalition leaders. His retraction came days after another witness, Zuhair Ibn Mohammed Said Saddik, allegedly was paid to testify by Rifaat al-Assad, Bashar's uncle, who still had an eye on the presidency.[5]

Syria also engaged in brinkmanship with the UN commission in November, baulking at a demand by the UN commission to interview in Beirut six Syrian officials, among them Assef Shawkat, the head of Syrian military intelligence, and to gain access to intelligence records on Lebanon. The commission was told that all military intelligence documentation related to Lebanon had been burned. Mehlis eventually backed down and agreed to Syria's demands that the interviews be held in the neutral setting of Vienna and guaranteed that the Syrian officials could return to Damascus afterwards. In the end, only five Syrians travelled to Vienna; Shawkat remained in Damascus.

Mehlis made it clear in his second interim report and in his statement to the Security Council on December 12 that Syria was still prevaricating.

But the Security Council avoided sanctions, instead issuing a tepid reso-lution that granted a six-month extension to the commission and merely 'took note' of a Lebanese request to include other killings in the investiga-tion and for the establishment of an international tribunal.

The Syrians had won some breathing space, helped by their sym-pathisers in the Security Council, Russia, China and Algeria. The quandary for those Security Council members who wanted to place additional pres-sure on Syria was that sanctions were a double-edged sword. While the imposition of sanctions would place additional pressure on Damascus, it would also end all Syrian cooperation with the UN commission, which risked the investigation grinding to a halt, causing even further stagnation in Lebanon's ability to shed the vestiges of Pax Syriana.

And for Walid Jumblatt, that would mean no imminent release from his self-imposed incarceration in his mountain refuge in the Chouf. The veteran Druze leader saw himself locked into a duel to the death with the Syrian regime, his only chance of survival dependent on the fall of his enemies in Damascus. But the odds were not in his favour. A few days before the author met Jumblatt in mid-December, a bundle of rocket-propelled grenades had been discovered on the side of a road near his castle in Mukhtara. The rockets were not rigged to explode, but it was interpreted as a death threat.[6]

'I can do nothing. I can wait. I can rely on destiny. That's it,' Jumblatt says with a rueful smile, his wiry frame hunched and his thin legs crossed on a stool in a small antechamber.[7] 'There's no means of protection against a terrorist regime with advanced technical ways of killing.'

Jumblatt's home is a testimony to his family's violent past. In his office, an old bolt-action rifle leans against a wall beside a modern assault rifle. On his desk, beside a laptop computer are four identical automatic pistols, all within easy reach. On one wall of a small reception room is a photograph of his father, Kamal Jumblatt, his tie loosened and top button undone, looking a little like a gaunt George Orwell. He is flanked by photographs of the two bodyguards who died with him in 1977. Nearby is a blurred photograph of Walid Jumblatt's grandfather, clutching a rifle and sitting astride a horse, the very picture of a traditional Druze warrior and proud chieftain. The sunlight streaming through the tiny windows fails to dispense the chill in this room of memorialised death.

'My father used to always say "A Jumblatt never dies in his bed," ' he says, repeating a favourite aphorism.

There was a certain bleak irony in the fate that had befallen Jumblatt. He had earned a reputation as one of Lebanon's great survivors, instinctively and unashamedly switching allegiances to stay one step ahead of the assassin's bullet or political irrelevance. But his vocal hostility toward the Syrian regime, which had steadily increased since the assassination attempt against his friend Marwan Hamade, for once had left him bereft of avenues of escape. He had taken to repeatedly calling Bashar a 'terrorist tyrant', and turned against Hizbullah, his erstwhile ally in the parliamentary elections the previous spring. From defending the right of Hizbullah to retain its weapons, he was now demanding the party's disarmament and in February even suggested that it might be planning to kill him.

In January, Jumblatt crossed perhaps the ultimate 'red line' with the Syrians. When asked in an interview with the *Washington Post* what America could do for Lebanon, he replied 'You came to Iraq in the name of majority rule. You can do the same thing in Syria.' Jumblatt had flouted the taboos of regime change in Damascus and the Alawites' minority status in Syria. No wonder he rarely left the safety of Mukhtara.

'This tension [with Syria] will continue,' he says with a sigh. 'Their aim is to change the [parliamentary] majority either by assassinating more MPs or fixing new elections where they will have the majority which will enable them to again forbid Lebanon to have an independent say.'

Jumblatt read Lebanon's travails within the broader context of shifting regional dynamics, where the Shiite Hizbullah was the 'vanguard' of the Syrian regime, part of an axis stretching from the 'shores of the Mediterranean' to Tehran, the Iranian capital.

'We are engulfed in a new dimension in the Middle East. The regional environment is not in Lebanon's favour,' he says gloomily.

So was it all for nothing? The independence intifada, the removal of Syrian forces, the overturning of the pro-Syrian majority in parliament?

Jumblatt pauses for several seconds and then gives his biggest sigh yet.

'No. We had to do it. We were convinced that we had to do it. We thought we could achieve some stability, some free will, but now we fear they [the Syrians] might come back. They never left in the sense of their [continuing] criminal deeds. If they create havoc, they will tell the rest of the world "Look, the Lebanese are unable to rule themselves. We are the only people who can guarantee stability." '

'Have you read the book by Bernard Lewis about the Ismailis?' he asks.

Jumblatt was referring to Lewis's history of the secretive Ismaili sect of Shiite Islam which, under the leadership of Rashid al-Din, the 'Old Man of the Mountain', achieved infamy in the twelfth century as the legendary Assassins. The Assassins, who introduced the art of political murder to the world and were feared by Crusaders and Muslims alike, lived in the same mountain chain in Syria inhabited by Syria's modern-day rulers, the Alawites.

'We have the same story today,' Jumblatt observed dryly. 'History repeats itself.'

The narrow, potholed road running due east from the Bekaa village of Nabi Sheet cuts across a sharp ridge before falling in a stomach-churning gradient into a narrow valley surrounded by jagged limestone peaks. In late spring, it is an impressively beautiful place. A shallow river winds along the valley floor, its churning waters flashing in the sunshine through the swaying poplars and walnut trees that line its course. The road crosses a small bridge at Janta and continues for another kilometre hugging the river before petering out at the ruins of the old Ottoman railway station at Yahfoufa, a hamlet of small stone houses clustered on the hillside. It is still possible to discern the path of the track as it passes the station and disappears down a narrow, tree-shrouded gorge to the border with Syria two kilometres further on.

Despite its pastoral ambience, the valley is effectively a military zone under the control of Hizbullah. It was in these craggy mountains and the dusty hill villages of Nabi Sheet and Janta that the organisation first emerged in the summer of 1982, spreading into the Bekaa, recruiting and training legions of resistance fighters to confront Israeli troops in the battlefields of south Lebanon.

'We are all over these hills. If you had come here in the dark, you would have been stopped by armed fighters,' says a young Hizbullah man sitting in the shade of his small home up the hill from the river. With an unusual lack of discretion for the normally secretive Hizbullah, he admits that training continues in the surrounding hills, although it has declined since Israel withdrew from south Lebanon in 2000.

'The level is about half what it used to be,' he says, pouring tea into tiny glasses and offering walnuts from a bowl. 'New recruits are still trained and the older fighters receive refresher courses to keep them in shape.'

What he does not discuss, however, is the reports of Hizbullah's arsenal of rockets which by 2005 Israel claimed numbered 13,000, many of them long-range variants capable of striking targets deep inside Israel.[8] Hizbullah traditionally declines to discuss details of its weapons inventory or military tactics, preferring to keep its Israeli enemy guessing.[9] If the reports are to be believed, then it is probably in these remote and rugged mountains that they are stashed away in natural caves or specially constructed underground bunkers.

Lebanese advocates of Hizbullah's disarmament are principally concerned with the continued existence of the Islamic Resistance itself – a well-organised and equipped, experienced and disciplined military force – rather than the party's long-range rocket arsenal. Non-Shiite Lebanese regard a militarised Hizbullah as giving the Shiites unfair leverage through the implicit threat of violence in the tussle for political influence. In the domestic political context, long-range rockets are irrelevant. Israel and the US, on the other hand, recognise that the rockets are a strategic asset for Hizbullah, having the potential to inflict serious damage on Israel. In the opinion of some American and Israeli military analysts, if Hizbullah was to hand over its rockets to the Lebanese Army or to a neutral third party, Israel could live with Hizbullah's armed presence along its northern border and even the periodic artillery bombardments of Israeli military positions in the Shebaa Farms pending the conclusion of Middle East peace.

Since the onset of the Shebaa Farms campaign in October 2000 with the kidnapping of three Israeli soldiers, Hizbullah has developed a complex, finely calibrated and multi-dimensional strategy in launching operations against Israeli forces along the Blue Line. The Blue Line serves as a locus of Hizbullah retaliation to Israeli-initiated actions, such as assassinations of resistance commanders and breaches of Lebanese territory by Israeli jets or ground forces.[10] Hizbullah can act with relative impunity because its long-range rocket arsenal grants the organisation a strategic parity with Israel, a 'balance of terror' that limits Israel's traditional freedom of action against its enemies in Lebanon. If Israel were to resort to punishing air strikes against Lebanese infrastructure, such as power stations and bridges, in response to resistance assaults in the Shebaa Farms, Hizbullah would retaliate with rocket bombardments of northern Israel.

However, the deterrence value of Hizbullah's rockets is not limited to the dynamics of the Lebanon–Israel border conflict. They also tacitly serve as part of Iran's deterrence against the possibility of a US or Israeli strike against its nascent nuclear industry, a prospect that has grown since the election in August 2005 of the confrontational Mahmoud Ahmadinejad as president of Iran, whose inflammatory rhetoric and threats against Israel had by early 2006 placed him on a collision course with the US and Europe.

US and Israeli military planners have to take into account the possibility that Hizbullah, acting on the orders of Tehran, would unleash its arsenal of rockets against northern Israel in the event of an attack against Iranian nuclear sites. However, while the existence of the rockets is intended to convey that threat, it is not a given that they would be immediately employed against Israel in a knee-jerk retaliation in the event of an attack on Iran. Hizbullah's domestic interests would be seriously jeopardised if it blindly followed Iranian orders to attack Israel. Lebanon's Shiites support Hizbullah's self-declared role as a defender of Lebanese sovereignty against Israeli aggression, but that support would tail off if Hizbullah dragged Lebanon into a war against Israel for the sake of Iran's nuclear ambitions. For what it is worth, Hizbullah has tried to reassure doubters that it is mindful of its responsibilities as an armed force. In a May 25, 2005 speech marking the fifth anniversary of Israel's withdrawal from south Lebanon, Sayyed Hassan Nasrallah said 'We do not want to attack anyone and will not allow anyone to attack Lebanon . . . We do not want to drag the region into a war . . . We want to protect our country.'

Hizbullah is constantly struggling to balance the often-conflicting agendas of abiding by its broader ideological aspirations as an exemplar of anti-Israel 'resistance' to a pan-Arab, pan-Islamic audience with its obligations and interests as a player on Lebanon's parochial political stage. It was able to contain both visions during the 1990s when under the umbrella of Pax Syriana it could freely wage its resistance campaign against the Israelis in south Lebanon while securing a foothold in the Lebanese parliament and building its political presence. It was able to weather the challenge posed to the continued existence of the Islamic Resistance following the withdrawal of Israeli forces from south Lebanon in May 2000, which threatened to deprive the party's military wing of its *raison d'être*. Even the danger represented by Resolution 1559 was in part ameliorated by Nasrallah's dialogue with Hariri in the months before the latter's murder.

Hizbullah regards Resolution 1559 as a blatant attempt by the US to defang an ardent and resilient foe of Israel. It is an argument that wins some sympathy. Resolution 1559 was principally intended to erode Syria's grip on Lebanon by opposing Lahoud's presidential extension and pressuring Damascus to withdraw its forces from Lebanon. But the US overreached by throwing in unrelated clauses calling for the deployment of the Lebanese Army along Lebanon's southern border with Israel and disarming Hizbullah and Palestinian groups in Lebanon. Initially, the Hariri–Nasrallah dialogue appeared to have resolved the potentially destabilising ramifications of 1559's demand for Hizbullah's disarmament. Hariri understood that forcing Hizbullah to disarm would have perilous consequences for Lebanon's stability. Instead, he pursued a gradualist approach in which Hizbullah's pretext for retaining weapons would subside over time as the party became more deeply entrenched within the Lebanese political framework. This is a process that has been under way since 1992 when Hizbullah reversed its original opposition to Lebanon's confessional political system and entered parliament for the first time. Some critics dismiss Hizbullah's 'Lebanonisation' as a mirage, a fig leaf to disguise its militant anti-Israel Islamist agenda, intact since the 1980s. Such criticism, however, misses the point. Although Hizbullah continues to adhere, on paper at least, to its core ideological pillars (the destruction of Israel, liberation of Jerusalem, Islamic state in Lebanon), the party has 'Lebanonised' because it now plays an important domestic political role and has a constituency to which it is answerable. It cannot afford to disregard its constituency if it wishes to maintain relevance in Lebanon's political arena. The Palestinian resistance movement, Hamas, may well undergo a similar process of pragmatisation after winning the Palestinian legislative elections in January 2006. Hamas will discover that there is little room for rigid ideological dogma when confronted with the grinding daily responsibilities of running the Palestinian territories.

Hizbullah is often regarded as a monolith, a well-oiled, disciplined party machine with a tight chain of command dancing to one tune. But hidden beneath that veneer of unanimity lies a constantly evolving discourse encompassing a wide variety of opinions. Some within Hizbullah understand that the role of the Islamic Resistance is finite and are more open to a purely political future for the party. One Hizbullah official told the author that there are non-violent means to continue the anti-Israel struggle.

In December 2004, Mohammed Raad, the Hizbullah MP, hinted that the party could one day trade the Islamic Resistance for greater political influence, in which Hizbullah would capitalise on the numerical superiority of the Shiites over other confessions. Raad told the author in an interview that, if a referendum was held in Lebanon, the majority of the population would support the continuation of the resistance.

Was he calling for such a referendum?

'No, but if you did, you would have to ask another questions as well,' he said.

What question was that?

'You should ask whether the presidency should still be reserved for the Maronites,' he replied with a sly smile.

That said, Hizbullah's priority is to maintain the Islamic Resistance, the party's beating heart, for as long as possible, and it is unlikely to countenance a trade-off until faced with no other option.

Ultimately, the conclusion of the Middle East peace process is the key that will unlock the door to Hizbullah's disarmament. Peace between Israel and its northern neighbours, Lebanon and Syria, will leave no room for Hizbullah's continued militancy and is the safest and most satisfactory means of disarming the party. In that context, the Bush administration has been criticised for disregarding the Israel–Syria track of the moribund peace process. In December 2003 and on several occasions in 2004, Bashar declared he was willing to resume peace talks with Israel without pre-conditions. The Syrian president may have been insincere and looking for an avenue of escape from the mounting international pressure, but the US declined to give Ariel Sharon the coercive nudge required to call Bashar's bluff.[11]

Hariri recognised that the ultimate solution to Hizbullah's disarming was a regional peace deal. Consequently, in his talks with Nasrallah in the months before his death, Hariri reached a compromise in which Hizbullah would be allowed to retain its weapons until the conclusion of the Middle East peace process on the understanding that the Shiite party would act wisely and not resort to actions that could seriously jeopardise the national good. Hariri's assassination destroyed that compromise and re-energised the international and domestic effort to disarm Hizbullah. Thus, by early 2006, unrelenting international pressure to fulfil Resolution 1559's disarmament clauses had catalysed a degree of political and sectarian polarisation in Lebanon unseen since the 1975–1990 war and, on a regional level, helped reinforce an anti-Western axis grouping Iran, Syria, Hizbullah, anti-Israel Palestinian groups and some Shiite elements in Iraq.

In the initial period following Hariri's death, with Lebanon in turmoil and Syria under intense pressure to disengage, Hizbullah trod warily while assessing what lay in store for the party. It co-opted and appeased other political actors in the run-up to the parliamentary elections, striking a tactical alliance with the March 14 coalition and a strategic alliance with erstwhile rival, the Amal movement, in a bid to retain them as allies and defenders of the resistance, rather than turn them into opponents through competition at the ballot box. The Hizbullah–Amal alliance effectively shifted the disarmament debate from one targeting Hizbullah into one perceived as targeting the Shiite community as a whole. The alliance strengthened Hizbullah's position, but at the expense of exacerbating an increasingly tense sectarian climate.

The participation by Hizbullah in the government of Fouad Siniora also represented an opportunity to defend its armed wing against pro-ponents of Resolution 1559 and resist the growing influence of the West in Lebanese affairs which it regarded as a threat to its interests.

Certainly, the level of international involvement in Lebanon since the Syrian disengagement has reached unprecedented levels, including a raft of UN Security Council resolutions and the involvement of at least three senior UN officials in Lebanese affairs.[12] The US, Britain and France have assisted in the process of overhauling Lebanon's cumbersome and unsophisticated security agencies while the FBI and French investigators provided technical assistance in the investigation of some of the bombings in Lebanon. A 'core group' was established in September 2005 bringing together the US, the UN, the World Bank, Britain, France, Italy, the European Union, Russia, Egypt and Saudi Arabia to examine and assist Lebanon's political, economic and administrative reform effort. A donor conference organised by the 'core group' was scheduled for late November to attract international funds to bankroll Lebanon's reform programme. Political turmoil pushed the date to December and then January. As of the time of writing in late February 2006, no date for the much-needed conference has been set, fuelling the belief that the holding of the event is conditional on the fulfilment of the remaining clauses of Resolution 1559.

'The Americans', Nasrallah said in September 2005, 'order the countries of the world not to meddle in Lebanon's internal affairs, but they allow themselves from the US president to the secretary of state to the US ambassador to Lebanon to interfere in every single detail in Lebanon. We reject that, since we don't need any tutelage. We want to be sovereign.'

In late October, Hizbullah began flexing its political muscles, emboldened by the overwhelming support of the Shiites, Lebanon's largest confession, and in tandem with Syria's counter-attack against the UN commission following the release of its first interim report into Hariri's murder. Nasrallah ignored a request from Siniora to cancel Hizbullah's annual 'Jerusalem Day' military parade in the southern suburbs of Beirut, defiantly staging the party's largest-ever march. In November, it led a walk-out by the five Shiite ministers from a cabinet meeting that was about to discuss Bashar's fiery speech earlier that day in which he called Siniora a 'slave'. On November 21, the eve of independence day, Hizbullah fighters launched the most ambitious assault against Israeli border positions since the Israeli withdrawal in 2000. Under the cover of an artillery barrage of nearby Israeli outposts, a Hizbullah squad attempted to capture Israeli soldiers from a position close to the Blue Line. The attack was thwarted when an Israeli sniper shot dead four members of the Hizbullah team.

In December, the Shiite ministers staged a six-week boycott of cabinet sessions to extract from the government an unambiguous declaration that Hizbullah's military wing was a 'resistance' organisation, rather than a 'militia', thus exempt from the provisions of Resolution 1559. An embattled Siniora eventually agreed on a compromise statement, declaring that Hizbullah was a 'national resistance', while making no reference whatsoever to the term 'militia'.

Hizbullah's domestic position was further strengthened in February when it struck an unlikely agreement with Michel Aoun, who not much earlier had been a champion of the party's disarmament. The relationship, cemented by a memorandum of understanding, brought Aoun's goal of winning the presidency a little closer by securing the backing of the Shiites, while Hizbullah had broadened its support base into Christian circles.

Hizbullah's growing sense of confidence in late 2005 was spurred by the emergence of the anti-Western axis centred on Damascus and Tehran, an alliance which ironically was cemented in part by the fallout from Hariri's assassination. Hariri's death not only changed the political landscape in Lebanon but resonated far beyond, a 'butterfly effect' where the shockwaves of a bomb blast on Beirut's seafront rippled across the Middle East to be felt in Damascus, Jerusalem, Tehran and the Gulf, adding its dynamic to the turmoil in Iraq, Sunni–Shiite tensions and the Israeli–Palestinian conflict.

The election of Mahmoud Ahmadinejad reinvigorated the long-standing alliance between Damascus and Tehran. Both countries were drawn to each other because of the pressure they faced from the international community over Iran's nuclear ambitions and Syria's hesitant cooperation with the Hariri murder investigation. Syria was the geostrategic linchpin connecting Tehran to Hizbullah, the conduit for the transfer of weapons from Iran to the Islamic Resistance. It was also regarded by Iran and Hizbullah as the weak link in the chain and required buttressing.

On January 20, 2006, Bashar hosted a summit in Damascus with Ahmadinejad, his first state visit. Also attending were Nasrallah, Nabih Berri and the leaders of several anti-Israel Palestinian groups, including Khaled Meshaal of Hamas and Ahmad Jibril of the Popular Front for the Liberation of Palestine – General Command. It was an explicit affirmation of the anti-Western 'rejectionist' axis and its preference for defiance toward the West rather than accommodation.

'The meeting between Ahmadinejad and Assad', commented Sateh Noureddine of Lebanon's *As Safir* newspaper, 'did not come as a sign of defeat, but rather as a joint warning to the world. A warning that the alliance between the two neighbours is on its way to becoming stronger.'

The following month Iran and Syria signed sweeping economic and trade agreements including one establishing gas, oil, railway and electrical links between Syria and Iran via Iraq. The electoral victory of Hamas in January gave Syria and Iran greater leverage in the Israeli–Palestinian arena, with Tehran vowing to provide funds to fill the void created by Washington's declaration not to support a Hamas-led government. The axis also reached into Iraq where Shiite factions close to Tehran dominated the elections in December.

The strengthening of this alliance, and its Shiite emphasis, contributed to the growing unease among Sunni-majority Arab countries, especially Jordan, Egypt and Saudi Arabia. In December 2004, King Abdullah of Jordan famously warned of a new 'crescent' of Shiite movements and nations stretching from Iran to Lebanon which could upset the traditional balance of power between Shiites and Sunnis and pose serious challenges to Washington's Middle East policies. The Sunni nervousness was aggravated by the presence of sizeable Shiite communities around the rim of the Arabian Gulf – in Kuwait, where they form about one-third of the population but do not enjoy the same privileges as the state's Sunni rulers, in the oil-rich Eastern Province of Saudi Arabia, and in Bahrain where Shiites constitute about 70 per cent of the population. The idea of an Iran armed with nuclear weapons manipulating discontented Shiite communities in the Gulf and enjoying an uninterrupted chain of allies all the way to the Mediterranean is a prospect that does not sit well with the region's Sunnis.

For some, Hariri's murder plays into this emerging dynamic. Hariri was a powerful Sunni whose influence spread well beyond Lebanon, a potential bulwark against the nascent rise of Shiite power and, for the minority Alawite-dominated Syrian regime, a dangerously inspirational model for Syria's majority Sunni population.

Although the 'Shiite crescent' appellation has become a familiar term and a perceived reality by many in the Middle East, it oversimplifies the trans-sectarian and political nature of the Tehran–Damascus–Hizbullah–Hamas alliance, perhaps a reflection more of Sunni fears rather than Shiite intentions.

'Are the Palestinians Shiites? Is the Palestinian issue a Shiite issue?' asks Sheikh Naim Qassem, Hizbullah's deputy secretary-general.[13] 'Our relationship with Syria is not based on religion, but on politics to fight Israeli aggression. In Iraq, we said that we are very clearly against American aggression [there] even though the Americans say that their occupation has helped the Shiites obtain political power. Whoever tries to draw a big Shiite picture will get muddled by all the contradictions.'

Based on a misconception or not, tensions between Sunnis and Shiites in the region are on the rise, hastened by the radicalisation of a generation of young Sunnis frustrated with the privations and inequities of life under dictatorial regimes, angered by Western interference in the Arab and Islamic world, the invasion and occupation of Iraq in particular, and inspired by the defiance of Osama bin Laden and the durability of the Iraqi resistance. The Shiite–Sunni friction has been aggravated by bomb attacks against Iraqi Shiites perpetrated by Al-Qaeda in Iraq headed by the Jordanian militant Abu Musab al-Zarqawi until his death in June 2006, in what is apparently an attempt to foster a civil war.

Lebanon has not been immune to the rise of a militant brand of jihadi Islam, which quietly has taken root in the poorer peripheral Sunni areas such as Dinnieh and Akkar in the far north, parts of the Bekaa valley and the predominantly Sunni cities of Tripoli and Sidon. The phenomenon first came to light in dramatic and bloody fashion in January 2000 when a small band of diehard militants belonging to Takfir wal-Hijra fought a brief but vicious insurrection against the Lebanese Army in the icy mountains of Dinnieh. Thousands of Lebanese troops backed by tanks and helicopters flooded into the mountains east of Tripoli after the militants ambushed an army patrol near their mountain hideaway. Pumped up on morphine to withstand the bitter cold and injuries, some of the militants had mounted a last stand in two houses they overran in a Christian village. Surrounded by Lebanese commandos, the militants cut the throats of their hostages, a mother and daughter, and prepared to die fighting. As dusk fell, tanks ground through the muddy olive groves to within 50 metres of the two houses and pounded both buildings into rubble while soldiers poured machine gun fire into the burning ruins.

'They mutilated the women with knives,' said a weary soldier, his face lit by flickering flames as he watched Lebanese Red Cross workers haul the mangled bodies from the rubble. 'I have never seen fighting like this. You shoot these terrorists and they won't die. They just keep shooting back.'

The Dinnieh rebellion, Lebanon's mini 'war on terrorism', sounded an ominous warning, but Hariri's dominance of the Sunni political scene and Syria's control of security matters in Lebanon helped keep the militants to the shadows. From time to time, the Lebanese authorities would announce the breaking of an 'Al-Qaeda cell', although sceptics noted that the arrests invariably occurred during periods of increased tension between Washington and Damascus. But the resurgent sectarianism in Lebanon since Hariri's death combined with a weak government and a disorganised state security system is giving rise to concern that Al-Qaeda sees Lebanon as ripe for the establishment of a presence. In July 2005, a statement purportedly from Al-Qaeda Jund al-Sham posted on a jihadist website threatened to kill several leading Shiite clerics, politicians and members of Hizbullah. The statement was dismissed by Sunni clerics as a fake. On December 29, Zarqawi's Al-Qaeda in Iraq organisation claimed responsibility for the firing two days earlier of four Katyusha rockets from south Lebanon into northern Israel. The attack replicated similar rocket firings in the past three years which were generally blamed on Palestinian militants.[14] Days later, the Lebanese authorities arrested 13 suspected Al-Qaeda militants who were accused of establishing 'a gang to carry out terrorist acts'. Al-Qaeda in Lebanon subsequently claimed responsibility for a bomb attack against a Lebanese Army barracks in Beirut which it said was in retaliation for the arrests.

Hizbullah has been observing the rise of Sunni radicals in Lebanon with barely concealed alarm. The Katyusha rocket attack from south Lebanon in particular was regarded by Hizbullah as a direct challenge to its tight operational control of the Blue Line.

'It's impossible to have stability with this Takfiri movement,' says Hizbullah's Qassem, referring to the branch of Sunni extremists who regard other Muslims as apostates. 'There are some in Lebanon but we don't know what their plans are or if they want to do operations here. It's important to caution everyone not to make Lebanon an arena for settling scores.'

The discord is exacerbated by Hizbullah's retention of an armed wing which perhaps is tolerated even less by Sunnis than by Christians. Muslim religious leaders routinely speak out against jihadist militancy and promote inter-Muslim coexistence. But the tensions between the two communities are palpable, even overshadowing Lebanon's traditional Christian–Muslim divide.

Dawood al-Sherian, a columnist for *Al-Hayat* newspaper, wrote in January that it was the first time in Lebanon's history that a crisis had emerged between Lebanese Sunnis and Shiites.

'Lebanon has paid the price of a civil war between Muslims and Christians, and is now preparing for another one between Sunnis and Shiites,' he wrote.

Any doubts about the extent of the Sunni militancy that had taken hold in some parts of Lebanon were shattered on February 5 when thousands of Sunni demonstrators rampaged through a quiet Christian neighbourhood in central Beirut, smashing cars and shop fronts, attacking a church and burning a building housing the Danish embassy. The violence came amid a wave of demonstrations in the Islamic world protesting against the publication in Danish and other European newspapers of cartoons depicting the Prophet Mohammed. Outnumbered troops and police retreated before the rioters as furious Christians dusted off weapons that had lain dormant for 16 years and prepared to defend their homes. Islamic clerics vainly appealed for calm as the mob stoned a Maronite church and ripped a metal cross from the entrance to the Greek Orthodox Bishop of Beirut's residence.

'What [Lebanese Sunni leaders] don't want to tell us is that they have, at best, nominal influence (if indeed any influence at all) over a swathe of radical Sunni Islamist groups,' wrote columnist Michael Young in Lebanon's English-language *Daily Star*. 'While a large majority of Sunnis accept the rules of the game . . . there are myriad splinter groups endorsing a far more aggressive, exclusivist ideology, supporting the establishment of an Islamic state.'

Lebanese officials were quick to condemn the riot and pointed the finger at 'fifth columnists'. For many Lebanese, the riot carried Syria's fingerprints, particularly as it came just a day after a similar demonstration in Damascus in which protestors attacked buildings housing the Danish, Swedish, Chilean and Norwegian embassies.

Although the Syrian demonstration appeared to be an impulsive and unplanned outpouring of anti-Western anger, spontaneous protests simply do not occur in Damascus. Indeed, witnesses noticed that plain-clothes agitators equipped with walkie-talkies were directing the crowd while the police stood to one side smoking cigarettes. The protest merely re-affirmed that Bashar was pursuing the path of confrontation with the West.

Bashar al-Assad is perhaps the most enigmatic leader in the Middle East, a conundrum who has confounded analysts, diplomats and journalists since coming to power in 2000. He was initially seen as a breath of fresh air, a young, British-trained doctor, married to an attractive and accomplished anglophone Syrian Sunni, a technocratic modernist who would reform the creaking, ossified Baathist state and usher his nation into the globalised economy of the twenty-first century. When the political and economic reforms took longer to materialise than expected, it was the fault of the 'old guard', the cronies of Hafez al-Assad who were resistant to change. Then gradually the doubts began to set in. Perhaps Bashar was a chip off the old block, his father's son who believed in the Baath party's Arab nationalist ideology, who unreservedly regarded Israel as an enemy and the US as a country to be distrusted.

Bashar's sympathisers blamed the Bush administration for taking too tough a stance against Syria, warning that too much stick and not enough carrot would force the young president to hunker down and flex his Arab nationalist muscles. His critics argued that Bashar was incapable or unwilling to reform his country, a weakling before the corrupt vested interests within his regime, an amateur who blundered from one diplomatic disaster to another.

Syria watchers adopted the 'Godfather' analogy to analyse the regime. If Hafez al-Assad was Vito Corleone, was Bashar the weak-kneed and ultimately doomed Fredo, the hot-headed and impulsive Sonny (a role often ascribed to his older brother, Basil) or the unassuming Michael whose ruthless leadership qualities only surfaced with time and adversity?

Bashar was never supposed to be president – that was a destiny selected for Basil – and he must have been conscious, as his father groomed him for power following his older brother's death, that his was an inheritance that was hard to justify in a republic. There were powerful and experienced potential rivals with stronger claims to the presidency lurking on the sidelines. Chief among them was Abdel-Halim Khaddam who could do little but silently seethe as his presidential ambitions withered before Assad's determination to hand over the reins of power to his son.

Not only did Bashar have to contend with the regime's discontented *éminences grises*, but Syria's strategic position had eroded by the time he took office in July 2000 owing to the collapse of the peace process and the Israeli withdrawal from Lebanon. The Clinton administration in its last months abandoned the Syria track to concentrate on finalising a peace deal between the Palestinians and Israelis. The Bush administration initially paid little attention to the Arab–Israeli conflict, and after 9/11 its policies toward Syria were seen through the prism of the 'war on terrorism'.

Consequently, although Bashar's reformist instincts are probably genuine, they were smothered beneath the weight of external and internal pressures augmented by an instinctive need to prove to his doubters and rivals that he was a strong and capable leader and deserving of the presidency.

'Bashar', says a childhood friend, 'is insecure. He always wants to prove himself as a tough guy who can take tough decisions. He is the opposite of his father. His father could be tough without being unpredictable. With Bashar, one moment you will say how nice and polite he is; the next he becomes unreasonably violent.'

Indeed, diplomatic and political U-turns have been a hallmark of Bashar's presidency, his actions contradicting earlier commitments, confounding and irritating his interlocutors and earning him a reputation as undependable.

'He tends to ramble on a bit, not terribly concise,' said Patrick Seale, the British biographer of Hafez al-Assad, in a conversation with the author in

June 2002. 'He probably has a rather high opinion of himself. I don't think he has much experience in power, how to hold it, how to run things, how to put his people in key positions.'

In the treacherous and unforgiving environment of the Middle East, character traits such as these tend to bring vultures circling overhead.

Fares Boueiz, the former Lebanese minister, received a telling glimpse into Bashar's mindset and the constraints upon him during a meeting he held with the Syrian president in 2002.[15]

Boueiz was explaining to Bashar that many Lebanese resented the heavy hand of Syria and its associated corruption which was 'destroying the principle of good brotherly relations'.

'I told him that I was afraid it would get worse and some moderate-minded people would not be able to stop it,' Boueiz says. 'Then Bashar al-Assad said "You know that I am also upset with many of our allies who are doing bad things and are corrupt. You know that I have started to withdraw the army [from Lebanon]. I want to institute relations only with the government and officials, not parties. I want to make a total reform [*islah*] of our relationship with Lebanon. But I can't do that under pressure, nor under threats and demonstrations, especially if it takes on a confessional [countenance]. In Syria we have many communities and, if I accept the pressure in Lebanon, I will have to accept it in Syria." '

'He hinted to me that he had a very sensitive situation in Syria and could demonstrate no weakness in Lebanon, although he could reform [the relationship],' Boueiz recalls.

The two men agreed that Boueiz would convey Bashar's message to Cardinal Sfeir, the Maronite patriarch, and, if the Lebanese opposition toned down its rhetoric, the bilateral relationship would be revised.

'The patriarch was impressed and used his authority to calm things down,' Boueiz says. 'So I was shocked to see [Bashar] going against what he told me when he extended Lahoud's mandate. We had waited two years. But Lahoud was a symbol of the same policy and Syria had no intention of changing.'

The intensifying American pressure on Syria in the two years between Boueiz meeting with Bashar and the Lahoud presidential extension left the Syrian president with little margin for manoeuvre on the internal and Lebanese fronts. The Syrian regime absorbed an unceasing barrage of hostile rhetoric from the US, and threats of 'regime change', targeted by the 'war on terror' and ranked in a second-tier 'Axis of Evil' of countries allegedly pursuing weapons of mass destruction. Reams of newsprint from American think-tanks and policy planners equated Baathism to

Fascism and Stalinism and promised that Saddam Hussein's removal would have a 'domino effect', toppling the Middle East's dictatorships and theocracies one by one.

In the paranoid Baathist mindset, yielding to external pressure was a sign of weakness, a fatal flaw that would be seized upon by the regime's internal and external enemies. Bashar adopted Bush's dictum in his dealings with the Lebanese: either they were with Syria, or they were against Syria. The kind of middle course compromise typically favoured by Hariri was unacceptable when the Syrian regime faced such existential threats from the US.

Lebanese and Syrian officials who know Bashar personally or have dealt with him professionally believe that today he is in charge in Syria and makes the final decisions. But those decisions are often heavily influenced by the opinions and advice he receives from the regime's inner core, an Assad family 'kitchen cabinet', the 'Alawite nucleus', in the words of one former Arab diplomat,[16] which represents the real source of power in Syria today. Among others, it includes his younger brother Maher, who heads the Republican Guard, Bushra, the eldest and by reputation the most formidable of the Assad siblings, her husband, Assef Shawkat, the ambitious and shrewd head of Syrian military intelligence, and the Makhlouf brothers, Rami and Ihab, Bashar's maternal cousins.

The loss of Lebanon following Hariri's assassination raised expectations that Bashar would capitalise upon that trauma to introduce sweeping reforms at the Baath party congress in June 2005. He gave an encouraging signal in his March 5 address to the Syrian parliament when he said that it was to be hoped that the conference 'will be a leap for development in this country'. Among the anticipated measures were the abolition of Article 8 of the Syrian constitution which enshrines the Baath party as the ruling party, a general amnesty for political prisoners and the creation of a multi-party system. But once again Bashar confounded the optimists. The new measures were limited to retiring many 'old guard' figures, among them Abdel-Halim Khaddam, former defence minister Mustafa Tlass and former prime minister Mustafa Miro, and adopting a law authorising independent political parties. The latter decision was tempered by a caveat that no party could be based on religion or ethnicity, dashing any chance of a revival of the Muslim Brotherhood or Kurdish nationalist parties.

'The message that emerged from the conference', wrote Syrian political analyst Sami Moubayed, 'was that the Baath would do what it took to survive, and was here to stay.'

Even the damning initial report released in October by the UN investigation into Hariri's murder failed to cow Bashar, indeed having the opposite effect of bolstering his status in Arab eyes as the 'anti-Bush', in the words of Syria expert Joshua Landis.

'Resistance and steadfastness or chaos. There is no third choice,' Bashar said in his speech to Damascus University on November 10. 'If [Western nations] believe they can blackmail Syria, we tell them they have got the wrong address.'

The speech continued a strategy that had commenced before the 2003 invasion of Iraq in which Bashar presented Syria as the last redoubt of Arab pride and defiance against the aggressive predations of the West. The subtext suggested that the Syrian regime was resigned to the near inevitability at some point of UN sanctions and was appealing to the instinctive nationalism of the Syrian people, deflecting their anger toward the West rather than at their own leadership.

Yet Bashar's stance ultimately is unsustainable, shackling desperately needed economic and administrative reforms to the war of wills with the US. Syrians are growing poorer as prices of basic commodities increase, the economy is in decline, and promises of multi-million-dollar investments from private Gulf institutions remain just promises. But there appears no imminent end to the confrontation so long as Bashar continues digging in his heels and the Bush administration remains undecided about what to do with Syria.

Although the spectre of US-imposed regime change has hovered above Damascus since the invasion of Iraq in 2003, Washington continues to insist that it seeks a 'change of behaviour' rather than a change of regime.

'We have been very clear that our concern is the behaviour of the Syrian regime,' said Condoleezza Rice in February 2006. 'The Syrian regime needs to change its behaviour. It is a negative force in the Middle East and it needs to become a positive force in the Middle East.'

The ace in Bashar's dwindling and increasingly threadbare deck of diplomatic cards is the lack of an organised and credible opposition which could ease into power if the ruling Baath party was overthrown. Syria's sectarian and ethnic mix is as tangled and potentially as turbulent as in neighbouring Iraq and it is the Baath party's ruthless grip that has kept it in check. The opposition in Syria, such as it is, consists of an ageing and disorganised group of liberal civil society activists and intellectuals who lack grassroots support, the banned Muslim Brotherhood whose leadership is in exile, and the marginalised Kurds in Syria's north-east who lack cross-ethnic appeal. Although Syrians are unhappy with the listless pace of reform and the economic hardships they must endure, no one wants Iraq's bloody sectarian and ethnic turmoil to be visited upon Syria in the event of the Baath party's removal. Although Syria is nominally a secular country, Islamic sentiment has been rising steadily for years, manifested by greater mosque attendance, the growth of Islamic study centres and the increased wearing among women of the hijab, or headdress. The phenomenon has been closely monitored by the state, which has carefully trodden a line between permitting a degree of religious freedom and stamping down on its more militant variations. In 2003 and 2004, the Syrian authorities turned a blind eye to young Sunnis who slipped across the remote 600-kilometre border with Iraq to join the insurgency. After all, was it not better to let the young Islamic hotheads kill themselves fighting American troops in Iraq than mobilise and plot against the Baathist regime? Washington repeatedly slammed Damascus's lack of cooperation in securing the border against infiltrators and for allegedly harbouring remnants of Saddam Hussein's regime in Syria.

But by mid-2005, the Syrian regime had tightened its physical security measures along the border, and, more importantly, had spread the word to the tribal smugglers that it was no longer permissible to earn a living conveying militants into Iraq. Several Muslim clerics were arrested for inciting young men to travel to Iraq, and relatives of Syrians fighting in Iraq were detained to dissuade other would-be volunteers. According to a Syrian intelligence report received by the author, the sand berm running the length of the border was increased in height from 2 to 4 metres, and the number of border positions was increased to 557 with some 4,500 to 5,000 personnel patrolling the frontier.

The policy of permitting Syrians to fight in Iraq may have boomeranged, however. Since 2004, there have been a number of clashes between Syrian security forces and armed Sunni militants, some of whom had fought in Iraq and appeared to be establishing a network of cells in staunch Sunni areas of the country. There is a suspicion that some of these incidents may have been deliberately staged by the authorities to remind the West of what might arise should external pressure lead to the collapse of Bashar's regime. But it does not alter the fact that militant Islamists would probably emerge as the main beneficiaries of Bashar's downfall if there is no credible and durable alternative.

Faced with unpalatable options, the US seemed undecided over how much pressure to place on Syria, which has effectively strengthened Bashar's hand in the stand-off with Washington. Some American voices called for stringent measures such as carving out a 'security zone' several kilometres deep on the Syrian side of the border with Iraq, launching air strikes and commando raids against suspected insurgent bases in Syria, and channelling funds to US-friendly external opposition groups. Others preferred the softer option of squeezing without breaking, hoping that the US and Syria could forge an understanding to help stabilise Iraq. In mid-October, *The Times* of London reported that Washington had proposed a 'Libya-style' deal in which Syria's diplomatic isolation would end if it agreed to at least four key demands.[17] They included full cooperation with the Hariri investigation, ceasing to meddle in Lebanese affairs, and ending its support for Iraqi insurgents, and Hizbullah. The information, which came from a senior Bush administration official, appeared to have been deliberately leaked to *The Times* to kill off any chance of the compromise working, illustrating the lack of unanimity in Washington over Syria.

Then, in early October, Beirut and Damascus were abuzz with the whispers of a high-ranking Syrian official who was complaining to the National Security Council and elsewhere in Washington about the disastrous state of affairs in Damascus. The rumours indicated that the search was on in Washington for a suitable replacement for Bashar, possibly drawn from the ranks of the army or intelligence services, a Syrian equivalent to Pakistan's Pervez Musharraf, an army general who seized power in 1999 and was an ally of the US.

The speculation climaxed on the morning of October 12 when Damascus announced that Ghazi Kanaan, the minister of interior and former long-serving viceroy of Lebanon, had committed suicide in his office.

The evening before Kanaan's death, Lebanon's New TV channel had broadcast a report claiming that the Syrian official had given details to the UN investigation commission of bribes he had received from Hariri during his tenure in Lebanon. The next morning, Kanaan read out a statement over the phone to the Voice of Lebanon radio station insisting that New TV's claims were 'baseless'. His monologue, in which he justified Syria's role in Lebanon, had all the attributes of a final testimony, and ended ominously with 'I believe this is the last statement I might make.'

Shortly after 10 a.m., a gunshot was heard in Kanaan's office in the interior ministry. A bodyguard found him lying on the floor in convulsions, having apparently fired a bullet from a .38 Smith & Wesson into his mouth. Kanaan was pronounced dead in hospital. The Syrian authorities blamed his suicide on the pressures he was facing because of the UN investigation and the anti-Syrian campaign in the Lebanese media. Few were persuaded that the redoubtable general had killed himself because of some bad press, however.

'He was of the calibre of strong security men, and strong people do not usually commit suicide during such moments,' wrote Sahar Baasiri in Lebanon's *An Nahar*.[18]

So was Kanaan the rumoured Syrian 'Musharraf'? Was he 'suicided' after the regime discovered he was plotting a coup with American support?

Kanaan was known to have had links to the US when in charge of Lebanon, and his two sons had studied at Georgetown University in Washington. Since returning from Lebanon to Damascus in 2002 when he became head of the political security department, he had mediated between the state and Syria's discontented Kurds and played a key role in building Syria's ties to neighbouring Turkey. But his attempt to reorganise the cluttered intelligence branches had brought him into conflict with Assef Shawkat, the then powerful deputy head of military intelligence. He was appointed minister of interior in a cabinet reshuffle in 2004, widely regarded as a demotion that cut him off from his powerbase in the army and intelligence services. Kanaan had advised against Lahoud's presidential extension, and must have watched aghast as Syria's position in Lebanon which he had spent so many years building crumbled following Hariri's murder.

Did Kanaan choose to take matters into his own hands to prevent Syria from sliding inexorably into the abyss? If so, he would have had to secure the cooperation of powerful allies in Syria as American support alone would not have facilitated a successful coup. Who were his Syrian partners?

The names that sprang to the mind of most people were Abdel-Halim Khaddam and Hikmat Shehabi. All three men had been part of the pro-Hariri clique who had overseen Lebanon in the 1990s. Shehabi had spent most of his time between the US and Britain since leaving Syria in 2004. After retiring as vice-president in June, Khaddam had moved to Paris, ostensibly to write his memoirs.

According to a Lebanese source with close ties to the Syrian leadership, in the two days before he died Kanaan had unsuccessfully tried to arrange an appointment with Bashar.[19] On the morning of October 12, he was out of the office for a brief period, which the Syrian authorities said he spent at home. According to the source, however, Kanaan went to the French embassy instead and placed two phone calls, the first to Khaddam in Paris and the second to Shehabi in Los Angeles. After he was unable to reach either of them, he returned to his office in the interior ministry and, shortly afterwards, was dead.

Abdel-Halim Khaddam's home in Paris lies in a secluded mews off Avenue Foch, about ten minutes' walk from the Arc de Triomphe. A police van was parked before the black steel-barred gate at the entrance to the mews and a couple of policemen in black military-style uniforms with submachine guns over their shoulders hovered in the shadows, ignoring the persistent drizzle of a cold winter's evening. The security was courtesy of the French government, and few doubted that the former Syrian vice-president needed protecting after a flurry of bombshell interviews he had given to the media over the New Year, in which he confirmed that Bashar had threatened Hariri, and averred that it was impossible for Syrian intelligence to assassinate Hariri without Bashar's knowledge.

For several days in early January 2006, Arab and Western journalists filed up to record Khaddam's increasingly damning allegations, which were widely believed to have been encouraged by the Saudis and French to force greater cooperation from Bashar on the UN investigation.

The Syrian authorities branded Khaddam a traitor and accused him of rampant corruption, but privately Bashar beseeched the Saudis to use their influence to stem the flow of damaging claims. Bashar's plea fell on receptive ears. At least three scheduled interviews for Saudi media were cancelled at the last minute and the French authorities half-heartedly tried to prevent Khaddam from meeting any more reporters.

'Don't tell the police you're a journalist,' Jamal Khaddam, Abdel-Halim's eldest son, advised the author on the phone. 'Just say that you are a friend of mine.'

But the two policemen guarding the front door of Khaddam's house were not fooled. As they flicked through the author's passport, one of them smirked and muttered 'journaliste' to his colleague, as Jamal stood by shuffling his feet guiltily.

Jamal led the author into a tall, brightly lit salon of white walls yellowing with time and covered with oil paintings. The house was once owned by the Greek shipping magnate Aristotle Onassis, and was allegedly purchased by Hariri and given to Khaddam as a gift. The salon was stuffed with marshmallow-soft sofas, stiff Louis XV-style armchairs, and marble-topped mahogany tables carrying brass or marble lamps, art nouveau figurines, and a porcelain ballerina. A broad staircase swept up one wall leading to a balcony overlooking the salon, which Khaddam used as his office judging from the persistent hum of computers and fax machines. From this luxurious headquarters, Khaddam was planning his campaign of revenge against Bashar.

Dressed casually in blue trousers and a matching sweater, Khaddam padded silently down the carpeted staircase and gave a brief but distant smile before sitting down in a stiff-backed chair. Jamal, an affable, rumpled figure with a thick mop of greying hair, lit another Marlboro and sat on a sofa next to his neater younger brother, Jihad.

'The regime cannot survive because it is against the interests of the people and [Bashar] works as if he is living in the past century,' Khaddam says, his two sons looking on. 'The regime does not have a future. I am 100 per cent convinced that it is going to break up.'

There was a certain formality in Khaddam's stiff and upright bearing. The only time he shifted position in his armchair was to place a small pillow behind his back. His hands cupped the ends of the arm rests and his feet were placed on the floor neatly before him. It was a pose that looked vaguely familiar. Then it dawned that this was exactly how Hafez al-Assad used to sit in those endless photographs of the old Syrian leader meeting visiting dignitaries at the presidential palace in Damascus.

The bitterness felt by the 77-year-old statesman was evident in his words, but there was not a trace of emotion on his grey, lined face as he savaged the young man who had dashed his presidential dreams.

'Bashar doesn't have any knowledge or experience,' he says. 'He inherited his father's position and this was one of the mistakes of Hafez al-Assad. Bashar acted the same way as a young man who inherits his father's company and then fritters it away and loses it all. He doesn't understand international politics . . . He knows nothing about Arab politics. He dealt with other Arab countries as if he is special and that they should accept all his ideas seriously. He doesn't even know the Syrian people . . . And now his family members and friends have become known for their widespread corruption . . . That's why we find Syria as it is after five years, despite lots of advice from Syrians, Arabs and foreigners. He was blinded and didn't see the facts. He didn't hear the voices of the people.'

Yet Khaddam was not exactly known for listening to the voices of the people either, having spearheaded the crackdown on the political discussion salons that flourished during the Damascus Spring in 2001, ending initial hopes that Bashar's presidency would lead to swift reforms.

Behind Khaddam's polite but fleeting smiles and the cool, dispassionate gaze lay an unbending self-belief in the virtue of his own convictions. This was not a man accustomed to being corrected or acknowledging his own contradictions.

At one point in the conversation when discussing how the failure of the Geneva summit between Assad and Clinton in March 2000 changed the political landscape of the Middle East, leading among other things to the outbreak of the Al-Aqsa intifada in September that year, Khaddam interjects, saying 'The intifada started before Geneva.'

Before Geneva? Did Khaddam not recall how the intifada broke out in September 2000 when Ariel Sharon took a controversial walk on the Muslim holy site of Haram al-Sharif in Jerusalem?

'No,' he replies in a voice of utmost certainty. 'The Al-Aqsa intifada was in September 1999.'

Jamal and Jihad stared blankly at the author from the opposite sofa.

Surely, it was 2000.

'Sharon visited Al-Aqsa in 1999,' Khaddam says again, with that chilly, self-confident stare.

Pause.

Okay. Let's move on.

Khaddam was hoping to build a government in exile and was reaching out to members of the opposition living in exile, and appeared to be forging a union with Ali Sadreddine Bayanuni, the head of the Muslim Brotherhood, strengthened perhaps by their mutual Sunni connection. The domestic opposition, however, was giving Khaddam a cold shoulder, sceptical of the former vice-president's apparent conversion to democracy and reform. The trigger for the regime's collapse, he believed, would be the conclusions of the UN investigation into Hariri's murder. But did he really think that Bashar had ordered the assassination of Hariri?

'I am convinced that, yes, he made the decision,' Khaddam says. 'Why would Rustom Ghazaleh kill Rafik Hariri? Was there any political struggle between Hariri and Ghazaleh? It's an obvious matter because in the security apparatus and structure in Syria no one would take such a decision but the president. This operation requires 1,000 kilogrammes of explosive. How can Ghazaleh get this by himself? It needed personnel to execute it. Can Ghazaleh order one of his generals to execute such a plan if he was not backed by the president? It needs jamming equipment and from where would Ghazaleh get jamming equipment? This was a big operation that no one could execute except an intelligence organisation and I feel confident that the international investigation will prove this.'

Khaddam said he was speaking out now because Kanaan's death had effectively closed the door to his returning to Syria.

'If I was in Syria now, I would meet the same fate as Hariri,' he says.

Or Ghazi Kanaan?

'Yes. Anyone charged with plotting against the president would automatically be eliminated.'

Had he plotted against the regime with Kanaan?

'No. When I used to meet him and talk about some of Bashar's mistakes, he used to defend Bashar. Maybe he shared my feelings, but we never discussed these things together.'

As for Bashar, Khaddam insisted that the Syrian president's days 'are very short'.

'Syria cannot tolerate a centralised system of rule,' he says. 'It doesn't need a president who regards the country as his own private farm. It needs a president who has the confidence that the people are the source of power.'

Someone like himself?

'My ultimate goal is simply to move Syria from a centralised rule to democratic system,' Khaddam says. 'The presidency is not important, not a priority for me. What is important for me is to save Syria.'

Khaddam may have been bashful about his own lingering presidential ambitions, but one person who was more than transparent about his aspirations to become a head of state was the Lebanese lawyer and democracy campaigner Chibli Mallat.

The momentum to unseat Lahoud as part of the anti-Syrian demonstrations of the Beirut Spring had fallen by the wayside following the Syrian disengagement in April and the subsequent parliamentary elections. Christian unease at the Maronite presidency coming under attack from a mainly Sunni–Druze alliance effectively ensured Lahoud would remain in Baabda palace, albeit vilified by most Lebanese and shunned by visiting foreign dignitaries.

But Mallat believed that leaving Lahoud in Baabda was a mistake and tarnished the achievements of the independence intifada. To hasten Lahoud's departure and inject a democratic edge into the debate, Mallat announced in October that he was running for the presidency and launched a small-scale but slick campaign to pursue what was a somewhat quixotic goal.

'We succeeded in our sovereignty revolution but we failed in our democratic revolution,' he says. 'If we had succeeded in unseating Lahoud it would have had a ten times greater effect on the Arab world. That is why I'm running for the presidency.'

Mallat, a bespectacled, 44-year-old Maronite expert on Islamic law, began his quest for the presidency armed with some impressive credentials as a human rights activist and democracy campaigner. He was a founder member of Indict, the campaign to bring Saddam Hussein to trial for crimes against humanity. He also was one of three lawyers acting on behalf of survivors of the 1982 massacre in the Sabra/Shatila Palestinian refugee camp in Beirut who launched a petition in 2001 in a Belgian court to indict Ariel Sharon on war crimes charges.[20]

Even though his chances of reaching Baabda palace were minimal, his action succeeded in giving new impetus to removing Lahoud. And as the country prepared to mark the first anniversary of Hariri's assassination, the parliamentary majority headed by Saad Hariri announced the launching of a new independence intifada which pledged to drive Lahoud from office by March 14, the one-year anniversary of the million man rally that had triggered Syria's troop withdrawal from Lebanon.

On February 14, 2006, Lebanon's 'Cedar revolutionaries' were back in Martyrs' Square, turning the city centre once more into a heaving sea of red and white flags, in a bid to recapture the heady spirit of the Beirut Spring after months of political tensions, violence and disillusion. They packed the square waving flags and brandishing portraits of Hariri, spilling into the surrounding streets like a vast red and white octopus. Sunlight glinted off the golden tips of the four minarets on the massive Mohammed al-Amine mosque overlooking Hariri's flower-bedecked tomb. Soldiers frisked participants at the entrance to the square and checked bags for explosives and weapons. But it was a peaceful and good-natured rally, with whole families having taken advantage of the day-long mobilisation of the Lebanese bus system to convey people from all over the country to Beirut.

Walid Jumblatt was there, making a rare foray from the safety of his castle in Mukhtara. Standing on a podium and protected by a screen of bullet-proof glass, the Druze leader delivered a typically harsh stream of invective against the 'terrorist tyrant' in Damascus, demanding Bashar 'take back his agent Emile Lahoud'. The crowd roared with delight, and Jumblatt's mouth creased into a mischievous smile.

And there too was Saad Hariri. His absence from Lebanon had become a political liability. How could the leader of the largest parliamentary bloc continue living in self-imposed exile with Lebanon politically gridlocked? So Saad had come back to show the Lebanese that he remained cognisant of the obligations incumbent upon him as the political heir of Rafik Hariri. The crowd held him aloft and conveyed him to the podium on a sea of hands, much like his father's coffin had travelled the last few metres to the grave almost exactly a year earlier.

'As Lebanese, rather than Christians and Muslims, let us cry "Lebanon First",' he told the crowd. 'I call on all Lebanese to adopt a historic position of unity on this day to show that our national unity is above all else.'

But he was speaking to an audience that, like the rallies of the Beirut Spring, was missing the Shiites. Even Michel Aoun's followers stayed away. Both Aoun and Hizbullah sent formal delegations to the rally but only out of respect for the memory of Rafik Hariri and certainly not to endorse the more fiery sentiments being expressed from the podium.

Thus, this is where Lebanon stood a year to the day after that deafening thunderclap and pall of thick black smoke marked the end of an era of Syrian tutelage and signalled the beginning of a new uncertain chapter in Lebanon's tortured history.

Rafik Hariri was a unique figure in Lebanese politics, a powerhouse driven by enormous financial resources and extensive diplomatic reach who initially was able to win over or buy up Syria's proconsuls in Lebanon and their clientelist networks to pursue his altruistic vision of a peaceful and prosperous Lebanon. Hariri gave new impetus to the war-enfeebled Sunni body politic at a time when the newly empowered and numerically superior Shiites were beginning to chip away at the traditional Sunni leadership of Lebanon's Muslim communities. Although he was the undisputed leader of Lebanon's Sunnis, his talent, charm and muscle resonated across the confessional divide, making him a national figure capable of transcending Lebanon's sectarian hurdles to steer the country independently from the clutches of Syria. While those attributes were regarded by many as an advantage, others saw them as a threat.

Hariri's murder was one of those political earthquakes which periodically ripple through the Middle East, triggering tectonic shifts and realignments along the region's political faultlines. The assassination broke Lebanon from Syria's grip, and a beleaguered Damascus chose to hunker down and confront the increased external pressure with defiance and a reinvigorated relationship with Iran and Shiite allies in Lebanon and Iraq. King Abdullah's notion of a 'Shiite crescent' is exaggerated, but not entirely fanciful. The strengthened alliance between Iran and Syria has thrown the seething regional tensions between Sunnis and Shiites into sharper relief and raised the stakes in the looming confrontation between the West and Tehran over the latter's nuclear ambitions. Hariri's murder helped crystallise these regional divisions, pitting those states and factions hostile to Israel and to Western interference against the Bush administration's goal of establishing a placid and compliant Middle East won through its formidable military, diplomatic and economic might and cloaked in a veneer of democratic values.

The tussle for control of the Middle East is played out in microcosm in Lebanon, its inherent weaknesses and confessional cleavages seemingly forever fating it to be a pawn of broader, more powerful interests. Indeed, after demonstrating such inspirational qualities during the Beirut Spring and evoking so much hope for change, how quickly the Lebanese had succumbed to their old ways. The embers of sectarianism that Pax Syriana had smothered or manipulated had flared into life once more, fanned by the fears and suspicions of Lebanon's confessional bosses who continue to plot and intrigue, moulding and breaking alliances, clawing for the fickle support of foreign patrons.

And what would Rafik Hariri have made of the Lebanon he left in such a terrible fashion a year earlier? Would he have wrung his hands in frustration perhaps, despairing at the inability of his fellow Lebanese to act as a nation rather than a group of feuding sects? Little wonder then that, 12 months after his death, whether one loved him or loathed him, the Lebanese missed the reassuring, larger-than-life presence of 'Mr Lebanon'.

The last of the speakers departed the podium and the masses slowly drifted away from Martyrs' Square, some pausing to pay their respects at Hariri's tomb. Lying discarded in the dust, stirred by the chill breeze, was a placard with that familiar portrait of a smiling Rafik Hariri, his eyes twinkling beneath those thick, bushy eyebrows. And beneath his picture, written by hand in Arabic, was the forlorn question 'Waynak?' Where are you?

Epilogue:
the return of war

The newly made coffins were stacked up six high and stretched down the hospital courtyard as the carpenter continued to labour beneath the sweltering midday sun to complete his melancholy task.

Their faces covered with surgical masks and with two men brandishing chemical sprays standing by, hospital workers swung open the back doors of a refrigerated truck exposing an untidy pile of bodies wrapped in blankets and plastic bags bound tightly with tape.

The initial victims of Israel's onslaught against south Lebanon had been stored in a makeshift morgue – a refrigerated meat transport truck brought from Tripoli in northern Lebanon at the outset of the conflict in anticipation of many fatalities. But the corpses had begun to rot, biology defeating the clattering generator that blew cold air into the rear compartment, and the local people had begun to complain. More ominously, officials at the government-run hospital feared they would soon need the space for what might come next.

For Hizbullah's battle-hardened fighters were displaying more tenacity than expected, despite 11 days of the most punishing air and artillery blitz against Lebanon since Israel's 1982 invasion. With Israeli soldiers being killed and Israeli tanks being knocked out by Hizbullah's anti-armour missiles, Israel had decided to ratchet up the pace of its offensive. The Israeli military broadcast warnings by radio and recorded voice messages in phone calls to local Lebanese officials instructing all residents of south Lebanon to abandon their homes and head north of the Litani river, which cuts across much of south Lebanon about 40 kilometres from the border.

The offensive had claimed over 300 lives. It had destroyed the southern suburbs of Beirut, and created a humanitarian disaster in the south with some 500,000 refugees fleeing the fighting and tens of thousands more trapped by bomb cratered impassable roads in villages under air strike and artillery shelling. Yet it promised to get much worse.

Israel has a long and bloody history of using disproportionate force against its enemies, more often than not found in Lebanon. At this time of writing it is unclear whether or not Hizbullah could foresee what was about to befall Lebanon when it dispatched a squad of fighters to kidnap Israeli soldiers along the border with Lebanon.

It was a well-coordinated operation, though, clearly one that had been studied and refined for months. They struck in a remote brush-covered section of the border south of Aitta Shaab village, a Hizbullah stronghold. The fighters blasted through the 3-metre-high border fence, hitting an Israeli jeep with a missile as rocket batteries further north staged a diversion by firing Katyushas into the area between the Israeli towns of Shetula and Zarit. Two soldiers were snatched by the Hizbullah squad and dragged across the border to disappear into the thick undergrowth. In the ambush and subsequent clashes, eight soldiers died, four of them when an anti-tank missile destroyed a Merkava tank, the highest Israeli military death toll in a confrontation with Hizbullah since 1997.

In the hours that followed, throughout the dusty hill villages of south Lebanon, Hizbullah supporters in convoys of cars sporting yellow party flags drove through the streets honking horns in celebration at the news. Others stood in the centre of main roads handing out fistfuls of sweets to motorists, a traditional symbol of celebration.

Israel's initial response was to destroy three key bridges crossing the Litani river, cutting off much of south-east Lebanon from Beirut. Harassed-looking Lebanese soldiers blocked the roads leading to the bridges instructing motorists to return north out of the area.

From Marjayoun, a Christian town of stone houses and terracotta roofs lying on the crest of a valley within sight of the border with Israel, the deep boom of Israeli artillery was heard as round after round exploded in a valley at the foot of the Shebaa Farms hills to the east. The roar of an Israeli jet was followed a moment later by a loud blast that echoed off the hills and down the valley as a towering column of dust and smoke gently rose into the sky from the far side of Khiam, Marjayoun's Shiite neighbour.

That evening as the sun bled into the Mediterranean, Lebanon held its breath. It was a moment of decision for Israel. Ever since it had withdrawn from south Lebanon in May 2000, it had turned the other cheek to each of Hizbullah's needling attacks along the Blue Line. By the same token, Hizbullah had been careful not to overstep a certain threshold that would compel the Israeli government to respond forcefully. It was always a precarious equation, however, one that both sides knew from the beginning would end in a showdown.

'This will happen and we are constantly preparing for it,' a Hizbullah official told the author as long ago as February 2002. He added that, when the confrontation finally occurred, 'the whole of the Middle East will change'.

Hizbullah's kidnapping operation was carefully timed to coincide with another abduction crisis, this one in Gaza where two weeks earlier Palestinian militants had tunnelled out of the Gaza Strip, attacked an Israeli position and snatched a soldier. Ehud Olmert, the Israeli prime minister, sent tanks and troops into Gaza to recover the missing soldiers but to no avail. Hamas, which was one of three groups that carried out the military operation, said the soldier would be released only in exchange for thousands of Palestinian detainees. Olmert was caught in a bind, suffering the traditional insecurity of an Israeli leader with a non-military background attempting to convey leadership and strength to an Israeli public wanting results in a difficult military situation.

In terms of compounding the pressure on Olmert, Hizbullah's kidnapping came at an opportune moment. It even had the bonus of Hizbullah outdoing Hamas by capturing two soldiers to the Palestinian movement's one.

Olmert could not afford to appear weak and indecisive before such a flagrant provocation. His inner security cabinet met that evening to decide the course of action. The Israeli military urged for a powerful response 'to teach Hizbullah a lesson once and for all'. Olmert agreed. The kidnapping, he said, was 'an act of war'. Israel's response would be 'restrained' but 'very very very painful'.

There was little evidence of restraint in what was to follow, however. Israeli jets launched the offensive by bombing the runway at Beirut airport, which had been renamed the Rafik Hariri International Airport. The runways cratered, the airport closed down and flights were diverted to Cyprus. Then the jets struck at the southern suburbs of Beirut itself, powerful guided missiles that turned apartment block after apartment block into dust and rubble. Hizbullah's entire headquarters in the sealed-off area of Haret Hreik was utterly destroyed as day after day the Israeli jets returned to drop tons of bombs on the area. The Shiite inhabitants fled the area seeking refuge with relatives, in schools and abandoned houses.

Beirut turned into a ghost town, shops closed and residents headed to homes in remote mountain villages. Foreigners made plans to evacuate the city. After a week, the US Marines were back in Beirut for the first time

since an older generation of Shiite fighters had suicide-bombed them out
of Lebanon more than 20 years earlier.

The air raids went as far north as Qlayaat on the coast near the border
with Syria where the runways of a disused military airport were bombed.
Most main roads were bombed and bridges destroyed or rendered
impassable, including the soaring road bridge, reputedly the highest in
the Middle East, spanning the Dahr al-Baidar pass on the main highway
linking Beirut to the Bekaa valley. The remaining bridges over the Litani
were destroyed, augmenting the south's isolation.

The destruction of the southern suburbs was breathtaking in its
magnitude, but what was happening in south Lebanon was something
else entirely. The politicians and generals in Israel spoke of 'neutralising'
Hizbullah's leadership and 'degrading' its military infrastructure, of
'pinpoint strikes' and temporary 'incursions'. But the rounded limestone
hills and swooping valleys of south Lebanon had turned into a killing
zone where Israeli jets pulverised hundreds of civilian houses and apartment blocks, killing entire families at a time. Vehicles packed with civilians escaping their villages were attacked by Israeli jets and helicopters,
blowing the occupants into pieces or incinerating them where they sat.
The dead rotted under the rubble of their demolished homes while the
wounded died in the street, unable to reach hospital because of the bomb-
cratered roads. By the end of the first week of the offensive, Lebanese Red
Cross workers in Tyre said they were seeing stray dogs eating the corpses
lying on the roads or protruding from debris.

This was not just about striking at Hizbullah. This was Israel taking
cold-blooded revenge for more than two decades of humiliation at the
hands of its Shiite adversaries in Lebanon.

Yelling for people to move aside, medics burst into the emergency room
of the Jabel Amel hospital in Tyre carrying a woman, her head lolling from
side to side, her body daubed in blood. 'Allah Akhbar,' God is greatest,
she moaned. She was one of five people – four women and one young
man – whose car had been targeted by an Israeli jet on a road near
Bourgheliyeh, a tiny ramshackle village off the coastal road just north of
Tyre.

'Two bombs fell next to each other 15 metres in front of the car,' said a
shaken Jihad Daoud, as he anxiously watched his relatives being treated
by doctors.

In the hospital's intensive care unit lay Alia Alieddine, 30, one of only
two casualties to make it to the hospital from the village of Srifa, 16 kilometres east of Tyre. Israeli jets flattened an entire neighbourhood in the
village. Residents initially recovered 10 bodies but at the time of writing it

was thought there could be another 60 to 80 people buried under the rubble.

Connected to breathing tubes and her head heavily bandaged, Alieddine's bruised and half-closed eyes stared sightlessly at the ceiling.

'She suffered major head wounds, her arm is broken and she lost a lot of blood,' said Dr Abdullah Abbas. 'Her chances are not good. It is in God's hands.'

The basement of the hospital was jammed with casualties and their anxious relatives who had fled their homes from neighbouring villages to sleep on thin mattresses in the corridors.

UNIFIL peacekeepers acknowledged that Israel was treating the south as a free-fire zone with any vehicle travelling the roads at risk of being hit. On the second day of the offensive, 21 people were killed when an Israeli helicopter gunship rocketed a three-vehicle convoy carrying residents of Marwahine, a hamlet on the border, to the relative safety of Tyre. Around 25 people had been packed into the back of an open-bed truck travelling in between two cars. The residents had been instructed by loudhailer from an Israeli military position a few hundred metres away on the other side of the border to vacate their homes immediately. Many heeded the call. The convoy was travelling along an open road running along the crest of a ridge between the villages of Biyada and Shamaa when the helicopter, whose pilot must have seen there were mainly women and children in the back of the uncovered truck, opened fire. The first missile hit the truck, killing all occupants but four. The second missile hit the rear car, killing one and wounding three.

The next day, a UNIFIL relief column attempting to rescue beleaguered residents of Marwahine and nearby villages came under Israeli shellfire, with 12 155mm rounds exploding nearby. A peacekeeper who was on the convoy said that body-armoured UN soldiers threw themselves on top of the villagers to protect them from flying shrapnel.

But what happened in Marwahine was to be repeated throughout south Lebanon in the days that followed.

The minibus had come to a stop on the side of a downhill road cut into the side of a steep valley midway between the villages of Siddiquine and Yater. Minutes earlier an Israeli helicopter gunship had fired a missile through the roof of the vehicle, blasting it off the road. One man, with the left half of his head torn off, sat almost upright, his yellowing hand hanging with seeming nonchalance out of the window. The bodies of two other people, their clothes sodden with blood, lay slumped over each other. Sitting beside the dead man, covered in the contents of his skull, a woman, dazed with shock, moved slowly back and forth.

'Can you stand?' asked a Lebanese Red Cross volunteer.

The woman mumbled an incoherent response. A few metres away, some of the survivors lay on the ground, moaning and crying. The driver, a thin man with a straggly beard, lay prostrate on the ground calling out to God. One woman, her black dress drenched in blood and her face a gory mask, writhed slowly while a medic treated her.

There had been 19 people on board the vehicle, most of them women and children, who were at the tail end of a convoy fleeing the village of Tiri, 10 kilometres to the south-east.

Abbas Shayter, a 12-year-old boy whose naked torso was speckled with dried blood, said that the village had been instructed by the Israelis to leave and his family had been waiting for transport.

'Someone came for us and we drove with other cars out of the village,' he said. 'We were trying to keep up with the others when we were hit.'

His grandmother and uncle were among those killed. Abbas' older brother, Ali, sobbed beside his prone mother whose bandaged left arm was streaked with blood. She raised her right hand and held her son's arm consolingly.

Hizbullah responded to Israel's intensifying air strikes with its first ever rocket attack against Haifa, Israel's third largest city lying 40 kilometres south of the border. That attack laid to rest once and for all the debate over whether Hizbullah possessed long-range weapons. On the evening of the third day, after the southern suburbs had been struck, Nasrallah gave a televised address, saying that if Israel wanted all-out war then they would get all-out war. He added that Hizbullah had many more surprises and if the residents of Beirut looked out to sea at that very minute they would see an Israeli ship burning and sinking. After his speech, the crackle of gunfire erupted from the southern suburbs in celebration, thin beads of red tracer arcing into the sky.

Nasrallah's claim was true. Of all the missiles speculated to be in Hizbullah's possession, no one had thought it might have acquired anti-ship radar-guided missiles. One had struck a navy patrol boat 10 kilometres off shore, killing four crew members and disabling the vessel so that it had to be towed back to Israel.

Israel responded the next day by hitting all the military radar sites along the Lebanese coast, having concluded that the army had helped Hizbullah attack the ship.

A series of loud bangs from trees close to the seashore north of Tyre signalled the unleashing of the latest barrage of long-range rockets, coils of smoke reaching into the blue sky charting their south-bound trajectory. Shortly afterwards, the Arabic television channels reported that Haifa had been struck again. It was taking Israel too long to disable Hizbullah's rocket batteries, and questions were beginning to be asked in the Israeli press about why more had not been achieved after a week and a half of bombing.

A hollow thump and a puff of smoke in the sky above the Christian quarter on the tip of Tyre's promontory signalled another leaflet drop from the Israelis. A cloud of yellow paper rippled down like confetti blown by the sea breeze inland east of Tyre, the plastic barrel which had contained the warning slips crashing next to the Catholic bishop of Tyre's residence.

An hour later, the Maronite and Catholic churches had closed and a convoy of more than 20 cars, most of them with white sheets fluttering from windows, departed the Christian quarter and headed out of town. Families lugged suitcases down the narrow alleys of the quarter to their cars. Not all wanted to leave, however. One exasperated man pleaded with his elderly mother to get in the car with the rest of his family, but she refused.

'How can I leave my home?' she asked.

Some other residents refused to leave, mainly the old who sat outside their front doors sipping tiny cups of coffee and gloomily watching their neighbours depart.

Food and petrol began to run low and despair set in among officials of Tyre's municipal council, who found themselves overwhelmed by the scale of the humanitarian disaster unfolding around them.

A crowd of anxious people thronged the reception area of the municipality's offices, begging for food handouts and bottled water.

'There's nothing for them. We have no supplies,' said Hassan Al-Husseini, the mayor, bitterly.

His staff castigated the government for abandoning them in their hour of need, asking why a Christian charity had managed to dispatch several truckloads of supplies down the dangerous coastal road from Beirut to Tyre while the government had sent nothing. During Israel's 16-day air and artillery blitz against south Lebanon in April 1996, convoys of humanitarian supplies had travelled from Beirut to the south, but not this time.

'That's because in 1996 there was a man called Rafik Hariri,' said Mohammed Al-Husseini, the mayor's son who was working at the municipality. 'He was a very big man in international relations. A very big man. But there is no more Rafik Hariri.'

No more Rafik Hariri to plead Lebanon's case before the world. And his absence was felt. Fouad Siniora, a decent man faced with an impossible task, watched in anguish as the efforts of 14 years reconstruction collapsed around him in days. He travelled to New York to deliver an emotional heart-felt plea to the United Nations for an immediate ceasefire, saying his country had been 'torn to shreds'.

The international community ignored him. The Bush administration, which had so swiftly adopted the 'independence uprising' as its own, dropped Lebanon like a hot brick when it came to Israel's war against Hizbullah. While Israel's air force dispassionately blasted civilians into bloody fragments in south Lebanon, American officials went on about Iranian and Syrian terrorism and the need for Hizbullah to stop firing rockets into Israel. The leading Arab states of Saudi Arabia, Jordan and Egypt muttered the usual platitudes about Israeli aggression but they had little taste for Hizbullah and hoped for its destruction almost as fervently as Israel. Lebanon was on its own, a victim once more of its own inherent weaknesses and international exploitation. Hariri had always feared that Hizbullah's hostility toward Israel would lead Lebanon into just this kind of slaughter and destruction. How he had bargained, negotiated and manoeuvred to avoid such a catastrophe. Yet it had all come to nothing. His death and the subsequent chain of events – the polarisation in Lebanon over Hizbullah's arms, resurgent sectarianism, government weakness, Syrian meddling and international manipulation – had led to this unfolding disaster.

Lebanon will rebuild. It always does. Its long-suffering, tenacious, resourceful, enterprising and resilient people will collectively shrug their shoulders and continue to live their lives, working hard to raise and educate their children while keeping a detached, half-amused eye on the ceaseless squabbles of Lebanese politicians.

And as Tyre awaits the next phase of this brutal war, the rumble of a passing Israeli jet high above is almost smothered by the reassuring ineluctable hiss of breaking waves as the timeless Mediterranean laps and foams gently against the green-algaed rocks and toppled ancient stone columns on the beach.

Notes

Chapter 1

1 The following account of the morning of February 14, 2006 is based on author interviews with Adnan Baba, Carole Farhat, Fadi Fawaz, Nejib Friji, Marwan Hamade, Rashid Hammoud, Fady Khoury, Ghattas Khoury, Samer Rida and Amer Shehadi.
2 See Report of the International Independent Investigation Commission, 19 October, 2005, paragraph 144.

Chapter 2

1 Interview with the author – August 3, 2005.
2 Interview with the author – August 3, 2005.
3 Interview with the author – August 3, 2005.
4 Interview with the author – January 27, 2006.
5 Interview with the author – August 3, 2005.
6 Interview with the author – July 5, 2005.
7 Interview with the author – January 13, 2006.
8 Interview with the author – July 5, 2005.
9 Interview with the author – January 27, 2006.
10 Interview with the author – August 3, 2005.
11 Interview with the author – November 23, 2005.
12 Interview with the author – January 13, 2006.
13 Interview with the author – January 17, 2006.
14 Interview with the author – June 23, 2005.
15 Interview with the author – August 4, 2005.
16 Ibid.
17 Interview with the author – June 23, 2005.
18 Ibid.
19 Interview with the author – October 20, 2005.
20 Interview with the author – June 23, 2005.
21 Interview with the author – January 27, 2006.

22 Interview with the author – September 18, 2005.
23 Interview with the author – August 22, 2005.
24 Interview with the author – January 17, 2006.
25 Interview with the author – September 18, 2005.
26 Interview with the author.
27 Interview with the author.
28 Interview with the author – December 16, 2005.
29 Interview with the author – August 4, 2005.
30 Ibid.
31 Interview with the author – June 23, 2005.
32 Interview with the author – August 22, 2005.
33 Interview with the author.
34 Interview with the author – January 17, 2006.
35 Interview with the author – January 27, 2006.
36 Interview with the author – August 4, 2005.
37 Interview with the author – August 22, 2005.
38 Interview with the author – January 17, 2006.
39 *Daw'i al-Asfar: Al-Siyassa al-Amrikiyyi Tijah Lubnan.* Beirut, Sharikat al-Matbu' at lil-Tawzi' wal-Nashr, 1991.
40 Interview with the author – August 22, 2005.
41 Interview with the author – January 13, 2006.

Chapter 3

1 Kamal Feghali. *Displacement in Lebanon: The Strategy of Return and Development* (in Arabic). Beirut, Lebanese Center for Policy Studies, 1997.
2 Boutros Labaki. 'The Postwar Economy: A Miracle That Didn't Happen'. In *Limbo: Postwar Society and State in an Uncertain Regional Environment.* (Eds) Theodor Hanf and Nawaf Salam. Baden-Baden, Nomos, 2003.
3 Interview with the author – December 16, 2005.
4 Interview with the author – November 21, 2005.
5 Interview with the author – January 13, 2006.
6 Interview with the author – September 20, 2005.
7 Interview with the author – August 29, 2005.
8 Interview with the author – September 19, 2005.
9 Interview with the author – November 21, 2005.
10 Interview with the author – January 13, 2006.
11 Interview with the author – December 18, 2005.
12 Interview with retired general in the Lebanese Army.
13 Interview with the author.
14 Interview with the author – January 27, 2006.
15 Interview with the author – December 16, 2005.
16 Interview with the author – January 14, 2006.
17 Ibid.
18 Interview with the author – December 16, 2005.
19 Interview with the author – November 21, 2005.

20 Interview with the author.

21 Interview with the author – November 18, 2005.

22 One prominent and influential MP is said to have secured $15 million for his endorsement.

23 Interview with the author – August 29, 2005.

24 Interview with the author – January 9, 2006.

25 Interview with the author.

26 Interview with the author – July 11, 2005.

27 Interview with Joe Faddoul – July 11, 2005. Allegations of corruption and fraud at the casino were repeatedly aired in the Lebanese media and cited by Lebanese politicians. In February 2006, President Emile Lahoud in a defence of his presidential record claimed that he had insisted on an 'honourable' person to run the Casino du Liban 'in order to avoid the illegal funnelling of cash'.

28 Interview with the author – July 11, 2005.

29 Interview with the author – August 29, 2005.

30 Fadlallah is often mistakenly described as Hizbullah's spiritual leader, but he has never held a formal position within the party even though he is a *marjaa* (model of emulation) for many Shiites, including Hizbullah members.

31 Interview with the author.

32 Interview with the author – July 20, 2005.

33 Interview with the author.

34 Interview with the author – October 20, 2005.

35 Interview with the author – December 16, 2005. Mashnouq fell victim to the pressure exerted on Hariri by Bashar and Lahoud in autumn 1998 when a 'file' was opened on him by Syrian military intelligence. Mashnouq was accused of being an Israeli spy, a false claim which he and Hariri recognised as a Syrian decision that Mashnouq should leave Lebanon. Mashnouq left for Paris in November 1998 and was able to return three years later after Taha Mikati, a prominent Sunni businessman and brother of former prime minister Najib Mikati, interceded with Bashar, a close friend. Another point of pressure against Hariri was the permission granted to the MP Najah Wakim to publish his book detailing allegations of corruption by Hariri and his aides. *Al-Ayadi as-Saud* (The Black Hands) (Beirut, 1978) was a huge bestseller.

36 Interview with the author – February 9, 2006.

37 Interview with the author – 10 October, 2005.

Chapter 4

1 Interviewed by the author – January 20, 2006.

2 Ehud Barak defeated Benjamin Netanyahu in the May 1999 Israeli general elections and took office in July. He promised that, if elected, he would withdraw Israeli troops from south Lebanon, adding it would happen within the framework of peace negotiations with Syria. For months after being elected, he refused to say what would happen if no peace deal with Syria was forthcoming, but the inference of his electoral pledge was that the troop pull-out would take precedence.

3 Interview with the author – January 14, 2006.

4 Interview with the author – January 13, 2006.

5 Interview with the author.

6 Interviews with current and former diplomats in Beirut.

7 Author interviews with retired and serving senior Lebanese Army officers – April–December 2005.

8 Interview with the author. According to Qanso, Lahoud subsequently contacted Bashar, saying he could no longer work with Kanaan and asked for his removal. Although Bashar chose not to satisfy Lahoud's request, Kanaan's days in Lebanon were numbered and he would depart Anjar in two years. Another incident that highlights the poor relations between Lahoud and Kanaan occurred when Bashar, accompanied by Kanaan, visited Lahoud at Baabda palace. According to a senior Lebanese Army officer, Mustafa Hamdan, Lahoud's closest aide, suggested to Kanaan that they wait outside while the two presidents conferred. But Bashar told Hamdan that Kanaan 'is me and I am him'. Instead, it was Hamdan who had to wait outside while Kanaan sat with Lahoud and Bashar, like a 'third president', according to the army officer. Several pro- and anti-Syrian sources told the author that Lahoud sponsored a whispering campaign against Kanaan, using his son, Emile Lahoud junior, and son-in-law, Elias Murr, to tell senior regime officials, such as Maher al-Assad, Bashar's younger brother, that Kanaan was a danger to the president.

9 Kanaan was rumoured to have received large sums of money from Hariri for tailoring the law to his advantage. The rumour resurfaced in October 2005 when Lebanon's New TV channel claimed that, in an interview with the UN commission investigating Hariri's murder, Kanaan had admitted to receiving a $10 million cheque from Hariri. 'Premier Hariri had at the time given me a $10 million cheque and another $10 million to General Jamil Sayyed,' New TV quoted Kanaan as telling the UN investigators. 'We were making money from Premier Hariri so how could we possibly kill him and close the flow of his riches?' The morning after the report was aired, Kanaan read out a statement to the Voice of Lebanon radio station insisting that New TV's allegations were 'baseless' and 'tendentious'. Hours later, Kanaan was dead, having apparently shot himself in the head.

10 Qassem Qanso, the then head of the Lebanese branch of the Baath party, said in a parliamentary debate on the Hariri government that Jumblatt's comments had 'exceeded all limits', adding that Israeli 'agents . . . will not be protected from the rifles of the resistance fighters by any red lines or by seeking refuge in embassies'. The Lebanese media interpreted Qanso's comments as tantamount to a death threat against Jumblatt. Two days later, Qanso attended a meeting of the Baath party National Command in Damascus and was berated by Abdel-Halim Khaddam, the Syrian vice-president, for attacking Jumblatt so strongly. Qanso told the author in an interview (February 8, 2006) that he retorted that Jumblatt was against Syria and the Lebanese resistance and deserved to be treated harshly. The two men argued heatedly until Farouq al-Sharaa, the Syrian foreign minister, who was also present, sided with Qanso against Khaddam, saying that he had discussed the incident with Bashar

al-Assad the day before. Bashar told Sharaa that Qanso was right to attack Jumblatt. 'Khaddam fell silent,' Qanso recalls. The Baath party meeting neatly illustrated Khaddam's declining influence in Damascus as well as his continuing ties to Jumblatt.

11 From taking office in November 2000 to mid-February 2001, Hariri travelled to Qatar, twice to Saudi Arabia, Morocco, Egypt (where he negotiated a $2 billion project to supply liquid gas to Lebanon, Syria and Turkey), Libya, Kuwait (which provided $550 million in development funds) and Japan (where he secured pledges of further loans and an offer to help launch a bond issue in yen).

12 Interview with the author.

13 Interviews with ministers in Hariri's 2000 and 2003 governments.

14 Interview with the author.

15 Interview with the author – November 23, 2005.

16 Interview with the author.

17 Interviews with former ministers in Hariri's 2000 and 2003 governments.

18 Interview with the author – May 24, 2005.

19 Interview with the author – September 24, 2005.

20 Interview with the author – February 9, 2006.

21 Interview with the author.

22 Interview with the author.

23 Interview with the author – December 16, 2005.

24 'Following the old money trail', *US News and World Report*. April 4, 2005.

25 Interview with the author – September 14, 2005.

26 Interview with a Lebanese official involved in the negotiations.

27 Interview with the author.

28 Interview with the author.

29 Interview with the author – January 14, 2006.

30 Ibid.

31 Ibid.

32 Interview with the author.

33 Interview with the author.

34 Interviews with aides to Hariri.

35 Author interview with Sheikh Naim Qassem, Hizbullah's deputy secretary-general.

36 Interview with the author – July 20, 2005.

37 Hariri's third son, Hussam, died aged 18 in 1991 in a car crash in the United States. Nasrallah's eldest son, Hadi, an 18-year-old resistance fighter, was killed in 1997 in a clash with Israeli commandos in the Israeli occupation zone in south Lebanon.

38 Interviews with the author.

39 Author interview with an American diplomat.

40 Interview with the author – January 14, 2006.

Chapter 5

1 Interview with the author – November 23, 2005.

2 Interviews with the author.

3 Interview with the author.

4 Interview with the author.

5 Interview with the author – November 23, 2005.

6 Interview with the author – October 10, 2005.

7 Author interview with Walid Jumblatt – December 18, 2005.

8 Interview with the author.

9 Author interview with a Hariri aide.

10 Interview with the author – January 10, 2006.

11 Interview with the author.

12 Interview with the author – December 17, 2005.

13 Interview with the author – October 10, 2005.

14 Interview with the author – February 9, 2006.

15 Interview with the author.

16 Interview with the author – August 9, 2005.

17 Author interviews with current and former Lebanese MPs.

18 Interview with the author.

19 Interview with the author.

20 Interview with the author.

21 Interview with the author – January 27, 2006.

22 Author interview with a source close to Hariri and Murr.

23 Elias Murr claimed that the bomb consisted of 300 kilograms of explosive, although the Italian government put the figure at 100 kilograms.

24 Murr, one of Syria's most dependable allies, swiftly lost Syria's good will following the discovery of the alleged Al-Qaeda plot. Marwan Hamade told the author that, a month after the arrests, Murr had predicted he would be the victim of a similar assassination attempt to the one that gravely wounded Hamade on October 1, 2004. On July 12, 2005, Murr was severely wounded when a car bomb exploded beside his convoy in a Beirut suburb. While recovering from his injuries in Zurich two months later, he revealed in a television programme that he had been repeatedly threatened by Ghazaleh before the Syrian troop withdrawal in April.

25 Interview with the author – March 9, 2005.

26 Interview with the author.

27 Interview with the author – September 24, 2005.

28 Interview with the author – December 18, 2005.

29 Author interview with one of the participants.

30 Interview with the author.

31 Interview with the author.

32 Interview with the author – August 9, 2005.

33 Interview with the author.

34 Interview with the author – July 22, 2005.

35 In an interview with Al-Manar television station on February 15, 2006, Nasral-

lah recounted in some detail the discussions he held with Hariri in the months before the former premier's death. 'We agreed that the resistance had a duty to protect Lebanon,' Nasrallah said. 'He made it clear that the resistance weapon is related to the [regional] political settlement rather than the [Shebaa] Farms or [freeing of Lebanese] prisoners [in Israeli prisons] . . . I even remember that he told me then that, even if there was a political settlement, he would sit with me to agree on addressing the issue of resistance weapons should I have any objections. He added that, if I had any objections, he would resign and quit his post because he was not willing to start a new Algeria-like experience. Of course, for me his words were great and I took them as a source of guarantee and reassurance by the Lebanese government, which he was expected to form after the elections, whether the Syrians stayed in the country or left. The course of political events was clear. The government will not be in conflict with the resistance and will not act against it. At the personal level, my colleagues and I took his words and guarantees as sufficient. He even told me that he was willing to write and sign a document to this effect. But I refused and told him that his verbal commitment was enough for us.'

36 Interview with the author – January 14, 2006.

37 Interview with the author – September 24, 2005.

38 Interview with the author – November 23, 2005.

39 Author interview with a Hariri advisor.

40 Author interview with a Hariri advisor.

41 Interview with the author – December 18, 2005.

42 The conversation in Koreitem was secretly taped by Hariri and the above statements were reproduced in the first interim report of the UN International Independent Investigation Commission into Hariri's assassination on October 19, 2005. The commission assessed that the recorded interview 'clearly contradicts' a statement given by Muallem to the commission 'in which he falsely described the 1 February meeting as "friendly and constructive" '. However, Muallem's recorded comment could just as easily be interpreted as being sympathetic to Hariri's plight, rather than a threat, more in keeping with his perceived less partisan status in the tensions between Hariri and the Syrian leadership. Furthermore, Fouad Siniora told the author that Muallem agreed at the meeting to attempt a reconciliation between Bashar and Hariri.

43 Interview with the author – January 27, 2006.

44 Interview with the author – January 14, 2006.

45 Interview with the author – January 26, 2006.

46 Author interview with sources familiar with the conversation between Larsen and Bashar. Larsen declined to confirm or deny to the author his suggestion to Bashar.

47 Interview with the author – January 26, 2006.

48 Author interview with Mustafa Nasr, the go-between for Hariri and Nasrallah – July 20, 2005.

49 Interview with the author – February 9, 2006.

50 Author interviews with Saad Hariri (January 13, 2006) and a bodyguard to Rafik Hariri.

51 Interview with the author – January 13, 2006.

Chapter 6

1 The following account of the aftermath of the explosion is based on author interviews with Abed Arab, Adnan Baba, Carole Farhat, Rami Farous, Nejib Friji, Rashid Hammoud, Ahmad Husari, Walid Jumblatt, Fady Khoury, Ghattas Khoury, Samer Rida and Amer Shehadi.
2 Interview with the author – January 13, 2006.
3 Author interviews with participants at the meeting.
4 Interview with the author – September 24, 2005.
5 See the 'Report of the International Independent Investigation Commission', October 19, 2005.
6 See the 'Fourth Report of the International Independent Investigation Commission', June 10, 2006.
7 Paula Dobriansky also coined the phrase 'Purple Revolution' to describe the first post-Saddam Hussein national election in Iraq in January 2005, the purple referring to the ink used to mark each voter's finger.
8 Negotiations for Aoun's return to Lebanon had been under way for some months in which pro-Syrian Lebanese travelled to France to mediate on behalf of Lahoud and the Syrian authorities. The unlikely negotiations between Damascus and the traditionally anti-Syrian Aoun go some way in explaining the general's subsequent choice of political alliances.
9 Allegations of vote-buying were widely aired during the election campaign, mainly directed at the Hariri camp. Vote-buying is a traditional feature of Lebanese elections and is widely practised. The European Union Election Observation Mission reported on June 20, 2005 that its observers had received 'a substantial number of allegations of vote-buying from rival candidates and political groups. Observers also witnessed a few attempts at vote-buying.'

Chapter 7

1 Interview with the author – December 18, 2006.
2 The names came to light because of an embarrassing blunder in which initial copies of the report sent to members of the UN Security Council left the document track changes intact. The track changes to the document includes the date and time of each alteration to the text. Most of the changes were from grammatical errors, but some parts of the report appeared to have been excised because of their sensitivity. Intriguingly, despite assurances from the UN that the UNIIIC report would not be changed, some of the most sensitive alterations occurred after the report was submitted to UN Secretary-General Kofi Annan on the morning of October 20, 2005. The UN subsequently, and somewhat unfairly, wheeled out Detlev Mehlis, who was not to blame for the release of the unedited report, to explain to the UN press corps what had gone wrong. He insisted that Kofi Annan had not pressured him into making any

changes to the report, but was unable to satisfactorily explain why the changes were made after the report was submitted to Annan.

3 Interview with the author – January 13, 2006.

4 Ibid.

5 Hussam Hussam, a Syrian Kurd who claimed to have worked for Syrian military intelligence in Lebanon and had made some of the most potent claims in the initial report, suddenly appeared on Syrian state television in late November declaring that Saad Hariri had attempted to bribe him with $1.3 million in cash to make false statements. He added that he had seen a veritable who's who of leading anti-Syrian Lebanese filing into the Monteverde headquarters of the UN commission to force him into implicating his Syrian masters. Hussam claimed that, to prevent him escaping, his captors would inject him with medication to keep him immobile for 12 days. The television interview and a press conference he gave the next day were a little too slick to be believable, but they succeeded in sowing doubt over the integrity of the Mehlis report. If Hussam was lying in Damascus, might he not have been lying to the UN commission as well? Zuhair Ibn Mohammed Said Saddik, who worked in the office of Hassan Khalil, the former head of Syrian military intelligence, told Mehlis he had seen the Mitsubishi van used in the Hariri assassination being fitted with explosives in a Syrian military base near the Lebanese border. He also claimed to have arranged planning meetings for the assassination. Germany's *Der Spiegel* news magazine reported that Saddik was a convicted swindler primed by Rifaat al-Assad. DNA tests carried out by the UN commission indicated Saddik had fabricated part of his testimony.

6 Bahiya Hariri, Rafik's sister and an MP, received a similar warning in February 2006 when several rocket-propelled grenades were found in a plastic bag on the side of a road near her home in Sidon.

7 Interview with the author – December 18, 2005.

8 In the summer of 2005, Israel said that Hizbullah had acquired in excess of 13,000 rockets, most of them standard 122mm Katyushas. Among the alleged long-range variants are the 240mm Fajr 3 with a 43-kilometre range, its big brother the 333mm Fajr 5, with a 70-kilometre range, and Syrian 220mm Katyusha-style rockets.

9 In a speech on May 25, 2005, marking the fifth anniversary of Israel's withdrawal from south Lebanon, Sayyed Hassan Nasrallah, Hizbullah's secretary-general, referred to the rocket allegations, saying 'Some people think we have 12,000 rockets. I tell you we have more than 12,000 . . . All of the north of occupied Palestine, its settlements, airports, seaports, fields, factories and farms is under the feet and hands of the Islamic Resistance.' While the comment was a typical example of Nasrallah's rhetorical flippancy rather than a sober affirmation of its rocket numbers, in the author's opinion Hizbullah has amassed a substantial arsenal of rockets both short- and long-range. Three months later, three long-range rockets – either 240mm Fajr 3s or 220mm Katyushas – were launched from south Lebanon to the border with Israel. One exploded just inside Israel; the other two fell short of the border and exploded harmlessly. Hizbullah denied responsibility for the rocket firing. It was the

first known time that long-range rockets had been fired at Israel from Lebanon.

10 For example, in January 2006, Israeli soldiers stationed in the Shebaa Farms shot and killed a Lebanese hunter who was on the Lebanese side of the Blue Line. Hizbullah responded to this breach of the Blue Line two days later by shelling Israeli army positions in the Shebaa Farms. An example of Hizbullah's quid pro quo policy elsewhere along the Blue Line came in July 2004. A day after a Hizbullah commander was killed in a car bomb explosion in Beirut, two Israeli soldiers fixing an antenna on the roof of a military position on the border were shot dead by a Hizbullah sniper. The sniper fired three rounds from a distance of about 500 metres, hitting one soldier in the head and the other in the chest and head. Security sources told the author at the time that they believed Hizbullah marksmen were deployed along the Blue Line with instructions to seek out targets of opportunity to revenge the assassination of the Hizbullah commander.

11 Several senior Israeli officials, including then Israeli foreign minister Silvan Shalom, urged Ariel Sharon to take up Bashar's offers, believing that Israel should take advantage of Syria's diplomatic isolation to cut the best possible deal. In January 2004, the head of Israeli military intelligence, Aharon Zeev Farkash, assessed that the Syrian president had 'serious intentions'. More controversially, Israeli chief of staff, Lieutenant General Moshe Yaalon, broke a taboo in August 2004 when he announced that Israel's military superiority was such that it could defend Israel without requiring the strategic depth offered by the Golan Heights. Sharon, however, saw no reason to enter negotiations with Bashar while Syria was under international pressure, especially when he was planning the controversial disengagement from Gaza.

12 The UN Security Council resolutions include 1559, 1595, which authorised the creation of the UN commission to investigate Hariri's murder, 1614, which called on the Lebanese government to deploy troops along the border with Israel, 1636, demanding Syrian cooperation with the UN commission and a cessation of meddling in Lebanese affairs, and 1664, authorising the creation of an international tribunal to try those found responsible for Hariri's murder. The three senior UN envoys were Detlev Mehlis (followed by Serge Brammertz when Mehlis resigned from the commission in December), Terje Roed Larsen, tasked with overseeing the implementation of Resolution 1559, and Geir Pederson, the UN Secretary-General's personal representative for southern Lebanon, who is based in Beirut.

13 Interview with the author – January 5, 2006.

14 The claim was initially greeted with some scepticism in Lebanon with anti-Syrian politicians believing that Syria had arranged for the rocket strike. But the Al-Qaeda connection hardened on January 8, 2006, with the posting on a website used by Al-Qaeda in Iraq of a recorded message attributed to Zarqawi, saying 'The rocket firing at the ancestors of monkeys and pigs from the south of Lebanon was only the start of a blessed in-depth strike against the Zionist enemy . . . [The attack] was on the instructions of the sheikh of the mujahidin, Osama bin Laden, may God preserve him.'

15 Interview with the author – January 5, 2006.

16 Interview with the author.

17 The author co-wrote the report with *The Times'* diplomatic editor, Richard Beeston.

18 The suspicions that Kanaan was murdered, or 'suicided', were only reinforced by some embarrassing slips of the tongue by Syrian officials. In a televised press conference, Mohammed al-Louji, Syria's chief public attorney, said to the delight of reporters that 'the act of killing, pardon, assassination, occurred at his office in the interior ministry at 9.15 a.m.'. During a eulogy at Kanaan's funeral two days later, Farouq al-Sharaa twice used the word 'assassination' to describe the interior minister's death, the second time, adding 'excuse me, suicide'.

19 Interview with the author.

20 The case against Ariel Sharon was filed in Brussels in 2001 under a 1993 law on universal jurisdiction, allowing suspected war criminals to be tried in Belgium regardless of the nationality of the accused and the victims and regardless of where the crime was committed. Under this law, the plaintiffs argued that Sharon could stand trial for his role in the 1982 Sabra/Shatila massacre. After making impressive headway, the case was killed off in 2003 when Donald Rumsfeld, the US defence secretary, threatened to move the NATO head-quarters from Brussels if the Belgian government did not change the law with retroactive effect. Although Rumsfeld's objections were to prevent American soldiers from being tried for war crimes, the intervention sealed the fate of the case against Sharon.

Index